# TIME
## 100

# TIME 100

| | |
|---|---|
| **Editor** | Kelly Knauer |
| **Art Director** | Anthony Wing Kosner |
| **Picture Editor** | Patricia Cadley |
| **Research Director** | Leah Shanks Gordon |
| **Copy Editor** | Bruce Christopher Carr |
| **Associate Copy Editors** | Bob Braine, Ellin Martens |
| **Production Director** | John Calvano |
| **Photo Technology** | Urbano Delvalle |
| **TIME Special Projects Editor** | Barrett Seaman |

## SPECIAL ISSUE STAFF

This book is based on two special issues of TIME. The editorial staff for those issues includes:

| | |
|---|---|
| **Managing Editor** | Walter Isaacson |
| **Editors: Leaders & Revolutionaries** | James Kelly, Joshua Cooper Ramo |
| **Editors: Artists & Entertainers** | Christopher Porterfield, Jan Simpson |
| **Picture Editor** | Jay Colton, Jessica Taylor Taraski (Assistant) |
| **Art Director** | Marti Golon |
| **Research Director: Leaders & Revolutionaries** | Ratu Kamlani |
| **Research Director: Artists & Entertainers** | William Tynan |

**Thanks to:** Gerard Abrahamsen, Ames Adamson, Andy Blau, Anne Considine, Elena Falaro, Kevin Kelly, Kin Wah Lam, Cornelis Verwaal, Anna Yelenskaya

## TIME INC. HOME ENTERTAINMENT

| | |
|---|---|
| **President** | David Gitow |
| **Director, Continuities and Single Sales** | David Arfine |
| **Director, Continuities and Retention** | Michael Barrett |
| **Director, New Products** | Alicia Longobardo |
| **Group Product Manager** | Robert Fox |
| **Product Managers** | Christopher Berzolla, Alison Ehrmann, Roberta Harris, Stacy Hirschberg, Kenneth Maehlum, Jennifer McLyman, Daniel Melore |
| **Manager, Retail and New Markets** | Thomas Mifsud |
| **Associate Product Managers** | Carlos Jiminez, Daria Raehse, Betty Su, Lauren Zaslansky, Cheryl Zukowski |
| **Assistant Product Managers** | Jennifer Dowell, Meredith Shelley |
| **Editorial Operations Director** | John Calvano |
| **Book Production Manager** | Jessica McGrath |
| **Book Production Coordinator** | Joseph Napolitano |
| **Fulfillment Director** | Michelle Gudema |
| **Assistant Fulfillment Manager** | Richard Perez |
| **Financial Director** | Tricia Griffin |
| **Associate Financial Manager** | Amy Maselli |
| **Assistant Financial Manager** | Steven Sandonato |
| **Marketing Assistant** | Ann Gillespie |

Copyright 1998 by Time Inc. Home Entertainment
Published by TIME Books
Time Inc., 1271 Ave. of the Americas, New York, NY 10020
ISSN: 1521-5008
ISBN: 1-883013-49-6

We welcome your comments and suggestions about TIME Books. Please write to us at:
TIME Books
Attention: Book Editors
P.O. Box 11016
Des Moines, IA 50336-1016

To order additional copies, please call 1-800-327-6388
(Monday through Friday 7:00 a.m.—8:00 p.m. or Saturday 7:00 a.m.—6:00 p.m. Central Time)

Printed in the United States of America

# LEADERS & REVOLUTIONARIES

# TIME 100

# ARTISTS & ENTERTAINERS

# TIME 100

## LEADERS & REVOLUTIONARIES

> When our children's children look back, they will see that above all else, the story of the 20th century is the story of the triumph of freedom.

**PRESIDENT BILL CLINTON, speaking at TIME's 75th anniversary party, March 1998**

# The Most Influential People Of the 20th Century

## ARTISTS & ENTERTAINERS

# Foreword

# The TIME 100

The two young men who founded TIME, Henry Luce and Briton Hadden, strongly believed in the power of the individual to influence history: week after week for many decades, the cover of the magazine always featured a portrait of a man or woman in the news. In the first issue of 1928, five years after TIME's debut, the editors named aviation pioneer Charles Lindbergh the "Man of the Year 1927. " This designation of the individual who had done the most in the past year to affect the news for good or for ill became the magazine's signature journalistic act, the annual embodiment of its belief in the power of individual deeds to affect the destiny of men and nations.

As the 20th century was drawing to a close, TIME managing editor Walter Isaacson conceived a project that reflected the magazine's deepest roots: to select and profile the 100 most influential people of the century. The list would be divided into five groups of 20 individuals: Leaders and Revolutionaries, Artists and Entertainers, Builders and Titans, Scientists and Thinkers, Heroes and Inspirations. The entire project would culminate in the naming of a Person of the Century.

To select the individuals for the list, TIME solicited nominations from editors and journalists around the world, consulted outside experts and historians and registered opinions from millions of readers who sent in suggestions by mail and e-mail. The final selection was made in a series of occasionally contentious (but always stimulating) meetings that included journalists from CBS News, which produced a series of television specials on the project.

With the final list in hand, the editors sought out a hall-of-fame collection of writers and thinkers to make the case for each of the TIME 100. The result is a series of biographical essays that are both authoritative and impressionistic, including speechwriter Peggy Noonan's personal glimpses of President Ronald Reagan, Holocaust survivor Elie Wiesel's reflections on Adolf Hitler, and composer Philip Glass's recollection of hearing Igor Stravinsky conducting his compositions at a concert that featured an all-star quartet of pianists—Aaron Copland, Samuel Barber, Lukas Foss and Roger Sessions.

This volume covers the first 40 individuals named to the TIME 100, the Leaders and Revolutionaries and Artists and Entertainers. In the process of transforming these special issues of the weekly magazine into book form, the stories have been completely redesigned, many new pictures have been added, and some minor factual errors (most of them caught by TIME's astute readers) have been corrected.

# Leaders

# &

# Revolutionaries

Heroes and villains, martyrs and tyrants, they inspired the common man and shaped the fate of nations in a century marked by false ideologies, brutal wars—and the lure of freedom

# Our Century
## ...And the Next One

By **WALTER ISAACSON**

**A**s centuries go, this has been one of the most amazing: inspiring, at times horrifying, always fascinating. Sure, the 15th was pretty wild, with the Renaissance and Spanish Inquisition in full flower, Gutenberg building his printing press, Copernicus beginning to contemplate the solar system and Columbus spreading the culture of Europe to the Americas. And of course there was the 1st century,

which if only for the life and death of Jesus may have had the most impact of any. Socrates and Plato made the 5th century B.C. also rather remarkable. But we who live in the 20th can probably get away with the claim that ours has been one of the top four or five of recorded history.

Let's take stock for a moment. To name just a few random things we did in a hundred years: we split the atom, invented jazz and rock, launched airplanes and landed on the moon, concocted a general theory of relativity, devised the transistor and figured out how to etch millions of them on tiny microchips, discovered penicillin and the structure of DNA, fought down fascism and communism, bombed Guernica and painted the bombing of Guernica, developed cinema and television, built highways and wired the world. Not to mention the peripherals these produced, such as sitcoms and cable channels, "800" numbers and websites, shopping malls and leisure time, existentialism and modernism, Oprah and Imus. Initials spread like graffiti: NATO, IBM, ABM, UN, WPA, NBA, NFL, CIA, CNN, PLO, IPO, IRA, IMF, TGIF. And against all odds, we avoided blowing ourselves up.

All this produced some memorable players. Look around. There's Lenin arriving at the Finland Station and Gandhi marching to the sea to make salt. Winston Churchill with his cigar, Louis Armstrong with his horn, Charlie Chaplin with his cane. Rosa Parks staying seated on her bus and a kid standing in front of a tank near Tiananmen Square. Einstein is in his study, and the Beatles are on *The Ed Sullivan Show*.

In this book, the first of three in which we'll select and profile the 100 most influential players of this century, we start

with two major categories: leaders and revolutionaries, artists and entertainers. Succeeding volumes will report on three other categories: business titans, scientists and thinkers, heroes and inspirations. The exercise of naming the most influential persons of our time will culminate in TIME's choice of the Person of the Century. It's not a simple task, but it helps to start by looking at what the great themes of this century have been.

Rarely does a century dawn so clearly and cleanly. In 1900 Freud published *The Interpretation of Dreams,* ending the Victorian era. Her Majesty, as if on cue, died the following January, after a 63-year reign. Her empire included one-quarter of the earth's population, but the Boer War in South Africa was signaling the end of the colonial era. In China, the Boxer Rebellion heralded the awakening of a new giant. In America, cars were replacing horses, 42% of workers were in farming (today it's 2%), and the average life-span was about 50 (today it's around 75).

The tape recorder was unveiled in 1900 at the Paris Exposition; visitors flocked to France to be

world. And German physicist Max Planck made one of the discoveries that would shape the century: that atoms radiate energy in bursts he called quanta.

From these seeds was born a century that can be summed up and labeled in a handful of ways:

**The Century of Freedom** If you had to pick a two-word summation, it would be: Freedom won. It beat back the two totalitarian alternatives that arose to challenge it, fascism and communism. By the 1990s, the ideals developed by centuries of philosophers from Plato to Locke to Mill to Jefferson— individual rights, civil liberties, personal freedoms and democratic participation in the choice of leaders—finally held sway over more than half the world's population.

**The Century of Capitalism** Democracy can exist without capitalism, and capitalism without democracy, but probably not for very long. Political and economic freedom tend to go

scandalized by Rodin's non-Victorian statues, and Kodak introduced the Brownie camera, an apt symbol of a century in which technology would at first seem magical, then become simple, cheap and personal. The Scholastic Aptitude Test was born that year, permitting a power shift from an aristocracy to a meritocracy. The Wright brothers went to Kitty Hawk to try out their gliders. Lenin, 30, published his first newspaper calling for revolution in Russia. Churchill, 25, was elected to the House of Commons. J.P. Morgan began working with a young executive named Charles Schwab to buy out Andrew Carnegie and conglomerate U.S. Steel, by far the biggest business in the

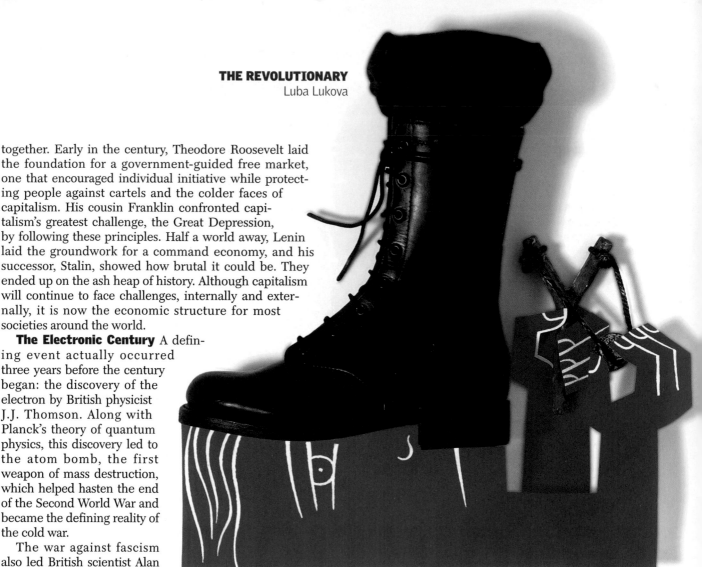

THE REVOLUTIONARY
Luba Lukova

together. Early in the century, Theodore Roosevelt laid the foundation for a government-guided free market, one that encouraged individual initiative while protecting people against cartels and the colder faces of capitalism. His cousin Franklin confronted capitalism's greatest challenge, the Great Depression, by following these principles. Half a world away, Lenin laid the groundwork for a command economy, and his successor, Stalin, showed how brutal it could be. They ended up on the ash heap of history. Although capitalism will continue to face challenges, internally and externally, it is now the economic structure for most societies around the world.

**The Electronic Century** A defining event actually occurred three years before the century began: the discovery of the electron by British physicist J.J. Thomson. Along with Planck's theory of quantum physics, this discovery led to the atom bomb, the first weapon of mass destruction, which helped hasten the end of the Second World War and became the defining reality of the cold war.

The war against fascism also led British scientist Alan Turing to harness electronics in devising the first digital computers. Five centuries earlier, Gutenberg's printing press had cut the cost of transmitting information by a factor of a thousand. That paved the way for the Reformation by allowing individuals to have their own Bibles, and for the progress of individual liberties, which became inevitable once information and ideas flowed freely. The transistor and the microchip have cut the cost of transmitting data by a factor of more than a million. The result has been a transition from an industrial age to an information age.

**The Global Century** Human society over the millenniums has evolved from villages to city-states to empires to nation-states. In this century, everything became global. Much of the first half was dominated by the death spasms of an international order that for 400 years was based on the shifting alliances of European nation-states, but this time the resulting wars were world wars. Now not only are military issues global, so are economic and even cultural ones. People everywhere are threatened by weapons anywhere, they produce and consume in a single networked economy, and increasingly they have access to the same movies and music and ideas.

**The Mass-Market Century** Yet another defining event of the century came in 1913, when Henry Ford opened his assembly line. Ordinary people could now afford a Model T (choice of color: black). Products were mass-produced and mass-marketed, with all the centralization and conformity that entails. Television sets and toothpaste, magazines and movies, shows and shoes: they were distributed or broadcast, in cookie-

cutter form, from central facilities to millions of people. In reaction, a modernist mix of anarchy, existential despair and rebellion against conformity motivated art, music, literature, fashion and even behavior for much of the century.

**The Genocidal Century** Then there was the dark side. Amid the glories of the century lurked some of history's worst horrors: Stalin's collectivization, Hitler's Holocaust, Mao's Cultural Revolution, Pol Pot's killing fields, Idi Amin's rampages. We try to personalize the blame, as if it were the fault of just a few madmen, but in fact it was whole societies, including advanced ones like Germany's, that embraced or tolerated madness. What they had in common was that they sought totalitarian solutions rather than freedom. Theologians have to answer the question of why God allows evil. Rationalists have one almost as difficult: Why doesn't progress make civilizations more civilized?

**The American Century** That's what TIME's founder Henry Luce called it in a 1941 essay. He was using the phrase to exhort his compatriots to prepare for war, to engage in the struggle for freedom. They did, yet again. And they won. Some countries base their foreign policy on realism or its Prussian-accented cousin, realpolitik: a cold and careful calculation of strategic interests. America is unique in that it is equally motivated by idealism. Whether it is the fight against fascism or communism, or even misconceived interventions like Vietnam, America's mission is to further not only its interests but also its values. And that idealist streak is a

# As centuries go, this has been one of the most amazing: inspiring, at times horrifying, always fascinating.

source of its global influence, even more than its battleships. As became clear when the Iron Curtain collapsed in 1989, America's clout in the world comes not just from its military might but from the power and appeal of its values. Which is why it did, indeed, turn out to be an American Century.

So what will the next century bring? The reams of guesses made as we approach the turn of the millennium are destined to be digitally retrieved decades hence and read with a smirk. But let's take that risk, peer into the haze and slap a few labels on the postmillennial period:

In the digital realm, the Next Big Advance will be voice recognition. The rudiments are already here but in primitive form. Ask a computer to "recognize speech," and it is likely to think you want it to "wreck a nice beach." But in a decade or so we'll be able to chat away and machines will soak it all in. Microchips will be truly embedded in our lives when we can talk to them. Not only to our computers; we'll also be able to chat with our cars, telephones, thermostats, VCRs, microwaves and any other devices we want to boss around.

That will open the way to the next phase of the digital age: artificial intelligence. By our providing so many thoughts and preferences to our machines each day, they'll accumulate enough information about how we think so that they'll be able to mimic our minds and act as our agents. Scary, huh? But potentially quite useful—at least until they decide they don't need us anymore and start building even smarter machines they can boss around.

The law powering the digital age up until now has been Gordon Moore's: that microchips will double in power and halve in price every 18 months or so. Bill Gates rules because early on he acted on the assumption that computing power— the capacity of microprocessors and memory chips—would become nearly free; his company kept churning out more and more lines of complex software to make use of this cheap bounty. The law that will power the next few decades is that bandwidth (the capacity of fiber-optic and other pipelines to carry digital communications) will become nearly free.

Along with the recent advances in digital switching and storage technologies, this means in the future we will have all forms of content—from newspapers, books and music to your aunt's recipes and home videos—instantly available anywhere on demand. Anyone will be able to be a producer of any content; you'll be able to create a movie or magazine, make it available to the world and charge for it, just like Time Warner!

The result will be a transition from a mass-market world to a personalized one. Instead of centralized factories and studios that distribute or broadcast the same product to millions, technology is already allowing products to be tailored to each user. You can subscribe to news sources that serve up only topics that fit your fancy. Everything from shoes to steel can be customized to meet individual wishes.

The digital revolution that burns so brightly today is likely to pale in comparison to the revolution in biotechnology that is just beginning. In early 1998 physicist Stephen Hawking, speaking at the White House on science in the next millennium, pointed out that for the past 10,000 years there has been no significant change in our human DNA. But over the next

hundred years, we will be able and tempted to tinker. We'll encode our dreams and vanities and hubris. We'll clone ourselves; we'll custom-design our kids. By playing Dr. Frankenstein, we'll have the chance to make miracles or monsters. The challenges will be not scientific but moral.

In the political realm, democratic capitalism, having defeated its twin foes, fascism and communism, is likely to face three others. The first is tribalism, as in Bosnia. This is, of course, nothing new. But democracies are often maladroit at dealing with minorities that seek group empowerment. The second challenge will be fundamentalism. Capitalism can be cold, consumption oriented and spiritless, alienating those who feel repelled by its modernity and its materialist values. Some will respond by embracing traditional religions or New Age spirituality, but there is also likely to be, especially in the Islamic world, a fierce religious challenge that rejects individual liberties as well as the materialism that comes with capitalism. Finally, there is the radical environmentalism of the Green movements, which could start seeming less radical and more urgent if the quest for economic growth that is inherent in capitalism continues to threaten the health of the planet. To counter this, *Homo sapiens* will have to become the first species to learn how to control its own population growth.

AMONG THE FEW THINGS CERTAIN ABOUT THE NEXT century is that it will be wired, networked and global. Because national borders will be unable to block the flow of information and innovation, the societies that thrive will be those that are comfortable with openness and with the free flow of services, goods and ideas. By these standards, the U.S. is rather well positioned. Ever since the days of the colonial pamphleteers, we've been comfortable with the cacophony that comes from freedom of information. We're used to being multicultural, and though we're constantly struggling with the consequences, we don't Balkanize because of it. Our disputes, such as those over affirmative action, may be divisive, but we have the political and constitutional means to resolve them peacefully.

But like other nations, the U.S. will have to adapt to a new century. With a global economy that will be increasingly knowledge based, we will no longer be able to condone unequal educational opportunities. Schools will need to be open to competition and subjected to standards so that we avoid creating a two-tiered society. We also must realize, as both Theodore and Franklin Roosevelt did, that capitalism can be efficient but it can also be cold. America's social fabric is strong when it weaves together rewards for individual initiative and neighborly compassion for all members of the community. The ultimate goal of democracy and freedom, after all, is not to pursue material abundance but to nurture the dignity and values of each individual. That is the fundamental story of this century, and if we're lucky and wise, it will be the story of the next one. ∎

*Walter Isaacson is the 14th managing editor of* TIME. *A former editor of new media for Time Inc., he is the author of* Kissinger: A Biography.

# Theodore Roosevelt

## With limitless energy and a passionate sense of the nation, he set the stage for the American century

**By EDMUND MORRIS**

THEY DON'T HOLD WHITE HOUSE LUNCHES THE WAY they used to at the beginning of the century. On Jan. 1, 1907, for example, the guest list was as follows: a Nobel prizewinner, a physical culturalist, a naval historian, a biographer, an essayist, a paleontologist, a taxidermist, an ornithologist, a field naturalist, a conservationist, a big-game hunter, an editor, a critic, a ranchman, an orator, a country squire, a civil service reformer, a socialite, a patron of the arts, a colonel of the cavalry, a former Governor of New York, the ranking expert on big-game mammals in North America and the President of the U.S.

All these men were named Theodore Roosevelt.

In his protean variety, his febrile energy (which could have come from his lifelong habit of popping nitroglycerin pills for a dicey heart), his incessant self-celebration and his absolute refusal to believe there was anything finer than to be born an American, unless to die as one in some glorious battle for the flag, the great "Teddy" was as representative of 20th century dynamism as Abraham Lincoln had been of 19th century union and George Washington of 18th century independence.

Peevish Henry Adams, who lived across the square from the White House and was always dreading that the President might stomp over for breakfast (T.R. thought nothing of guzzling 12 eggs at a sitting), tried to formulate the dynamic theory of history that would explain, at least to Adams' comfort, why America was accelerating into the future at such a frightening rate. His theory was eventually published in *The Education of Henry Adams* but makes less sense today than his brilliant description of the President as perhaps the fundamental motive force of

our age: "Power when wielded by abnormal energy is the most serious of facts ... Roosevelt, more than any other man living within the range of notoriety, showed the singular primitive quality that belongs to ultimate matter—he was pure Act."

In his youth, as indeed during his infamous "White House walks," which usually culminated in a nude swim across the Potomac, Theodore Roosevelt hewed to a cross-country motto: "Over, Under or Through—But Never Around." That overmastering directness—that focus upon his objective, be it geological or political or personal—was the force that Adams identified. But T.R., unlike so many other active (as opposed to reactive) Presidents, also had a highly sophisticated, tactical mind. William Allen White said that Roosevelt "thought with his hips"—an aperçu that might better be applied to Ronald Reagan, whose intelligence was intuitive, and even to Franklin Roosevelt, who never approached "Cousin Theodore" in smarts. White probably meant that T.R.'s mental processor moved so fast as to fuse thought and action.

He was, after all, capable of reading one to three books daily while pouring out an estimated 150,000 letters in his lifetime. He conducted the business of the presidency with such dispatch that he could usually spend the entire afternoon goofing off, if his kind of mad exercise can be euphemized as goofing off. "Theodore!" Senator Henry Cabot Lodge was once heard shouting, "if you knew how ridiculous you look up that tree, you'd come down at once!"

The obvious example of T.R.'s "Never Around" approach to statesmanship was the Panama Canal, which he ordered built in 1903, after what he called "three centuries of conver-

**BORN Oct. 27, 1858, in New York City**

**1897 Named Assistant Secretary of the Navy**

**1900-01 Elected Vice President. McKinley shot; T.R. becomes President**

**1906 Wins Nobel Peace Prize**

| 1858 | | | | | 1919 |
|---|---|---|---|---|---|

**ROUGH RIDER T.R., a happy warrior, gloried in battle**

**1898 Leads Rough Riders in Spanish-American War. Elected Governor of New York**

**1904 Elected President; begins Panama Canal**

**1912 Loses third-party bid for the presidency**

**1919 Dies in his sleep**

"He was so alive at all points, and so gifted with the rare faculty of living intensely ... in every moment ...

EDITH WHARTON, at Roosevelt's burial, January 1919

Charge! T.R. leads a family corps on Long Island, 1914

sation." If a convenient revolution had to be fomented in Colombia (in order to facilitate the independence of Panama province and allow construction to proceed p.d.q.), well, that was Bogotá's bad luck for being obstructionist and good fortune for the rest of world commerce. Being a historian, T.R. never tired of pointing out that his Panamanian revolution had been merely the 53rd anti-Colombian insurrection in as many years, but he was less successful in arguing that it was accomplished within the bounds of international law. "Oh, Mr. President," his Attorney General, Philander Knox, sighed, "do not let so great an achievement suffer from any taint of legality."

Dubious or not as a triumph of foreign policy, the canal has functioned perfectly for most of the century, and still does so to the honor of our technological reputation, although its control has reverted to the country T.R. allowed to sprout alongside, like a glorified right of way.

BUT T.R. DESERVES TO BE REMEMBERED, I THINK, FOR some acts more visionary than land grabbing south of the border. He fathered the modern American Navy, for example, while his peacemaking between Russia and Japan in 1905 elevated him to the front rank of presidential diplomats. He pushed through the Pure Food and Meat Inspection laws of 1906, forcing Congress to acknowledge its responsibility as consumer protector.

Many other Rooseveltian acts loom larger in retrospect than they did at the time, when they passed unappreciated. For example, T.R. was the first President to perceive, through his own pince-nez, that this nation's future trade posture must be toward Asia and away from the Old World entanglements of its past. Crossing the Sierra Nevada on May 7, 1903, he boggled at the beauty and otherworldliness of California. New York—his birthplace—seemed impossibly far away, Europe antipodean. "I felt as if I was seeing Provence in the making."

There was no doubt at all in T.R.'s leaping mind which would be the world's next superpower. Less than five years before, he had stormed San Juan Heights in Cuba and felt what he described as the "wolf rising in the heart"—that primal lust for victory and power that drives all conquerors. "Our place ... is and must be with the nations that have left indelibly their impress on the centuries!" he shouted in San Francisco.

It's tempting to speculate how T.R. would behave as President if he were alive today. The honest answer, of course, is that he would be bewildered by the strangeness of everything, as people blind from birth are said to be when shocked by the "gift" of sight. But he certainly would be appalled by contemporary Americans' vulgarity and sentimentality, particularly the way we celebrate nonentities. Also by our lack of respect for officeholders and teachers, lack of concern for unborn children, excessive wealth and deteriorating standards of physical fitness.

Abroad he would admire our willingness to challenge foreign despots and praise the generosity with which we finance the development of less fortunate economies. At home he would want to do something about Microsoft, since he had been passionate about monopoly from the moment he entered politics. Although no single trust a hundred years ago approached the monolithic immensity of Mr. Gates' empire, the Northern Securities merger of 1901 created the greatest transport combine in the world, controlling commerce from Chicago to China.

T.R. busted it. In doing so he burnished himself with instant glory as the champion of individual enterprise against corporate "malefactors of great

A man, a plan, a big digging machine, a canal: Panama!

A North Carolina audience falls under Roosevelt's spell during his eventful first term

wealth." That reputation suited him just fine, although he privately believed in Big Business and was just as wary of unrestrained, amateurish competition. All he wanted to establish, early in his first term, was government's right to regulate rampant entrepreneurship.

Most of all, I think, Theodore Roosevelt would use the power of the White House in 1998 to protect our environment. His earliest surviving letter, written at age 10, mourns the cutting down of a tree, and he went on to become America's first conservationist President, responsible for five new national parks, 18 national monuments and untold millions of acres of national forest. Without a doubt, he would react toward the

great swaths of farmland that are now being carbuncled over with "development" as he did when told that no law allowed him to set aside a Florida nature preserve at will. "Is there any law that prevents me declaring Pelican Island a National Bird Sanctuary?" T.R. asked, not waiting long for an answer. "Very well, then," reaching for his pen, "I do declare it." ∎

*Edmund Morris, whose biography of Ronald Reagan will be published in the fall of 1998, won a Pulitzer Prize for his biography of Theodore Roosevelt, which was published in 1980.*

# Vladimir Ilyich
# Lenin

## A zealot driven by ideology, he reshaped Russia and made communism into a global force

**By DAVID REMNICK**

**N**OT LONG AFTER THE BOLSHEVIKS HAD SEIZED power in 1917, Vladimir Ilyich Lenin filled out a bureaucratic questionnaire. For occupation, he wrote "man of letters." So it was a son of the Russian intelligentsia, a radical straight from the pages of Dostoyevsky's novel *The Possessed*, who became the author of mass terror and the first concentration camps ever built on the European Continent.

Lenin was the initiator of the central drama—the tragedy—of our era, the rise of totalitarian states. A bookish man with a scholar's habits and a general's tactical instincts, Lenin introduced to the 20th century the practice of taking an all-embracing ideology and imposing it on an entire society rapidly and mercilessly; he created a regime that erased politics, erased historical memory, erased opposition. In his short career in power, from 1917 until his death in 1924, Lenin created a model not merely for his successor, Stalin, but for Mao, for Hitler, for Pol Pot.

And while in this way Lenin may be the central actor who begins the 20th century, he is the least knowable of characters. As a boy growing up in Simbirsk, Lenin distinguished himself in Latin and Greek. The signal event of his youth—the event that radicalized him—came in 1887, when his eldest brother Alexander, a student at the University of St. Petersburg, was hanged for conspiring to help assassinate Czar Alexander III. As a lawyer, Lenin became increasingly involved in radical politics, and after completing a three-year term of Siberian exile, he began his rise as the leading theorist, tactician and organizer of the Communist Party.

In his personal relations with colleagues, family and friends, Lenin was relatively open and generous. Unlike many tyrants, he did not crave a tyrant's riches. Even when we strip Lenin of the cult that was created all around him after his death, when we strip away the myths of his "superhuman kindness," he remains a peculiarly modest figure who wore a shabby waistcoat, worked 16-hour days and read extensively. (By contrast, Stalin did not know that the Netherlands and Holland were the same country, and no one in the Kremlin inner circle was brave enough to set him straight.)

Before he became the general of the revolution, Lenin was its pedant, the journalist-scholar who married Marxist theory to an incisive analysis of insurrectionist tactics. His theories of what society ought to be and how that ideal must be achieved were the products of thousands of hours of reading.

"The incomprehensibility of Lenin is precisely this all-consuming intellectuality—the fact that from his calculations, from his neat pen, flowed seas of blood, whereas by nature this was not an evil person," writes Andrei Sinyavsky, one of the key dissidents of the 1960s. "On the contrary, Vladimir Ilyich was a rather kind person whose cruelty was stipulated by science and incontrovertible historical laws. As were his love of power and his political intolerance."

For all his learning, Lenin began the Bolshevik tradition of waging war on intellectual dissidents—of exiling, imprisoning and executing thinkers and artists who dared oppose the regime. He was a "man of letters" of a particular sort. In the years before and after the October 1917

**BORN**
**April 22, 1870**

**STUDENT** Lenin was bright, boisterous and quarrelsome at 15

**1870**

**1903 Forms the Marxist Bolshevik Party in Brussels**

**1917 Leads Russia into revolution and is elected head of the Russian Soviet Republic**

**1918 Civil war between czarist "Whites" and Lenin's "Reds" breaks out**

**1920 Defeats the "Whites"**

**1923 Warns against Stalin as successor**

**1924**

**1924 Dies after a series of strokes**

coup, Lenin was the avatar of a group of radical intellectuals who sought a revolution that did not merely attempt to redress the economic balances under czarism. Instead, Lenin made a perverse reading of the Enlightenment view of man as modeling clay and sought to create a new model of human nature and behavior through social engineering of the most radical kind.

"Bolshevism was the most audacious attempt in history to subject the entire life of a country to a master plan," writes Richard Pipes at the end of his two-volume history of the revolution. "It sought to sweep aside as useless rubbish the wisdom that mankind had accumulated over millennia. In

that sense, it was a unique effort to apply science to human affairs; and it was pursued with the zeal characteristic of the breed of intellectuals who regard resistance to their ideas as proof that they are sound."

It is, perhaps, impossible to calculate just how many tens of millions of murders "flowed" from Leninism. Certainly Stalin differed from Lenin in the length of his time as dictator—some 25 years to Lenin's six—and he also had the advantage of greater technology. As a result, Stalin's murderous statistics are superior to Lenin's. And yet Lenin contributed so very much.

In some scholarly circles in the West, Stalin was seen as an

## He laughs a great deal... his laugh seems friendly & jolly, but gradually one finds it grim.

**BERTRAND RUSSELL, first impression upon meeting Lenin, May 19, 1920**

"aberration," a tyrant who perverted Lenin's intentions at the end of Lenin's life. But as more and more evidence of Lenin's cruelty emerged from the archives, that notion of the "good Lenin" and the "bad Stalin" became an academic joke. Very few of Stalin's policies were without roots in Leninism: it was Lenin who built the first camps; Lenin who set off artificial famine as a political weapon; Lenin who disbanded the last vestige of democratic government, the Constituent Assembly, and devised the Communist Party as the apex of a totalitarian structure; Lenin who first waged war on the intelligentsia and on religious believers, wiping out any traces of civil liberty and a free press.

SINCE THE SOVIET ARCHIVES BECAME public, we have been able to read the extent of Lenin's cruelty, the depths of its vehemence. Here he is in 1918, in a letter instructing Bolshevik leaders to attack peasant leaders who did not accept the revolution: "Comrades! … Hang (hang without fail, so that people will see) no fewer than one hundred known kulaks, rich men, bloodsuckers … Do it in such a way that … for hundreds of versts around, the people will see, tremble, know, shout: 'They are strangling and will strangle to death the bloodsucker kulaks' … Yours, Lenin."

Among those artists and writers who survived the revolution and its aftermath, many wrote paeans to Lenin's intelligence that sound like nothing so much as religious songs of praise. The poet Mayakovsky would write, "Then over the world loomed/ Lenin of the enormous head." And later, the prose writer Yuri Olesha would say, "Now I live in an explained world. I understand the causes. I am filled with a feeling of enormous gratitude, expressible only in music, when I think of those who died to make the world explained."

By the Brezhnev era, Lenin's dream state had devolved into a corrupt and failing dictatorship. Only the Lenin cult

**Lenin, with Stalin behind him in 1917, grew to distrust his eventual successor**

persisted. The ubiquitous Lenin was a symbol of the repressive society itself. Joseph Brodsky, the great Russian poet of the late 20th century, began to hate Lenin at about the time he was in the first grade, "not so much because of his political philosophy or practice … but because of the omnipresent images which plagued almost every textbook, every class wall, postage stamps, money, and what not, depicting the man at various ages and stages of his life … This face in some ways haunts every Russian and suggests some sort of standard for human appearance because it is utterly lacking in character … coming to ignore those pictures was my first lesson in switching off, my first attempt at estrangement."

When Mikhail Gorbachev instituted his policy of *glasnost* in the late 1980s, the Communist Party tried to practice a policy of regulated criticism. The goal was to "de-Stalinize" the Soviet Union, to resume Khrushchev's liberalization in the late 1950s. But eventually, *glasnost* led to the image of Lenin, not least with the publication of Vassily Grossman's *Forever Flowing,* a novel that dared compare Lenin's cruelty to Hitler's. While he was in office, Gorbachev always called himself a "confirmed Leninist"; it was only years later that he too—the last General Secretary of the Communist Party—admitted, "I can only say that cruelty was the main problem with Lenin."

After the collapse of the anti-Gorbachev coup in August 1991, the people of Leningrad voted to call their city St. Petersburg once more. When Brodsky, who had been exiled from the city in 1964, was asked about the news, he smiled and said, "Better to have named it for a saint than a devil." ∎

*David Remnick, the editor of the* New Yorker, *wrote* Lenin's Tomb: The Last Days of the Soviet Empire, *which won the Pulitzer Prize in 1994.*

**Lenin rouses a group of factory workers during the revolutionary year 1917**

# Fellow Travelers
## Communism attracted sophisticates, visionaries—and tyrants

### Joseph Stalin
A more terrible tyrant than Ivan the Terrible, Stalin enslaved millions in the name of freedom. His word was gospel, his will law; he repealed truth and denied God. A Georgian, he was radicalized at an early age; at 23 he was sent to Siberia for agitating against the Czar. He met Lenin in 1905 and rose quickly in party ranks, directing the purges that followed victory in the civil war. After Lenin's death he starved millions of farmers in a vain effort to collectivize agriculture, then brutally purged the Party. In wartime he signed a cynical pact with Hitler, who betrayed him. At his death in 1953 he ruled an immense communist empire—by sheer terror.

### Che Guevara
Fidel Castro was the heart, soul, voice and beard of the Cuban revolution—but Che Guevara was its brain. With his vast competence, high intelligence, idealistic fervor and a perceptive sense of humor, the Argentine doctor was the hemisphere's charismatic champion of Marxist revolt—until he was shot in 1967 by Bolivian troops while he waged guerrilla war there with rebels.

### Nikita Khrushchev
A shrewd man who carefully preserved his peasant touch, an unabashed ham who pounded his shoe on a desk at the U.N., Khrushchev was the first Soviet ruler to admit a touch of humanism into communism. The earthy Ukrainian was a leading proponent of peaceful coexistence between East and West—when he wasn't gloating that communism would "bury" America.

### Zhou Enlai
As the chief architect of China's foreign policy under Mao Zedong, Zhou charted Beijing's course of independence from the two superpowers, creating in the process a new world center of power and influence. Suave, subtle and enduring, he advanced China's cause on the global stage with dexterity—and survived the Cultural Revolution to restore sanity to a nation in chaos. Henry Kissinger once called him "the greatest statesman of our era."

# Margaret Sanger

## Her crusade to legalize birth control spurred the movement toward women's liberation

**By GLORIA STEINEM**

"T HE MOVEMENT SHE STARTED WILL GROW TO BE, A hundred years from now, the most influential of all time," predicted futurist and historian H.G. Wells in 1931. "When the history of our civilization is written, it will be a biological history, and Margaret Sanger will be its heroine."

Though this prophecy of nearly 70 years ago credited one woman with the power that actually came from a wide and deep movement of women, no one person deserves it more. Now that reproductive freedom is becoming accepted and conservative groups are fighting to maintain control over women's bodies as the means of reproduction, Sanger's revolution may be even more controversial than during her 50-year career of national and international battles. Her experience can teach us many lessons.

She taught us, first, to look at the world as if women matered. Born into an Irish working-class family, Margaret witnessed her mother's slow death, worn out after 18 pregnancies and 11 live births. While working as a practical nurse and midwife in the poorest neighborhoods of New York City in the years before World War I, she saw women deprived of their health, sexuality and ability to care for children already born. Contraceptive information was so suppressed by clergy-influenced, physician-accepted laws that it was a criminal offense to send it through the mail. Yet the educated had access to such information and could use subterfuge to buy "French" products, which were really condoms and other barrier methods, and "feminine hygiene" products, which were really spermicides.

It was this injustice that inspired Sanger to defy church and state. In a series of articles called "What Every Girl Should Know," then in her own newspaper *The Woman Rebel* and finally through neighborhood clinics that dispensed woman-controlled forms of birth control (a phrase she coined), Sanger put information and power into the hands of women.

While in Europe for a year to avoid severe criminal penalties—partly due to her political radicalism, partly for violating postal obscenity laws—she learned more about contraception, the politics of sexuality and the commonality of women's experience. Her case was dismissed after her return to the States. Sanger continued to push legal and social boundaries by initiating sex counseling, founding the American Birth Control League (which became, in 1942, the Planned Parent-

"She made people accept that women had
the right to control their own destinies.

**Grandson ALEXANDER SANGER, head of Planned Parenthood of New York City**

hood Federation of America) and organizing the first international population conference. Eventually her work would extend as far as Japan and India, where organizations she helped start still flourish.

Sanger was past 80 when she saw the first marketing of a contraceptive pill, which she had helped develop. But legal change was slow. It took until 1965, a year before her death, for the Supreme Court to strike down a Connecticut law that prohibited the use of contraception, even by married couples. Extended to unmarried couples only in 1972, this constitutionally guaranteed right to privacy would become as important to women's equality as the vote. In 1973 the right to privacy was extended to the abortion decision of a woman and her physician, thus making abortion a safe and legal alternative—unlike the $5 illegal butcheries of Sanger's day.

**Speak no evil: Sanger is banned in Boston**

One can imagine Sanger's response to the current anti-choice lobby and congressional leadership that opposes abortion, sex education in schools, and federally funded contraceptive programs that would make abortion less necessary; that supports ownership of young women's bodies through parental-consent laws; that limits poor women's choices by denying Medicaid funding; and that holds hostage the entire U.S. billion-dollar debt to the United Nations in the hope of attaching an antiabortion rider. As in her day, the question seems to be less about what gets decided than who has the power to make the decision.

One can also imagine her response to the pro-life rhetoric that today is used to justify an average of one clinic bombing or arson per month—sometimes the same clinics Sanger helped found—and the murder of six clinic staff members, the attempted murder of 15 others, and assault and battery against 104 more. In each case, the justification is that potential fetal life is more important than a living woman's health or freedom.

Which mistakes in our era parallel those of Sanger's? There is still an effort to distort her goal of giving women control over their bodies by attributing such quotes to

Sanger as "More children from the fit, less from the unfit—that is the chief issue of birth control." Sanger didn't say those words; in fact, she condemned them as a eugenicist argument for "cradle competition." To her, poor mental development was largely the result of poverty, overpopulation and the lack of attention to children. She correctly foresaw racism as the nation's major challenge, conducted surveys that countered stereotypes regarding the black community and birth control, and established clinics in the rural South with the help of such African-American leaders as W.E.B. DuBois and Mary McLeod Bethune.

Nonetheless, expediency caused Sanger to distance herself from her radical past; for instance, she used soft phrases such as "family planning" instead of her original, more pointed argument that the poor were being manipulated into producing an endless supply of cheap labor. She also adopted the mainstream eugenics language of the day, partly as a tactic, since many eugenicists opposed birth control on the ground that the educated would use it more. Though her own work was directed toward voluntary birth control and public health programs, her use of eugenics language probably helped justify sterilization abuse. Her misjudgments should cause us to wonder what parallel errors we are making now and to question any tactics that fail to embody the ends we hope to achieve.

Sanger led by example. Her brave and joyous life included fulfilling work, three children, two husbands, many lovers and an international network of friends and colleagues. She was charismatic and sometimes quixotic, but she never abandoned her focus on women's freedom and its larger implications for social justice. Indeed, she lived as if she and everyone else had the right to control her or his own life. By word and deed, she pioneered the most radical, humane and transforming political movement of the century. ∎

*Gloria Steinem is a co-founder of* Ms. *magazine and author of* Revolution from Within.

---

**BORN
Sept. 14,
1879, in
Corning, N.Y.**

**1914 Launches *The Woman Rebel*, a feminist monthly that advocates birth control; is indicted for inciting violence and promoting obscenity**

**1921 Founds the American Birth Control League, precursor to the Planned Parenthood Federation**

**1879**

**1966**

**MOTHER With her two sons in 1916**

**1916 Opens the U.S.'s first family-planning clinic, in Brooklyn, N.Y.; is later jailed for 30 days**

**1966 Dies in Tucson, Ariz.**

# The New Faces of Power
## Long disenfranchised, women finally ascend to leadership roles

### Indira Gandhi

"If I die today," Indira Gandhi told a crowd of followers in 1984, "every drop of my blood will invigorate the nation." The next day, India's Prime Minister was slain by her own Sikh bodyguards, who were angered by her decision to send Indian troops to confront rebels sheltered in the Sikhs' holiest shrine, the Golden Temple of Amritsar. Daughter of J.P. Nehru, India's first Prime Minister, Indira reluctantly entered politics after her father's death but proved to be a proud, stubborn and courageous figure who gave India decisive leadership for almost 18 years, including the controversial period in the 1970s when she met civil unrest by declaring a state of emergency that gave her vast powers.

### Benazir Bhutto

Only 35 years old when elected Prime Minister of Pakistan in 1988, Benazir Bhutto was smart, beautiful and brave: she fought the dictator who had hanged her father, a beloved leader, and she restored democracy after years of military rule. But her legacy was tarnished by charges of corruption in office.

### Golda Meir

Her face was an apt symbol of Israel itself: strong, disarmingly homely, above all tough. It was a face that inspired love but also demanded respect—and the operative word is "demanded." Golda Meir was of that generation of pioneers who built the Jewish state; she served as its Prime Minister through five years and the 1973 war that drove her from office. A fierce Zionist, a driving organizer, a persuasive advocate, she made up for her lack of stylish eloquence with a peasant's shrewdness—and heart.

> I don't want a long life. I don't mind if my life goes in the service of my nation.
>
> **INDIRA GANDHI,**
> **in a speech the night before**
> **she was assassinated**

## Violeta Barrios de Chamorro

Like Corazon Aquino, Nicaragua's Violeta Chamorro rose to power as a surrogate for a martyred husband: newspaper publisher Pedro Chamorro was murdered in 1978, leading to the downfall of the brutal Somoza regime. After years of civil war and divisive rule by the leftist Sandinistas, Chamorro was elected President of her nation in 1990. Though she halted hyper-inflation during her six-year term, Nicaragua still lagged economically.

## Corazon Aquino

When Benigno Aquino, a leading critic of the corrupt regime of Philippine strongman Ferdinand Marcos, was slain on his return from exile in 1983, his wife Corazon stepped into his shoes and led one of the most memorable eruptions of People Power in the century. Swathed in her trademark yellow, the woman who listed her occupation as "housewife" when she entered the presidential election in 1986 rallied Filipinos when Marcos tried to steal the election. Voters—and then the army—rose up and swept Marcos out of power.

He was the only person I ever knew,
anywhere, who was never afraid.
God, how he could take it for us all.

LYNDON JOHNSON, April 1945

# Franklin Delano
# Roosevelt

## He lifted the United States out of economic despair and revolutionized the American way of life. Then he helped make the world safe for democracy

### By ARTHUR SCHLESINGER JR.

ERHAPS NO FORM OF GOVERNMENT," OBSERVED LORD Bryce, "needs great leaders as much as democracy." For democracy is not self-executing. It takes leadership to bring democracy to life. Great democratic leaders are visionaries. They have an instinct for their nation's future, a course to steer, a port to seek. Through their capacity for persuasion, they win the consent of their people and call forth democracy's inner resources.

Democracy has been around for a bit, but the 20th century has been the crucial century of its trial, testing and triumph. At the century's start, democracy was thought to be spreading irresistibly across the world. Then the Great War, the war of 1914-18, showed that democracy could not ensure peace. Postwar disillusion activated democracy's two deadly foes: fascism and communism. Soon the Great Depression in the 1930s showed that democracy could not ensure prosperity either, and the totalitarian creeds gathered momentum.

The Second World War found democracy fighting for its life. By 1941 there were only a dozen or so democratic states left on earth. But great leadership emerged in time to rally the democratic cause. Future historians, looking back at this most bloody of centuries, will very likely regard the 32nd President of the U.S., Franklin Delano Roosevelt, as the leader most responsible for mobilizing democratic energies and faith first against economic collapse and then against military terror.

F.D.R. was the best loved and most hated American President of the 20th century. He was loved because, though patrician by birth, upbringing and style, he believed in and fought for plain people—for the "forgotten man" (and woman),

**F.D.R., Eleanor and their five children in 1920, the year he campaigned unsuccessfully for the vice presidency**

for the "third of the nation, ill-housed, ill-clad, ill-nourished." He was loved because he radiated personal charm, joy in his work, optimism for the future. Even Charles de Gaulle, who well knew Roosevelt's disdain for him, succumbed to the "glittering personality," as he put it, of "that artist, that seducer." "Meeting him," said Winston Churchill, "was like uncorking a bottle of champagne."

But he was hated too—hated because he called for change, and the changes he proposed reduced the power, status,

---

**BORN Jan. 30, 1882 in Hyde Park, N.Y.**

**1913 Named Assistant Secretary of the Navy**

**1928-32 Serves as Governor of New York**

**1940-44 Elected to an unprecedented third term; U.S. enters World War II**

**1882** ————————————————————————————————— **1945**

**1921 Contracts polio**

**1932-36 Elected President; begins enacting New Deal legislation**

**1936-40 Re-elected to office; continues New Deal**

**1945 Attends Yalta Conference; dies two months later on April 12**

**MAMA'S BOY F.D.R. in girls' clothes, age 2**

income and self-esteem of those who profited most from the old order. Hatred is happily more fleeting than love. The men who sat in their clubs denouncing "that man in the White House," that "traitor to his class," have died off. Their children and grandchildren mostly find the New Deal reforms familiar, benign and beneficial.

When pollster John Zogby recently asked people to rate the century's Presidents, F.D.R. led the pack, even though only septuagenarians and their elders can remember him in the White House. Historians and political scientists are unanimous in placing F.D.R. with Washington and Lincoln as our three greatest Presidents. Even Republicans have come to applaud this most successful of Democrats. Ronald Reagan voted four times for F.D.R. Newt Gingrich calls F.D.R. the greatest President of the century. Bob Dole praises F.D.R. as an "energetic and inspiring leader during the dark days of the Depression; a tough, single-minded Commander in Chief during World War II; and a statesman."

F.D.R. was not a perfect man. In the service of his objectives, he could be, and often was, devious, guileful, manipulative, evasive, dissembling, underhanded, even ruthless. But he had great strengths. He relished power and organized, or disorganized, his Administration so that conflict among his subordinates would ensure that the big decisions would come to him. A politician to his fingertips, he rejoiced in party combat. "I'm an old campaigner, and I love a good fight," he

would say, and "Judge me by the enemies I have made." An optimist who fought his own brave way back from polio, he brought confidence and hope to a scared and stricken nation.

He was a realist in means but an idealist in ends. Above all, F.D.R. stood for humanity against ideology. The 20th was the most ideological of centuries. Adolf Hitler and Joseph Stalin systematically sacrificed millions to false and terrible dogmas. Even within the democracies, ideologues believed that the Great Depression imposed an either/or choice: if you abandon laissez-faire, you are condemned to total statism. "Partial regimentation cannot be made to work," said Herbert Hoover, "and still maintain live democratic institutions."

Against the worship of abstractions, F.D.R. wanted to find practical ways to help decent men and women struggling day by day to make a happier world for themselves and their children. His technique was, as he said, "bold, persistent experimentation … Take a method and try it. If it fails, admit it frankly and try another. But above all, try something." Except for the part about admitting failure frankly, that was the practice of his Administration.

When he came to office in 1933, laissez-faire had undermined the temples of capitalism, thrown a quarter of the labor force out of work, cut the gross national product almost in half and provoked mutterings of revolution. No one knew why things had gone wrong or how to set them right. Only communists were happy, seeing in the Great Depression

> "The presidency is not merely an administrative office. That's the least of it ... It is pre-eminently a place of moral leadership.
>
> **FRANKLIN DELANO ROOSEVELT**
> September 1932

decisive proof of Karl Marx's prophecy that capitalism would be destroyed by its own contradictions.

Then F.D.R. appeared, a magnificent, serene, exhilarating personality, buoyantly embodying new ideas, new courage, new confidence in America's ability to regain control over its future. His New Deal swiftly introduced measures for social protection, regulation and control. Laissez-faire ideologues and Roosevelt haters cried that he was putting the country on the road to communism, the only alternative permitted by the either/or creed. But Roosevelt understood that Social Security, unemployment compensation, public works, securities regulation, rural electrification, farm-price supports, reciprocal trade agreements, minimum wages and maximum hours, guarantees of collective bargaining and all the rest were saving capitalism from itself.

THE TEST OF OUR PROGRESS," HE SAID IN HIS SECOND Inaugural, "is not whether we add more to the abundance of those who have much; it is whether we provide enough for those who have too little." The job situation improved in the 1930s, aided by the Works Progress Administration, the famous WPA, with which government as employer of last resort built schools, post offices, airfields, parks, bridges, tunnels and sewage systems; protected the environment; and fostered the arts. By the 1940 election, the anticapitalist vote, almost 1 million in 1932, had dwindled to 150,000.

The New Deal never quite solved the problem of unemployment. Though F.D.R. was portrayed as a profligate spender, his largest peacetime deficit was a feeble $3.6 billion in 1936— far less, even when corrected for inflation, than deficits routinely produced 50 years later by Ronald Reagan. It took World War II and the Defense Department to create deficits large enough to wipe out unemployment, proving the case for a compensatory fiscal policy.

Before F.D.R., the U.S. had had a depression every 20 years or so. The built-in economic stabilizers of the New Deal, vociferously denounced by business leaders at the time, have preserved the country against major depressions for more than a half-century. F.D.R.'s signal domestic achievement was to rescue capitalism from the capitalists.

"We are fighting," he said in 1936, "to save a great and precious form of govern-

ment for ourselves and for the world." F.D.R.'s brilliant (and sometimes not so brilliant) improvisations restored America's faith in democratic institutions. Elsewhere on the planet, democracy was under assault. Hitler was on the march in Europe. Japan had invaded China and dreamed of a Greater East Asia Co-Prosperity Sphere under Japanese domination.

F.D.R.'s education in foreign affairs had been at the hands of two Presidents he greatly admired. Theodore Roosevelt, his kinsman (a fifth cousin), taught him national-interest, balance-of-power geopolitics. Woodrow Wilson, whom he served as Assistant Secretary of the Navy, gave him the vision of a world beyond balances of power, an international order founded on the collective maintenance of the peace. F.D.R.'s internationalism used T.R.'s realism as the heart of Wilson's idealism.

But Americans, disenchanted with their participation in the Great War, had turned their backs on the world and reverted to isolationism. Rigid neutrality acts denied the President authority to discriminate between aggressor states and their victims and thereby prevented the U.S. from throwing its weight against aggression.

To awaken his country from its isolationist slumber, Roosevelt began a long, urgent, eloquent campaign of popular education, warning that unchecked aggression abroad would ultimately endanger the U.S. itself. "Let no one imagine that America will escape, that America may expect mercy," he said. The debate in 1940-41 between isolationists and

**Roosevelt's refusal to be beaten by crippling polio was central to his inner strength. Here he greets a wounded veteran in 1942**

Four years after polio struck, Roosevelt relaxes at his favorite spa in Warm Springs, Ga.

interventionists was the most passionate political argument of my lifetime. It came to an abrupt end when Japanese bombs fell on Pearl Harbor. As war leader, F.D.R. picked an extraordinary team of generals and admirals. In partnership with Churchill, he presided over the vital strategic decisions. And also, in the footsteps of Wilson, he was determined that victory should produce a framework for lasting world peace.

He saw the war as bringing about historic changes—the rise of Russia and China, for example, and the end of Western colonialism. He tried to persuade the British to give India its independence and tried to stop the French from repossessing Indochina. In the Four Freedoms and, with Churchill, in the Atlantic Charter, he proclaimed war aims in words that continue to express the world's aspirations today.

Remembering America's reversion to isolationism after World War I, he set out to involve the U.S. in postwar structures while the war was still on and the country still in an internationalist frame of mind. "Anybody who thinks that isolationism is dead in this country is crazy," he said privately. "As soon as this war is over, it may well be stronger than ever."

In a series of conferences in 1944, he committed the country to international mechanisms in a variety of fields—finance and trade, relief and reconstruction, food and agriculture, civil aviation. Most of all, he saw the United Nations, in the words of the diplomat Charles E. Bohlen, as "the only device that could keep the U.S. from slipping back into isolationism." He arranged for the U.N.'s founding conference to take place in San Francisco before the war was over (though it turned out to be after his own death in April 1945 at the age of 63).

The great riddle for the peace was the Soviet Union. Perhaps Roosevelt, as some argue, should have conditioned aid to Russia during the war on pledges of postwar good behavior. But the fate of the second front in the west depended on the Red Army's holding down Nazi divisions in the east, and neither Roosevelt nor Churchill wanted to delay Stalin's military offensives—or to drive him to make a separate peace with Hitler.

With the war approaching its end, the two democratic leaders met Stalin at Yalta. Some say that this meeting brought about the division of Europe. In fact, far from endorsing Soviet control of Eastern Europe, Roosevelt and Churchill secured from Stalin pledges of "the earliest possible establishment through free elections of governments responsive to the will of the people." Stalin had to break the Yalta agreements to achieve his ends—which would seem to prove the agreements were more in the Western than the Soviet interest. In fact, Eastern Europe today is what the Yalta Declarations mandated in 1945.

Take a look at our present world. It is manifestly not Adolf Hitler's world. His Thousand-Year Reich turned out to have a brief and bloody run of a dozen years. It is manifestly not Joseph Stalin's world. That ghastly world self-destructed before our eyes. Nor is it Winston Churchill's world. Empire and its glories have long since vanished into history.

The world we live in today is Franklin Roosevelt's world. Of the figures who for good or evil dominated the planet 60 years ago, he would be least surprised by the shape of things at the millennium. And confident as he was of the power and vitality of democracy, he would welcome the challenges posed by the century to come. Roosevelt, said Isaiah Berlin, was one of the few statesmen in any century "who seemed to have no fear at all of the future." ∎

*Historian Arthur Schlesinger Jr., who won Pulitzer Prizes for his books on Presidents Jackson and Kennedy, is the author of* The Age of Roosevelt. *He is currently at work on his memoirs.*

# In the Crucible of History

## A quartet of memorable Presidents helped shape the century

### Harry S Truman

Truman's nondescript appearance, his shoot-from-the-hip diatribes, his taste for mediocre cronies—all the old cavils against him have faded over the years, as Americans realize he inherited a world's worth of tough problems and reacted decisively and wisely.

### Woodrow Wilson

Wilson created the Federal Reserve System, guided the U.S. through World War I and devised the League of Nations. But the stern idealist failed to convince Americans to forgo isolationism and join his visionary League.

### Richard Nixon

Nixon's bold diplomacy and sure feel for the pulse of the "silent majority" made him TIME'S Man of the Year in 1971 and '72. But triumphant breakthroughs like his visit to China were overshadowed by his self-induced downfall.

### Lyndon B. Johnson

Larger than life—almost larger than his native Texas—Johnson was one of the most gifted politicians to serve as President. He capitalized on the nation's shock over the murder of John F. Kennedy to pass historic civil rights legislation and a cornucopia of liberal federal programs he called the "Great Society." But his legacy was dimmed when he led America ever deeper into an unwinnable war in the jungles of Vietnam.

# Adolf
# Hitler

## The avatar of fascism posed the century's greatest threat to democracy and redefined the meaning of evil for all time

**By ELIE WIESEL**

NOT BEING A PROFESSIONAL HISTORIAN, I TAKE ON this essay with fear and trembling. That's because, although defeated, although dead, this man is frightening. What was the secret of his power over his listeners? His demagogic appeal to immoderation, to excess and to simplifying hate? They spoke of his intuitive powers and his "luck" (he escaped several attempts on his life).

Adolf Hitler or the incarnation of absolute evil: this is how future generations will remember the all-powerful Führer of the criminal Third Reich. Compared with him, his peers Mussolini and Franco were novices. Under his hypnotic gaze, humanity crossed a threshold from which one could see the abyss.

At the same time that he terrorized his adversaries, he knew how to please, impress and charm the very interlocutors from whom he wanted support. Diplomats and journalists insist as much on his charm as they do on his temper tantrums. The savior admired by his own as he dragged them into his madness, the Satan and exterminating angel feared and hated by all others, Hitler led his people to a shameful defeat without precedent. That his political and strategic ambitions have created a dividing line in the history of this turbulent and tormented century is undeniable: there is a before and an after. By the breadth of his crimes, which have attained a quasi-ontological dimension, he surpasses all his predecessors: as a result of Hitler, man is defined by what makes him inhuman. With Hitler at the head of a gigantic laboratory, life itself seems to have changed.

How did this Austrian without title or position manage to get himself elected head of a German nation renowned for its civilizing mission? How to explain the success of his cheap demagogy in the heart of a people so proud of having inherited the genius of a Wolfgang von Goethe and an Immanuel Kant?

Was there no resistance to his disastrous projects? There was. But it was too feeble, too weak and too late to succeed. German society had rallied behind him: the judicial, the educational, the industrial and the economic establishments gave him their support.

Few politicians of this century have aroused, in their lifetime, such love and so much hate; few have inspired so much historical and psychological research after their death. Even today, works on his enigmatic personality and his cursed career are best sellers everywhere. Some are good, others are less good, but all seem to respond to an authentic curiosity on the part of a public haunted by memory and the desire to understand.

We think we know everything about the nefarious forces that shaped his destiny: his unhappy childhood, his frustrated adolescence; his artistic disappointments; his wound received on the front during World War I; his taste for spectacle, his constant disdain for social and military aristocracies; his relationship with Eva Braun, who adored him; the cult of the very death he feared; his lack of scruples with regard to his former comrades of the SA, whom he ordered assassinated in 1934; his endless hatred of Jews, whose survival enraged him—each and every phase of his official and private life has found its chroniclers, its biographers.

And yet. There are, in all these givens, elements that escape us. How did this unstable paranoid find it within himself to impose gigantic hope as an immutable ideal that motivated his nation almost until the end? Would he have come to power if Germany were not going through endless economic crises, or if the winners in 1918 had not imposed on it conditions that represented a national humiliation against which the German patriotic fiber could only revolt?

We would be wrong to forget: Hitler came to power in January 1933 by the most legitimate means. His

**BORN** April 20, 1889, in Braunau, Austria

**1889**

**INFANT**
The Austrian would move to Germany at 24

**1919 Helps form the Nazi Party in war-weakened Germany**

**1923 Leads an abortive putsch in Munich beer hall**

**1924 Starts writing** *Mein Kampf* **in prison**

**1933 Becomes dictator of Germany, prepares the nation for war and a "Final Solution" to the "Jewish question"**

**1945**

**1939 Invades Poland and starts World War II**

**1945 Commits suicide**

Nationalist Socialist Party won a majority in the parliamentary elections. The aging Field Marshal Paul von Hindenburg had no choice but to allow him, at age 43, to form the new government, marking the end of the Weimar Republic. And the beginning of the Third Reich, which, according to Hitler, would last 1,000 years.

From that moment on, events cascaded. The burning of the Reichstag came only a little before the openings of the first concentration camps, established for members of the opposition. Fear descended on the country and squeezed it

**" If Hitler invaded hell, I would make at least a favorable reference to the devil in the House of Commons. "**

**SIR WINSTON CHURCHILL, 1941, justifying his support for Stalin after Hitler invaded Russia**

> ## " This war... is one of those elemental conflicts which usher in a new millennium and which shake the world. "
>
> **HITLER, in speech to the Reichstag, 1942**

in a vise. Great writers, musicians and painters went into exile to France and the U.S. Many Jews with foresight emigrated toward Palestine. The air of Hitler's Germany was becoming more and more suffocating. Those who preferred to wait, thinking that the Nazi regime would not last, could not last, would regret it later, when it was too late.

The fact is that Hitler was beloved by his people—not the military, at least not in the beginning, but by the average Germans who pledged to him an affection, a tenderness and a fidelity that bordered on the irrational. It was idolatry on a national scale. One had to see the crowds that acclaimed him. And the women who were attracted to him. And the young who in his presence went into ecstasy. Did they not see the hateful mask that covered his face? Did they not divine the catastrophe he bore within himself?

VIOLATING THE TREATY OF VERSAILLES, WHICH limited the German army to 100,000 men, Hitler embarked on a rearmament program of massive scale: fighter planes, tanks, submarines. His goal? It was enough to read *Mein Kampf,* written in prison after the abortive coup of 1923 in Munich, to divine its contours: to become, once again, a global superpower, capable and desirous of reconquering lost territory, and others as well.

And the free world let it happen.

His army entered the Rhineland in 1936. A tangible reaction from France and Britain would have led to his fall. But since nothing happened, Hitler played on the "cowardice" of democratic principles. That cow-

ardice was confirmed by the shameful 1938 Munich Agreement, by which France and Britain betrayed their alliance with Czechoslovakia and abandoned it like a dead weight. At every turn, Hitler derided his generals and their lack of audacity. In 1939 he stupefied the entire world by reaching a nonaggression pact with Stalin. Though they had never met, the two dictators appeared to get along perfectly; it was said that a sort of empathy existed between them. Poland paid the price of this unnatural "friendship"; cut in two, it ceased to exist as a state.

Hitler also counted on Stalin's naiveté. In a sense he was right. According to all witnesses, Stalin had total confidence in Hitler. To humor Hitler's extreme anti-Semitic sensibilities, the Soviet hierarchy withdrew certain Jews, such as Maxim Litvinov, the Soviet Foreign Minister, from the international scene. Stalin's order to honor the commercial agreements between the two countries was scrupulously executed, at all levels, until the beginning of hostilities: the day of German aggression, one still saw Soviet trains stuffed with raw materials heading toward German factories.

Was Hitler shrewder than Stalin? Certainly he was more tenacious than his French and British adversaries. Winston Churchill was the only man of state who unmasked Hitler immediately and refused to let himself be duped by Hitler's repeated promises that this time he was making his "last territorial demand."

And yet. In his own "logic," Hitler was persuaded for a

**Hitler celebrates a Harvest Day Festival with worshipping Germans, 1937**

fairly long time that the German and British people had every reason to get along and divide up spheres of influence throughout the world. He did not understand British obstinacy in its resistance to his racial philosophy and to the practical ends it engendered.

In fact, he wanted to swallow up Russia, Poland, Ukraine and the Baltic countries to augment *lebensraum:* Germany's vital space. But then why did he launch his destructive war against London? Why did he declare war against the U.S.? Solely to please his Japanese ally? Why did he mandate a policy of cruelty in the Soviet territories occupied by his armies, when certain segments of the population there were ready to greet them with flowers? And finally, why did he invest so much energy in his hatred of Jews? Why did the night trains that took them to their death have priority over the military convoys that were taking badly needed troops to the front? His dark obsession with the "Jewish question" and its "Final Solution" will be long remembered, for it has evocative names that paralyze men's hearts with terror: Treblinka, Auschwitz and Belzec.

After Erwin Rommel's defeat in North Africa, after the debacle at Stalingrad and even when the landings in Normandy were imminent, Hitler

**The music lover at an orchestra rehearsal in Munich, 1938**

and his entourage still came up with the Final Solution. In his testament, drafted in an underground bunker just hours before his suicide in Berlin, Hitler returns again to this hatred of the Jewish people that had never left him.

But in the same testament, he settles his score with the German people. He wants them to be sacked, destroyed, reduced to misery and shame for having failed him by denying him his glory. The former corporal become commander in chief of all his armies and convinced of his strategic and political genius was not prepared to recognize his own responsibility for the defeat of his Reich.

His kingdom collapsed after 12 years in a war that remains the most atrocious, the most brutal and the deadliest in history. But which, by the same token, allowed several large figures to emerge. Their names have become legendary: Eisenhower, Montgomery, De Gaulle, Patton ...

But when later we evoke the 20th century, among the first names that will surge to mind will be that of a fanatic with a mustache who thought to reign by selling the soul of his people to the thousand demons of hate and of death. ∎

**The Führer's great gamble— waging war on two fronts— proved to be his downfall**

*Elie Wiesel, a Holocaust survivor and Nobel laureate, is a professor in the humanities at Boston University.*

Victory! Churchill is hailed by cheering Londoners after the German surrender, 1945

# Winston Churchill

## The master statesman stood alone against fascism and renewed the world's faith in the superiority of democracy

**By JOHN KEEGAN**

THE POLITICAL HISTORY OF THE 20TH CENTURY CAN be written as the biographies of six men: Lenin, Stalin, Hitler, Mao Zedong, Franklin Roosevelt and Winston Churchill. The first four were totalitarians who made or used revolutions to create monstrous dictatorships. Roosevelt and Churchill differed from them in being democrats. And Churchill differed from Roosevelt—while both were war leaders, Churchill was uniquely stirred by the challenge of war and found his fulfillment in leading the democracies to victory.

Churchill came of a military dynasty. His ancestor John Churchill had been created first Duke of Marlborough in 1702 for his victories against Louis XIV early in the War of the Spanish Succession. Churchill was born in 1874 in Blenheim Palace, the house built by the nation for Marlborough. As a young man of undistinguished academic accomplishment—he was admitted to Sandhurst after two failed attempts—he entered the army as a cavalry officer. He took enthusiastically to soldiering (and perhaps even more enthusiastically to regimental polo playing) and between 1895 and 1898 managed to see three campaigns: Spain's struggle in Cuba in 1895, the North-West Frontier campaign in India 1897 and the Sudan campaign of 1898, where he took part in what is often described as the British Army's last cavalry charge, at Omdurman.

Even at 24, Churchill was steely: "I never felt the slightest nervousness," he wrote to his mother. "[I] felt as cool as I do now." In Cuba he was present as a war correspondent, and in India and the Sudan he was present both as a war correspon-

dent and as a serving officer. Thus he revealed two other aspects of his character: a literary bent and an interest in public affairs.

He was to write all his life. His life of Marlborough is one of the great English biographies, and *The History of the Second World War* helped win him a Nobel Prize for Literature. Writing, however, never fully engaged his energies. Politics consumed him. His father Lord Randolph Churchill was a brilliant political failure. Early in life, Winston determined to succeed where his father had failed. His motives were twofold. His father had despised him. Writing in August 1893 to Winston's grandmother, the dowager Duchess of Marlborough, he said the boy lacked "cleverness, knowledge and any capacity for settled work. He has a great talent for show-off, exaggeration and make-believe." His disapproval surely stung, but Churchill reacted by venerating his father's memory. Winston fought to restore his father's honor in Parliament (where it had been dented by the Conservative Party). Thirty years after Lord Randolph's death, Winston wrote, "All my dreams of comradeship were ended. There remained for me only to pursue his aims and vindicate his memory."

Churchill entered Parliament in 1901 at age 26. In 1904 he left the Conservative Party to join the Liberals, in part out of calculation: the Liberals were the coming party, and in its ranks he soon achieved high office. He became Home Secretary in 1910 and First Lord of the Admiralty in 1911. Thus it was as political head of the Royal Navy at the outbreak of the First World War in 1914 that he stepped onto the world stage.

A passionate believer in the navy's historic strategic role,

**BORN Nov. 30, 1874, in Oxfordshire, England**

**1874**

**FAME Captured by Boers in South Africa in 1899, he escapes and is lionized**

**1901 Enters House of Commons**

**1908 Marries Clementine Hozier**

**1911-15, 1939-40 Serves as First Lord of the Admiralty**

**1940-45, 1951-55 Prime Minister of Great Britain**

**1953 Knighted; wins Nobel Prize for Literature**

**1964 Retires from House of Commons**

**1965**

**1965 Dies in London**

> # "It was the nation... that had the lion's heart. I had the luck to be called upon to give the roar."
>
> **WINSTON CHURCHILL, celebrating his 80th birthday in 1954**

he immediately committed the Royal Naval Division to an intervention in the Flanders campaign in 1914. Frustrated by the stalemate in Belgium and France that followed, he initiated the Allies' only major effort to outflank the Germans on the Western Front by sending the navy, and later a large force of the army, to the Mediterranean. At Gallipoli in 1915, this Anglo-French force struggled to break the defenses that blocked access to the Black Sea. It was a heroic failure that forced Churchill's resignation and led to his political eclipse.

It was effectively to last nearly 25 years. Despite his readmission to office in 1917, after a spell commanding an infantry battalion on the Western Front, he failed to re-establish the reputation as a future national statesman he had won before the war. Dispirited, he chose the issue of the Liberal Party's support for the first government formed by the Labour Party in 1924 to rejoin the Conservatives, after a spell when he had been out of Parliament altogether. The Conservative Prime Minister appointed Churchill Chancellor of the Exchequer, but when he returned the country to the gold standard, it proved financially disastrous, and he further weakened his political position by opposing measures to grant India limited self-government. He resigned office in 1931 and entered what appeared to be a terminal political decline.

Churchill was truly a romantic, but also truly a democrat. He had returned to the gold standard, for instance, because he cherished, for romantic reasons, Britain's status as a great financial power. He had opposed limited self-government for India because he cherished, for equally romantic reasons, Britain's imperial history. It was to prove more important that as a democrat, he was disgusted by the rise of totalitarian systems in Europe. In 1935 he warned the House of Commons of the importance not only of "self-preservation but also of the human and the world cause of the preservation of free governments and of Western civilization against the ever advancing sources of authority and despotism."

**Churchill's colorful bulldog tenacity gave Britons—like these sailors in 1943—an icon to rally around**

His anti-Bolshevik policies had failed. By espousing anti-Nazi policies in his wilderness years between 1933 and 1939, he ensured that when the moment of final confrontation between Britain and Hitler came in 1940, he stood out as the one man in whom the nation could place its trust. He had decried the prewar appeasement policies of the Conservative leaders Baldwin and Chamberlain. When Chamberlain lost the confidence of Parliament, Churchill was installed as Prime Minister.

Churchill campaigning with his wife Clementine and daughter Diana, center, in 1931. He would be out of power until May 1940

His was a bleak inheritance. Following the total defeat of France, Britain truly, in his words, "stood alone." It had no substantial allies and, for much of 1940, lay under threat of German invasion and under constant German air attack. He nevertheless refused Hitler's offers of peace, organized a successful air defense that led to the victory of the Battle of Britain and meanwhile sent most of what remained of the British army, after its escape from the humiliation of Dunkirk, to the Middle East to oppose Hitler's Italian ally, Mussolini.

THIS WAS ONE OF THE BOLDEST STRATEGIC DECISIONS in history. Convinced that Hitler could not invade Britain while the Royal Navy and its protecting Royal Air Force remained intact, he dispatched the army to a remote theater of war to open a second front against the Nazi alliance. Its victories against Mussolini during 1940-41 both humiliated and infuriated Hitler, while its intervention in Greece, to oppose Hitler's invasion of the Balkans, disrupted the Nazi dictator's plans to conclude German conquests in Europe by defeating Russia.

Churchill's tendency to conduct strategy by impulse infuriated his advisers. His chief of staff Alan Brooke complained that every day Churchill had 10 ideas, only one of which was good—and he did not know which one. Yet Churchill the romantic showed acute realism in his reaction to Russia's predicament. He reviled communism. Required to accept a communist ally in a struggle against a Nazi enemy, he did so not only willingly but generously. He sent a large proportion of Britain's war production to Russia by Arctic convoys, even at a time when the convoys from America to Britain, which alone spared the country starvation, suffered devastating U-boat attacks.

From the outset of his premiership, Churchill, half American by birth, had rested his hope of ultimate victory in U.S. intervention. He had established a personal relationship with President Roosevelt that he hoped would flower into a war-winning alliance. Roosevelt's reluctance to commit the U.S. beyond an association "short of war" did not dent his optimism. He always hoped events would work his way. The

decision by Japan, Hitler's ally, to attack the American Pacific fleet at Pearl Harbor on Dec. 7, 1941, justified his hopes. That evening he confided to himself, "So we had won after all."

America's entry into the Second World War marked the high point of Churchill's statesmanship. Britain, demographically, industrially and financially, had entered the war weaker than either of its eventual allies, the Soviet Union and the U.S. Defeats in 1940 had weakened it further, as had the liquidation of its international investments to fund its early war efforts. During 1942, the prestige Britain had won as Hitler's only enemy allowed Churchill to sustain parity of leadership in the anti-Nazi alliance with Roosevelt and Stalin.

Churchill understandably exulted in the success of the D-day invasion when it came in 1944. By then it was the Russo-American rather than the Anglo-American nexus, however, that dominated the alliance, as he ruefully recognized at the last Big Three conference in February 1945. Shortly afterward he suffered the domestic humiliation of losing the general election and with it the premiership. He was to return to power in 1951 and remain until April 1955, when ill health and visibly failing powers caused him to resign.

It would have been kinder to his reputation had he not returned. He was not an effective peacetime Prime Minister. His name had been made, and he stood unchallengeable, as the greatest of all Britain's war leaders. It was not only his own country, though, that owed him a debt. So too did the world of free men and women to whom he had made a constant and inclusive appeal in his magnificent speeches from embattled Britain in 1940 and 1941. Churchill did not merely hate tyranny, he despised it. The contempt he breathed for dictators—renewed in his Iron Curtain speech at Fulton, Mo., at the outset of the cold war—strengthened the West's faith in the moral superiority of democracy and the inevitability of its triumph. ∎

*Historian John Keegan, the author of* A History of Warfare, *is the defense and military specialist for London's* Daily Telegraph.

# Great Speeches of the Century
In moments of crisis, words became beacons of freedom

### Franklin Delano Roosevelt
## The 1933 Inauguration
This is pre-eminently the time to speak the truth, the whole truth, frankly and boldly. Nor need we shrink from honestly facing conditions in our country today. This great nation will endure as it has endured, will revive and will prosper. So, first of all, let me assert my firm belief that the only thing we have to fear is fear itself—nameless, unreasoning, unjustified terror which paralyzes needed efforts to convert retreat into advance. In every dark hour of our national life a leadership of frankness and vigor has met with that understanding and support of the people themselves which is essential to victory. I am convinced that you will again give that support to leadership in these critical days... We face the arduous days that lie before us in the warm courage of national unity; with the clear consciousness of seeking old and precious moral values; with the clean satisfaction that comes from the stern performance of duty by old and young alike... In this dedication of a nation we humbly ask the blessing of God. May He protect each and every one of us. May He guide me in the days to come.

### Winston Churchill
## Before Parliament, June 1940
I have, myself, full confidence that if all do their duty, if nothing is neglected... we shall prove ourselves once again able to defend our island home, to ride out the storm of war, and to outlive the menace of tyranny, if necessary for years, if necessary alone... The British Empire and the French Republic, linked together in their cause and in their need, will defend to the death their native soil, aiding each other like good comrades to the utmost of their strength. Even though large tracts of Europe... have fallen or may fall into the grip of the Gestapo and all the odious apparatus of Nazi rule, we shall not flag or fail. We shall go on to the end, we shall fight in France, we shall fight on the seas and oceans, we shall fight with growing confidence and growing strength in the air, we shall defend our island, whatever the cost may be, we shall fight on the beaches, we shall fight on the landing grounds, we shall fight in the fields and in the streets, we shall fight in the hills; we shall never surrender.

## John F. Kennedy
### The 1961 Inauguration

In the long history of the world, only a few generations have been granted the role of defending freedom in its hour of maximum danger. I do not shrink from this responsibility—I welcome it. I do not believe that any of us would exchange places with any other people or any other generation... And so, my fellow Americans, ask not what your country can do for you— ask what you can do for your country. My fellow citizens of the world, ask not what America will do for you, but what together we can do for the freedom of man. Finally, whether you are citizens of America or citizens of the world, ask of us here the same high standards of strength... which we ask of you. With a good conscience our only sure reward, with history the final judge of our deeds, let us go forth to lead the land we love ... knowing that here on earth God's work must be truly our own.

## Martin Luther King Jr.
### On the Mall in Washington, 1963

I say to you today, my friends, that in spite of the difficulties and frustrations of the moment I still have a dream. It is a dream deeply rooted in the American Dream... I have a dream that one day on the red hills of Georgia the sons of former slaves and the sons of former slave owners will be able to sit down together at the table of brotherhood... I have a dream that my four little children will one day live in a nation where they will not be judged by the color of their skin but by the content of their character. I have a dream today... And if America is to be a great nation this must become true. So let freedom ring from the prodigious hilltops of New Hampshire. Let freedom ring from the mighty mountains of New York... From every mountainside, let freedom ring. When we let freedom ring... we will be able to speed up that day when all God's children, black men and white men, Jews and Gentiles, Protestants and Catholics, will be able to join hands and sing in the words of the old Negro spiritual, "Free at last! Free at last! Thank God Almighty, we are free at last!"

Honoring the boys
back from the
front, June 1942

# Eleanor
# Roosevelt

## America's most influential First Lady blazed paths for women and led the battle for social justice everywhere

By DORIS KEARNS GOODWIN

**W**HEN ELEANOR ROOSEVELT JOURNEYED TO New York City a week after her husband's funeral in April 1945, a cluster of reporters were waiting at the door of her Washington Square apartment. "The story is over," she said simply, assuming that her words and opinions would no longer be of interest once her husband was dead and she was no longer First Lady. She could not have been more mistaken. As the years have passed, Eleanor Roosevelt's influence and stature have continued to grow. Today she remains a powerful inspiration to leaders in both the civil rights and women's movements.

Eleanor shattered the ceremonial mold in which the role of the First Lady had traditionally been fashioned, and reshaped it around her own skills and deep commitment to social reform. She gave a voice to people who did not have access to power. She was the first woman to speak in front of a national convention, to write a syndicated column, to earn money as a lecturer, to be a radio commentator and to hold regular press conferences.

The path to this unique position of power had not been easy. The only daughter of an alcoholic father and a beautiful but aloof mother who was openly disappointed by Eleanor's lack of a pretty face, Eleanor was plagued by insecurity and shyness. An early marriage to her handsome fifth cousin once removed, Franklin Roosevelt, increased her insecurity and took away her one source of confidence: her work in a New York City settlement

**A honeymoon gondola ride in Venice, 1905; picture by F.D.R.**

**BORN Oct. 11, 1884, in New York City**

**EQUESTRIAN An early family picture, undated**

**1905 Marries distant cousin Franklin Delano Roosevelt**

**1918 Discovers F.D.R.'s affair with Lucy Mercer**

**1932 F.D.R., crippled by polio since 1921, is elected President. Eleanor becomes his eyes and ears**

**1948 Helps secure passage of the U.N.'s Universal Declaration of Human Rights**

**1962**

**1962 Dies in New York City on Nov. 7**

# "Can't you muzzle that wife of yours?... Do you have lace on your panties for allowing her to speak out so much?... Why can't she stay home and tend to her knitting?

**QUESTIONS put to F.D.R. about his wife's unrelenting outspokenness on political issues**

house. "For 10 years, I was always just getting over having a baby or about to have another one," she later lamented, "so my occupations were considerably restricted."

But 13 years after her marriage, and after bearing six children, Eleanor resumed the search for her identity. The voyage began with a shock: the discovery in 1918 of love letters revealing that Franklin was involved with her young social secretary, Lucy Mercer. "The bottom dropped out of my own particular world," she later said. "I faced myself, my surroundings, my world, honestly for the first time." There was talk of divorce, but when Franklin promised never to see Lucy again, the marriage continued. For Eleanor a new path had opened, a possibility of standing apart from Franklin. No longer would she define herself solely in terms of his wants and needs. A new relationship was forged, on terms wholly different from the old.

She turned her energies to a variety of reformist organizations, joining a circle of postsuffrage feminists dedicated to the abolition of child labor, the establishment of a minimum wage and the passage of legislation to protect workers. In the process she discovered that she had talents—for public speaking, for organizing, for articulating social problems. She formed an extraordinary constellation of lifelong female friends, who helped to assuage an enduring sense of loneliness. When Franklin was paralyzed by polio in 1921, her activism became an even more vital force. She became Franklin's

"eyes and ears," traveling the country gathering the grass-roots knowledge he needed to understand the people he governed.

They made an exceptional team. She was more earnest, less devious, less patient, less fun, more uncompromisingly moral; he possessed the more trustworthy political talent, the more finely tuned sense of timing, the better feel for the citizenry, the smarter understanding of how to get things done. But they were linked by indissoluble bonds. Together they mobilized the American people to effect enduring changes in the political and social landscape of the nation.

NOWHERE WAS ELEANOR'S INFLUENCE GREATER THAN in civil rights. In her travels around the country, she developed a sophisticated understanding of race relations. When she first began inspecting New Deal programs in the South, she was stunned to find that African Americans were being systematically discriminated against at every turn. Citing statistics to back up her story, she would interrupt her husband at any time, barging into his cocktail hour when he wanted only to relax, cross-examining him at dinner, handing him memos to read late at night. But her confrontational style compelled him to sign a series of Executive Orders barring discrimination in the administration of various New Deal projects. From that point on, blacks' share in the work projects expanded, and Eleanor's independent legacy began to grow.

**At the U.N., Eleanor fought the cold war alongside John Foster Dulles (left) and George Marshall, 1947**

After F.D.R.'s death, Eleanor stayed in the public eye; here she enjoys a picnic in 1948

She understood, for instance, the importance of symbolism in fighting discrimination. In 1938, while attending the Southern Conference for Human Welfare in Birmingham, Ala., she refused to abide by a segregation ordinance that required her to sit in the white section of the auditorium, apart from her black friends. The following year, she publicly resigned from the Daughters of the American Revolution after it barred the black singer Marian Anderson from its auditorium.

During World War II, Eleanor remained an uncompromising voice on civil rights, insisting that America could not fight racism abroad while tolerating it at home. Progress was slow, but her continuing intervention led to broadened opportunities for blacks in the factories and shipyards at home and in the armed forces overseas. Her positions on civil rights were far in advance of her time. Ten years before the Supreme Court rejected the "separate but equal" doctrine, Eleanor argued that equal facilities were not enough: "The basic fact of segregation, which warps and twists the lives of our Negro population, [is] itself discriminatory."

There were other warps and twists that caught her eye. Long before the contemporary women's movement provided ideological arguments for women's rights, Eleanor instinctively challenged institutions that failed to provide equal opportunity for women. As First Lady, she held more than 300 press conferences that she cleverly restricted to women journalists, knowing that news organizations all over the country would be forced to hire their first female reporter in order to have access to the First Lady.

Through her speeches and her columns, she provided a powerful voice in the campaign to recruit women workers to the factories during the war. "If I were of debutante age, I would go into a factory, where I could learn a skill and be useful," Eleanor told young women, cautioning them against marrying too hastily before they had a chance to expand their horizons. She was instrumental in securing the first government funds ever allotted for the building of child-care centers. And when women workers were unceremoniously fired as the war came to an end, she fought to stem the tide. She argued on principle that everyone who wanted to work had a right to be productive, and she railed against the closing of the child-care centers as a shortsighted response to a fundamental social need. What the women workers needed, she said, was the courage to ask for their rights with a loud voice.

For her own part, she never let the intense criticism that she encountered silence her. "If I ... worried about mudslinging, I would have been dead long ago." Yet she insisted that she was not a feminist. She did not believe, she maintained, that "women should be judged, when it comes to appointing them or electing them, purely because they are women." She wanted to see the country "get away from considering a man or woman from the point of view of religion, color or sex." But the story of her life—her insistence on her right to an identity of her own apart from her husband and her family, her constant struggle against depression and insecurity, her ability to turn her vulnerabilities into strengths—provides an enduring example of a feminist who transcended the dictates of her times to become one of the century's most powerful and effective advocates for social justice. ∎

*Doris Kearns Goodwin is a Pulitzer-prizewinning author, historian and political analyst.*

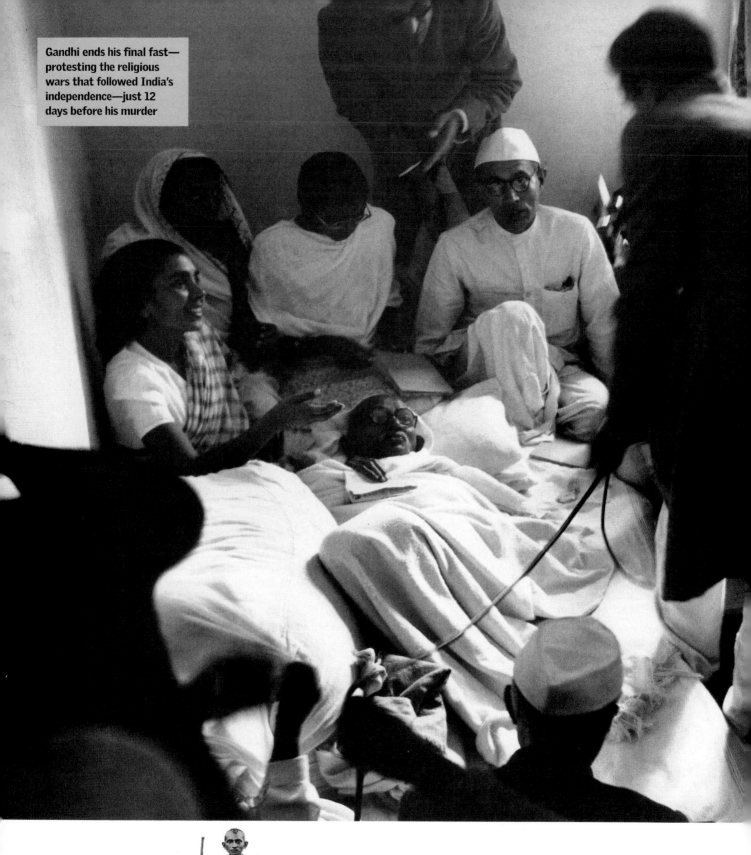

Gandhi ends his final fast—protesting the religious wars that followed India's independence—just 12 days before his murder

**BORN**
Oct. 2, 1869, in Porbandar, India

1869

**PROTESTER** In 1914, fighting British racial laws in South Africa

**1893** Goes to South Africa and battles for the rights of Indians

**1930** Leads hundreds on a long Salt March to Dandi to protest a tax on salt

**1947** Negotiates an end to 190 years of British colonial rule in India

1948

**1915-20** Begins his struggle for India's independence

**1948** Killed by a fanatic opposed to Gandhi's tolerance of other religions

# Mohandas
# Gandhi

## His philosophy of nonviolence and his passion for independence began a drive for freedom that doomed colonialism

### By SALMAN RUSHDIE

A THIN INDIAN MAN WITH NOT MUCH HAIR SITS ALONE ON A bare floor, wearing nothing but a loincloth and a pair of cheap spectacles, studying the clutch of handwritten notes in his hand. The black-and-white photograph takes up a full page in the newspaper. In the top left-hand corner of the page, in full color, is a small rainbow-striped apple. Below this, there's a slangily American injunction to "Think Different." Such is the present-day power of international Big Business. Even the greatest of the dead may summarily be drafted into its image ad campaigns. Once, a half-century ago, this bony man shaped a nation's struggle for freedom. But that, as they say, is history. Now Gandhi models for Apple. His thoughts don't really count in this new incarnation. What counts is that he is considered to be "on message," in line with the corporate philosophy of Apple.

The advertisement is odd enough to be worth dissecting a little. Obviously it is rich in unintentional comedy. M.K. Gandhi, as the photograph itself demonstrates, was a passionate opponent of modernity and technology, preferring the pencil to the typewriter, the loincloth to the business suit, the plowed field to the belching manufactory. Had the word processor been invented in his lifetime, he would almost certainly have found it abhorrent. The very term word processor, with its overly technological ring, is unlikely to have found favor.

"Think Different." Gandhi, in his younger days a sophisticated and Westernized lawyer, did indeed change his thinking more radically than most people do. Ghanshyam Das Birla, one of the merchant princes who backed him, once said, "He was more modern than I. But he made a conscious decision to go back to the Middle Ages." This is not, presumably, the revolutionary new direction in thought that the good folks at Apple are seeking to encourage.

Gandhi today is up for grabs. He has become abstract, ahistorical, postmodern, no longer a man in and of his time but a freeloading concept, a part of the available stock of cultural symbols, an image that can be borrowed, used, distorted, reinvented to fit many different purposes, and to the devil with historicity or truth.

Richard Attenborough's much-Oscared movie *Gandhi* struck me, when it was first released, as an example of this type of unhistorical Western saintmaking. Here was Gandhi-as-guru, purveying that fashionable product, the Wisdom of the East; and Gandhi-as-Christ, dying (and, before that, frequently going on hunger strike) so that others might live. His philosophy of nonviolence seemed to work by embarrassing the

Prophet motive: the Apple Gandhi ad

The advocate of the poorest everywhere, Gandhi visits textile mills in Lancashire, 1931

he was as rich and devious a figure as that glorious name suggests.

Entirely unafraid of the British, he was nevertheless afraid of the dark, and always slept with a light burning by his bedside. He believed passionately in the unity of all the peoples of India, yet his failure to keep the Muslim leader Mohammed Ali Jinnah within the Indian National Congress's fold led to the partition of the country. (For all his vaunted selflessness and modesty, he made no move to object when Jinnah was attacked during a Congress session for calling him "Mr. Gandhi" instead of "Mahatma," and booed off the stage by Gandhi's supporters. Later, his withdrawal, under pressure from Jawaharlal Nehru and Vallabhbhai Patel, of a last-ditch offer to Jinnah of the prime ministership itself, ended the last faint chance of avoiding partition.)

He was determined to live his life as an ascetic, but, as the poet Sarojini Naidu joked, it cost the nation a fortune to keep Gandhi living in poverty. His entire philosophy privileged the village way over that of the city, yet he was always financially dependent on the support of industrial billionaires like Birla. His hunger strikes could stop riots and massacres, but he also once went on a hunger strike to force the employees of one of his capitalist patrons to break their strike against the harsh conditions of employment.

He sought to improve the conditions of the untouchables, yet in today's India, these peoples, now calling themselves Dalits and forming an increasingly well-organized and effective political grouping, have rallied around the memory of their own leader, Bhimrao Ramji Ambedkar, an old rival of Gandhi's. As Ambedkar's star has risen among the Dalits, so Gandhi's stature has been reduced. The creator of the political philosophies of passive resistance and constructive non-violence, he spent much of his life far from the political arena, refining his more eccentric theories of vegetarianism, bowel movements and the beneficial properties of human excrement.

Forever scarred by the knowledge that, as a 16-year-old youth, he'd been making love to his wife Kasturba at the moment of his father's death, Gandhi later forswore sexual relations but went on into his old age with what he called his "brahmacharya experiments," during which naked young women would be asked to lie with him all night so that he could prove that he had mastered his physical urges. (He believed that total control over his "vital fluids" would enhance his spiritual powers.)

He, and he alone, was responsible for the transformation of the demand for independence into a nationwide mass

British into leaving; freedom could be won, the film appeared to suggest, by being more moral than your oppressor, whose moral code could then oblige him to withdraw.

But such is the efficacy of this symbolic Gandhi that the film, for all its simplifications and Hollywoodizations, had a powerful and positive effect on many contemporary freedom struggles. South African antiapartheid campaigners and democratic voices all over South America have enthused to me about the film's galvanizing effects. This posthumous, exalted "international Gandhi" has apparently become a totem of real inspirational force.

The trouble with the idealized Gandhi is that he's so darned dull, little more than a dispenser of homilies and nostrums ("An eye for an eye will make the whole world go blind") with just the odd flash of wit (asked what he thought of Western civilization, he gave the celebrated reply, "I think it would be a great idea"). The real man, if it is still possible to use such a term after the generations of hagiography and reinvention, was infinitely more interesting, one of the most complex and contradictory personalities of the century. His full name, Mohandas Karamchand Gandhi, was memorably—and literally—translated into English by the novelist G.V. Desani as "Action-Slave Fascination-Moon Grocer," and

> # Generations to come ... will scarce believe that such a one as this ever walked upon this earth.
> **ALBERT EINSTEIN**

movement that mobilized every class of society against the imperialist, yet the free India that came into being, divided and committed to a program of modernization and industrialization, was not the India of his dreams. His sometime disciple, Nehru, was the archproponent of modernization, and it was Nehru's vision, not Gandhi's, that was eventually—and perhaps inevitably—preferred.

Gandhi began by believing that the politics of passive resistance and nonviolence should be effective in any situation, at any time, even against a force as malign as Nazi Germany. Later, he was obliged to revise his opinion, and concluded that while the British had responded to such techniques because of their own nature, other oppressors might not.

GANDHIAN NONVIOLENCE IS WIDELY BELIEVED TO be the method by which India gained independence. (The view is assiduously fostered inside India as well as outside it.) Yet the Indian revolution did indeed become violent, and this violence so disappointed Gandhi that he stayed away from the independence celebrations in protest. Moreover, the ruinous economic impact of World War II on Britain, and—as British writer Patrick French says in his book *Liberty or Death: India's Journey to Independence and Division*—the gradual collapse of the Raj's bureaucratic hold over India from the mid-'30s onward did as much to bring about freedom as any action of Gandhi's. It is probable, in fact, that Gandhian techniques were not the key determinants of India's arrival at freedom. They gave independence its outward character and were its apparent cause, but darker and deeper historical forces produced the desired effect.

These days, few people pause to consider the complex character of Gandhi's personality, the ambiguous nature of his achievement and legacy, or even the real causes of Indian independence. These are hurried, sloganizing times, and we don't have the time or, worse, the inclination to assimilate many-sided truths. The harshest truth of all is that Gandhi is increasingly irrelevant in the country whose "little father"—Bapu—he was. As the analyst Sunil Khilnani has pointed out, India came into being as a secularized state, but Gandhi's vision was essentially religious. However, he "recoiled" from Hindu nationalism. His solution was to forge an Indian identity out of the shared body of ancient narratives. "He turned to the legends and stories from India's popular religious traditions, preferring their lessons to the supposed ones of history." It

didn't work. In today's India, Hindu nationalism is rampant in the form of the Bharatiya Janata Party. During the recent elections, Gandhi and his ideas have scarcely been mentioned.

Twenty-one years ago, the writer Ved Mehta spoke to one of Gandhi's leading political associates, a former Governor-General of independent India, C. Rajagopalachari. His verdict on Gandhi's legacy is disenchanted, but in today's India, on the fast track to free-market capitalism, it still rings true: "The glamour of modern technology, money and power is so seductive that no one—I mean no one—can resist it. The handful of Gandhians who still believe in his philosophy of a simple life in a simple society are mostly cranks."

What, then, is greatness? In what does it reside? If a man's project fails, or survives only in irredeemably tarnished form, can the force of his example still merit the extreme accolade? For Jawaharlal Nehru, the defining image of Gandhi was "as I saw him marching, staff in hand, to Dandi on the Salt March in 1930. Here was the pilgrim on his quest of Truth, quiet, peaceful, determined and fearless, who would continue that quest and pilgrimage, regardless of consequences." Nehru's daughter Indira Gandhi later said, "More than his words, his life was his message." These days, that message is better heeded outside India. Albert Einstein was one of many to praise Gandhi's achievement; Martin Luther King Jr., the Dalai Lama and all the world's peace movements have followed in his footsteps. Gandhi, who gave up cosmopolitanism to gain a country, has become, in his strange afterlife, a citizen of the world: his spirit may yet prove resilient, smart, tough, sneaky and, yes, ethical enough to avoid assimilation by global McCulture (and Mac culture too). Against this new empire, Gandhian intelligence is a better weapon than Gandhian piety. And passive resistance? We'll see. ■

*Salman Rushdie, born in Bombay, India, is the author of* Midnight's Children *and* The Moor's Last Sigh.

**Gandhi's beloved granddaughters would later see him murdered**

# David
# Ben-Gurion

## Part Washington, part Moses, he brought forth a new nation that altered the destiny of the Jewish people—and the Middle East

**By AMOS OZ**

EVER SINCE HE WAS A FRAIL CHILD WITH A DISPROPORTIONATELY BIG HEAD, David Ben-Gurion was always clear about his next move, about the Jewish people's destination, about the link between his steps and the deliverance of the Jews in their biblical homeland. Ben-Gurion ached to be an intellectual: during the most dramatic years of his leadership, he gulped philosophy books, commented on the Bible, flirted with Buddhism, even taught himself ancient Greek in order to read Plato in the original; he had a relentless curiosity about the natural sciences (but no taste for fiction or the fine arts). He would quote Spinoza as if throwing rocks at a rival. Verbal battle, not dialogue, was his habitual mode of communication. Rather than a philosopher, he was a walking exclamation mark, a tight, craggy man with a halo of silvery hair and a jawbone that projected awesome willpower and a volcanic temper.

He came from the depressed depths of small-town Polish-Jewish life, which he left behind in 1906. Inspired by a Hebrew-Zionist upbringing, shocked by anti-Semitic pogroms in Eastern Europe, he went to Turkish Palestine "to build it and be rebuilt by it," as was the motto of those days. He became a pioneer, a farmhand, active with early Zionist-socialist groups. At age 19 he was what he would remain all his life: a secular Jewish nationalist who combined Jewish Messianic visions with socialist ideals, a man with fierce ambition for leadership, extraordinary tactical-political skills and a sarcastic edge rather than a sense of humor.

In 1915 Ben-Gurion, expelled from Palestine for his nationalist and socialist activities, chose to go to New York City, where he hastily taught himself English and plunged head on into perpetrating the local Zionist-socialist movement. Yet his authoritative, almost despotic character and his enchantment with Lenin's revolution and leadership style were tempered during his three years in the U.S. by the impact American democracy left on him. Many years later, Ben-Gurion, who was urged by some countrymen to "suspend" democracy more than once, refused to do so.

**BORN Oct. 16, 1886, in czarist-ruled Poland**

**1906 Settles in Palestine**

**1948 Elected as first Prime Minister of the new state of Israel**

**1956 Back in power, orders invasion of Gaza Strip and Sinai peninsula**

**1886**

**1973**

**SOLDIER After three years in the U.S., he returns to Palestine and fights in a Jewish battalion against Turks, 1918**

**1953 Resigns as Prime Minister**

**1973 Dies on Dec. 1**

After World War I he returned to Palestine, now governed by Britain and—after 1920—designated by the League of Nations as a "National Home" for the Jewish people. He rose to prominence in the growing Zionist-socialist movement. The increasing anti-Semitism in Europe during the 1920s and '30s sent waves of Jewish immigrants into the country. Furious Arab leaders launched a rebellion against the British and a holy war on the Jews. Much earlier than others, Ben-Gurion recognized the depth and rationale of Arab objection to Zionism: he was aware of the tragic nature of a clash between two genuine claims to the same land. His position on this can be described as neither hawkish nor dovish: he saw the creation of an independent homeland for the homeless Jewish people as, first and foremost, a crucial provision for the survival of persecuted Jews.

At the cost of being labeled a traitor (by extremists on the right) and an opportunist (by the dogmatic left), he was ready to go a long way to accommodate the Arabs. Yet he was one of the first to foresee that in order for the Jews to avoid a showdown with the Arabs or to survive such a showdown, they must set up a shadow state and a shadow military force.

Ben-Gurion was the great architect and builder of both. Throughout the tragic years from 1936 to 1947, while millions

# Mao
## Zedong

His ruthless vision united a fractured people and inspired revolutions far beyond China's borders

**By JONATHAN D. SPENCE**

**M**AO ZEDONG LOVED TO SWIM. In his youth, he advocated swimming as a method of strengthening the bodies of Chinese citizens, and one of his earliest poems celebrated the joys of beating a wake through the waves. As a young man, he and his close friends would often swim in local streams before they debated together the myriad challenges that faced their nation. But especially after 1955, when he was in his early 60s and at the height of his political power as leader of the Chinese People's Republic, swimming became a central part of his life.

Mao swam so often in the large pool constructed for the top Party leaders in their closely guarded compound that the others eventually left him as the pool's sole user. He swam in the often stormy ocean off the north China coast, when the Communist Party leadership gathered there for its annual conferences. And, despite the pleadings of his security guards and his physician, he swam in the heavily polluted

**BORN** Dec. 26, 1893, in Hunan province

**1893**

**OLD SCHOOL** As a young student, Mao dressed in traditional garments

**1921 Attends first congress of Chinese Communist Party**

**1934 Sets out on the Long March**

**1949 Proclaims the People's Republic of China and becomes its first leader**

**1958 Launches the Great Leap Forward**

**1966 Begins the Cultural Revolution**

**1972 Meets Nixon in Beijing**

**1976**

**1976 Dies of heart attack**

**The advocate of Marxist equality was treated as an idol by young Chinese in 1958**

rivers of south China, drifting miles downstream with the current, head back, stomach in the air, hands and legs barely moving, unfazed by the globs of human waste gliding gently past. "Maybe you're afraid of sinking," he would chide his companions if they began to panic in the water. "Don't think about it. If you don't think about it, you won't sink. If you do, you will."

Mao was a genius at not sinking. His enemies were legion: militarists, who resented his journalistic barbs at their incompetence; party rivals, who found him too zealous a supporter of the united front with the Kuomintang nationalists; landlords, who hated his pro-peasant rhetoric and

activism; Chiang Kai-shek, who attacked his rural strongholds with relentless tenacity; the Japanese, who tried to smash his northern base; the U.S., after the Chinese entered the Korean War; the Soviet Union, when he attacked Khrushchev's anti-Stalinist policies. Mao was equally unsinkable in the turmoil—much of which he personally instigated—that marked the last 20 years of his rule in China.

Mao was born in 1893, into a China that appeared to be falling apart. The fading Qin dynasty could not contain the spiraling social and economic unrest, and had mortgaged

China's revenues and many of its natural resources to the apparently insatiable foreign powers. It was, Mao later told his biographer Edgar Snow, a time when "the dismemberment of China" seemed imminent, and only heroic actions by China's youth could save the day.

Mao's earliest surviving essay, written when he was 19, was on one of China's most celebrated early exponents of cynicism and realpolitik, the fearsome 4th century B.C. administrator Shang Yang. Mao took Shang Yang's experi-

ences as emblematic of China's crisis. Shang Yang had instituted a set of ruthlessly enforced laws designed "to punish the wicked and rebellious, in order to preserve the rights of the people." That the people continued to fear Shang Yang was proof to Mao they were "stupid." Mao attributed this fear and distrust not to Shang Yang's policies but to the perception of those policies: "At the beginning of anything out of the ordinary, the mass of the people always dislike it."

After the communist victory over Chiang Kai-shek in 1949, and the establishment of the People's Republic of China, Mao's position was immeasurably strengthened. Despite all that the Chinese people had endured, it seems not to have been too hard for Mao to persuade them of the visionary force and practical need for the Great Leap Forward of the late 1950s. In Mao's mind, the intensive marshaling of China's energies would draw manual and mental labor together into a final harmonious synthesis and throw a bridge across the chasm of China's poverty to the promised socialist paradise on the other side.

In February 1957, Mao gathered his thoughts on China together in the form of a rambling speech on "The Correct Handling of Contradictions Among the People." Mao's notes for the speech reveal the curious mixture of jocularity and cruelty, of utopian visions and blinkered perceptions,

Notes from the underground: Mao strategizing in his cave headquarters in Yenan, 1944

> ## " A revolution is not a dinner party... or doing embroidery; it cannot be so refined, so leisurely. "
>
> **MAO ZEDONG, 1927**

that lay at the heart of his character. Mao admitted that 15% or more of the Chinese people were hungry and that some critics felt a "disgust" with Marxism. He spoke too of the hundreds of thousands who had died in the revolution so far, but firmly rebutted figures—quoted in Hong Kong newspapers—that 20 million had perished. "How could we possibly kill 20 million people?" he asked.

It is now established that at least that number died in China during the famine that followed the Great Leap between 1959 and 1961. In the Cultural Revolution that followed only five years later, Mao used the army and the student population against his opponents. Once again millions suffered or perished as Mao combined the ruthlessness of Shang Yang with the absolute confidence of the long-distance swimmer.

Rejecting his former party allies, and anyone who could be accused of espousing the values of an older and more gracious Chinese civilization, Mao drew his sustenance from the chanting crowds of Red Guards. The irony here was that from his youthful readings, Mao knew the story of how Shang Yang late in life tried to woo a moral administrator to his service. But the official turned down Shang Yang's blandishments, with the words that "1,000 persons going 'Yes, yes!' are not worth one man with a bold 'No!'"

MAO DIED IN 1976, AND with the years those adulatory cries of "Yes, yes!" have gradually faded. Leaders Mao trained, like Deng Xiaoping, were able to reverse Mao's policies even as they claimed to revere them. They gave back to the Chinese people the opportunities to express their entrepreneurial skills, leading to astonishing rates of growth and a complete transformation of the face of Chinese cities.

Are these changes, these moves toward a new flexibility, somehow Mao's legacy? Despite the agony he caused, Mao was both a visionary and a realist. He learned as a youth not only how Shang Yang brought harsh laws to the Chinese people, even when they saw no need for them, but also how Shang Yang's rigors helped lay the foundation in 221 B.C. of the fearsome centralizing state of Qin. Mao knew too that the Qin rulers had been both hated and feared and that their dynasty was soon toppled, despite their monopoly of force and efficient use of terror. But in his final years,

Mao seems to have welcomed the association of his own name with these distant Qin precursors. The Qin, after all, had established a united state from a universe in chaos. They represented, like Mao, not the best that China had to offer, but something ruthless yet canny, with the power briefly to impose a single will on the scattered emotions of the errant multitude. It is on that grimly structured foundation that Mao's successors have been able to build, even as they struggle, with obvious nervousness, to contain the social pressures that their own more open policies are generating. Surely Mao's simple words reverberate in their ears: As long as you are not afraid, you won't sink. ■

*Jonathan D. Spence teaches at Yale University and is the author of a number of acclaimed books on China's history and culture.*

**After you: Mao with Khrushchev in 1959; their alliance was already teetering**

LEADERS & REVOLUTIONARIES

# Ho Chi Minh

## He married nationalism to communism and perfected the deadly art of guerrilla warfare

**By STANLEY KARNOW**

To Western eyes, it seemed inconceivable that Ho would make the tremendous sacrifices he did. But in 1946, as war with the French loomed, he cautioned them, "You can kill 10 of my men for every one I kill of yours, yet even at those odds, you will lose and I will win." The French, convinced of their superiority, ignored his warning and suffered grievously as a result. Senior American officers similarly nurtured the illusion that their sophisticated weapons would inevitably break enemy morale. But, as Ho's brilliant commander, General Vo Nguyen Giap, told me in Hanoi in 1990, his principal concern had been victory. When I asked him how long he would have resisted the U.S. onslaught, he thundered, "Twenty years, maybe 100 years—as long as it took to win, regardless of cost." The human toll was horrendous. An estimated 3 million North and South Vietnamese soldiers and civilians died.

The youngest of three children, Ho was born Nguyen Sinh Cung in 1890 in a village in central Vietnam. The area was indirectly ruled by the French through a puppet emperor. Its impoverished peasants, traditional dissidents, opposed France's presence; and Ho's father, a functionary at the imperial court, manifested his sympathy for them by quitting his position and becoming an itinerant teacher. Inheriting his father's rebellious bent, Ho participated in a series of tax revolts, acquiring a reputation as a troublemaker. But he was familiar with the lofty French principles of *liberté, égalité, fraternité* and yearned to see them in practice in France. In 1911 he sailed for Marseilles as a galley boy aboard a passenger liner. His record of dissent had already earned him a file in the French police dossiers. It was scarcely flattering: "Appearance awkward ... mouth half-open."

In Paris, Ho worked as a photo retoucher. The city's fancy restaurants were beyond his means, but he indulged in one luxury—American cigarettes, preferably Camels or Lucky Strikes. Occasionally he would drop into a music hall to listen to Maurice Chevalier, whose charming songs he would never forget.

In 1919 Woodrow Wilson arrived in France to sign the treaty ending World War I, and Ho, supposing that the American President's doctrine of self-determination applied to Asia, donned a cutaway coat and tried to present Wilson with a lengthy list of French abuses in Vietnam. Rebuffed,

**A**N EMACIATED, GOATEED FIGURE IN A THREADBARE bush jacket and frayed rubber sandals, Ho Chi Minh cultivated the image of a humble, benign "Uncle Ho." But he was a seasoned revolutionary and passionate nationalist obsessed by a single goal: independence for his country. Sharing his fervor, his tattered guerrillas vaulted daunting obstacles to crush France's desperate attempt to retrieve its empire in Indochina; later, built into a largely conventional army, they frustrated the massive U.S. effort to prevent Ho's communist followers from controlling Vietnam. For Americans, it was the longest war—and the first defeat—in their history, and it drastically changed the way they perceived their role in the world.

Ho joined the newly created French Communist Party. "It was patriotism, not communism, that inspired me," he later explained.

Soon Ho was roaming the earth as a covert agent for Moscow. Disguised as a Chinese journalist or a Buddhist monk, he would surface in Canton, Rangoon or Calcutta—then vanish to nurse his tuberculosis and other chronic diseases. As befit a professional conspirator, he employed a baffling assortment of aliases. Again and again, he was reported dead, only to pop up in a new place. In 1929 he assembled a few militants in Hong Kong and formed the Indochinese Communist Party. He portrayed himself as a celibate, a pose calculated to epitomize his moral fiber, but he had at least two wives or perhaps concubines. One was a Chinese woman; the other was Giap's sister-in-law, who was guillotined by the French.

IN 1940 JAPAN'S LEGIONS SWEPT INTO Indochina, and French officials in Vietnam, loyal to the pro-German Vichy administration in France, collaborated with them. Nationalists in the region greeted the Japanese as liberators, but to Ho they were no better than the French. Slipping across the Chinese frontier into Vietnam—his first return home in three decades—he urged his disciples to fight both the Japanese and the French. There, in a remote camp, he founded the Viet Minh, an acronym for the Vietnam Independence League, from which he derived his nom de guerre, Ho Chi Minh—roughly "Bringer of Light."

The charismatic guerrilla rallies the faithful at a party gathering in 1966

What he brought was a spirit of rebellion—against first the French and later the Americans. As Ho's war escalated in the mid-1960s, it became clear to Lyndon Johnson that Vietnam would imperil his presidency. In 1965 Johnson tried a diplomatic approach. Accustomed to dispensing patronage to recalcitrant Congressmen, he was confident that the tactic would work. "Old Ho can't turn me down," L.B.J. said. But Ho did. Any settlement, he realized, would mean accepting a permanent partition and forfeiting his dream to unify Vietnam under his flag.

There was no flexibility in Ho's beliefs, no bending of his will. Even as the war increasingly destroyed the country, he remained committed to Vietnam's independence. And millions of Vietnamese fought and died to attain the same goal.

Ho died in 1969, at the age of 79, some six years before his battalions surged into Saigon. Aspiring to bask in the reflected glory of his posthumous triumph, his heirs put his embalmed body on display in a hideous granite mausoleum copied from Lenin's tomb in Moscow. They violated his final wishes. In his will he specified that his ashes be buried in urns on three hilltops in Vietnam, saying, "Not only is cremation good from the point of view of hygiene, but it also saves farmland." ∎

*Stanley Karnow, who won a Pulitzer Prize in 1990 for* In Our Image: America's Empire in the Philippines, *is the author of* Vietnam: A History, *which was published in 1983.*

**BORN 1890 in Hoang Tru in rural Vietnam**

**1911 Sails to France to study and work**

**1954 Defeats the French at Dien Bien Phu. Vietnam is divided, and Ho becomes first President of North Vietnam**

**1967 Tells L.B.J., "We will never negotiate"**

1890

1969

**RADICAL At a Socialist Party meeting in France, 1920**

**1941 Forms the Vietnam Independence League, or Viet Minh**

**1959 Begins armed revolt against South Vietnam**

**1969 Dies of a heart attack in Hanoi**

# Martin Luther
# King

## He led a mass struggle for racial equality that doomed segregation and changed America for the better, forever

**By JACK E. WHITE**

IT IS A TESTAMENT TO THE GREATNESS OF Martin Luther King Jr. that nearly every major city in the U.S. has a street or school named after him. It is a measure of how sorely his achievements are misunderstood that most of them are located in black neighborhoods.

Three decades after King was gunned down in Memphis, Tenn., he is still regarded mainly as the black leader of a movement for black equality. That assessment, while accurate, is far too restrictive. For all King did to free blacks from the yoke of segregation, whites may owe him the greatest debt, for liberating them from the burden of America's centuries-old hypocrisy about race. It is only because of King and the movement that he led that the U.S. can claim to be the leader of the "free world" without inviting smirks of disdain and disbelief. Had he and the blacks and whites who marched beside him failed, vast regions of the U.S. would have remained morally indistinguishable from South Africa under apartheid, with terrible consequences for America's standing among nations. How could America have convincingly inveighed against the Iron Curtain while an equally oppressive Cotton Curtain remained draped across the South?

Even after the Supreme Court struck down segregation in 1954, what the world now calls human-rights offenses were both law and custom in much of America. Before King and his movement, a tired and thoroughly respectable Negro seamstress like Rosa Parks could be thrown into jail and fined simply because she refused to give up her seat on an Alabama bus so a white man could sit down. A six-year-old black girl like Ruby Bridges could be hectored and spit on by a white New Orleans mob simply because she wanted to go to the same school as white children. A 14-year-old black boy like Emmett Till could be hunted down and murdered by a Mississippi gang simply because he had supposedly made suggestive remarks to a white woman. Even highly educated blacks were routinely denied the right to vote or serve on juries. They could not eat at lunch counters, register in motels or use whites-only rest rooms; they could not buy or rent a home wherever they chose. In some rural enclaves in the South, they were even compelled to get off the sidewalk and stand in the street if a Caucasian walked by.

The movement that King led swept all that away. Its victory was so complete that even though those outrages took place within the living

**BORN**
Jan. 15, 1929, in Atlanta

**1957 Founds Southern Christian Leadership Conference advocating nonviolent struggle against racism**

**1964 Awarded Nobel Peace Prize**

**1983 Birthday declared a national holiday**

1929

1968

**YOUTH** At age six

**1963 Organizes March on Washington supporting proposed civil rights legislation**

**1968 Assassinated in Memphis, Tenn.**

"King made ... assuming personal responsibility for alleviating social harm ordinary and irresistible."

TONI MORRISON, Nobel prizewinner

King is booked after trying to attend a trial in Montgomery, Ala., in 1958

Marching with wife Coretta during the 1965 campaign for voting rights in Selma, Ala.

the defining moment of his life came during the early days of the bus boycott. A telephone call at midnight alarmed him: "Nigger, we are tired of you and your mess now. And if you aren't out of this town in three days, we're going to blow your brains out and blow up your house." Shaken, King went to the kitchen to pray. "I could hear an inner voice saying to me, 'Martin Luther, stand up for righteousness. Stand up for justice. Stand up for truth. And lo I will be with you, even until the end of the world.'"

In recent years, however, King's most quoted line—"I have a dream that my four little children will one day live in a nation where they will not be judged by the color of their skin but by the content of their character"—has been put to uses he would never have endorsed. It has become the slogan for opponents of affirmative action like California's Ward Connerly, who insist, incredibly, that had King lived he would have been marching alongside them. Connerly even chose King's birthday last year to announce the creation of his nationwide crusade against "racial preferences."

Such would-be kidnappers of King's legacy have chosen a highly selective interpretation of his message. They have filtered out his radicalism and sense of urgency. That most famous speech was studded with demands. "We have come to our nation's capital to cash a check," King admonished. "When the architects of our Republic wrote the magnificent words of the Constitution and the Declaration of Independence, they were signing a promissory note to which every American was to fall heir. Instead of honoring this sacred obligation, America has given the Negro people a bad check; a check which has come back marked 'insufficient funds.'" These were not the words of a cardboard saint advocating a Hallmark card–style version of brotherhood. They were the stinging phrases of a prophet, a man demanding justice not just in the hereafter, but in the here and now. ∎

TIME *national correspondent Jack E. White has covered civil rights issues in America and abroad for 30 years.*

memory of the baby boomers, they seem like ancient history. And though this revolution was the product of two centuries of agitation by thousands upon thousands of courageous men and women, King was its culmination. It is impossible to think of the movement unfolding as it did without him at its helm. He was, as the cliché has it, the right man at the right time.

To begin with, King was a preacher who spoke in biblical cadences ideally suited to leading a stride toward freedom that found its inspiration in the Old Testament story of the Israelites and the New Testament gospel of Jesus Christ. Being a minister not only put King in touch with the spirit of the black masses but also gave him a base within the black church, then as now the strongest and most independent of black institutions.

Moreover, King was a man of extraordinary physical courage whose belief in nonviolence never wavered. From the time he assumed leadership of the Montgomery, Ala., bus boycott in 1955 to his murder 13 years later, he faced hundreds of death threats. His home in Montgomery was bombed, with his wife and young children inside. He was hounded by J. Edgar Hoover's FBI, which bugged his telephone and hotel rooms, circulated salacious gossip about him and even tried to force him into committing suicide after he won the Nobel Peace Prize in 1964. As King told it,

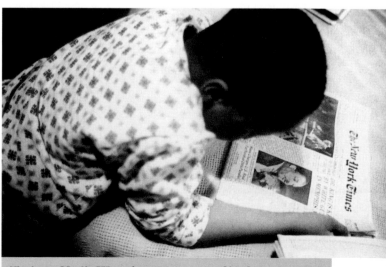

**King's son Martin III reads news accounts of his father's murder**

# Pope
# John Paul II

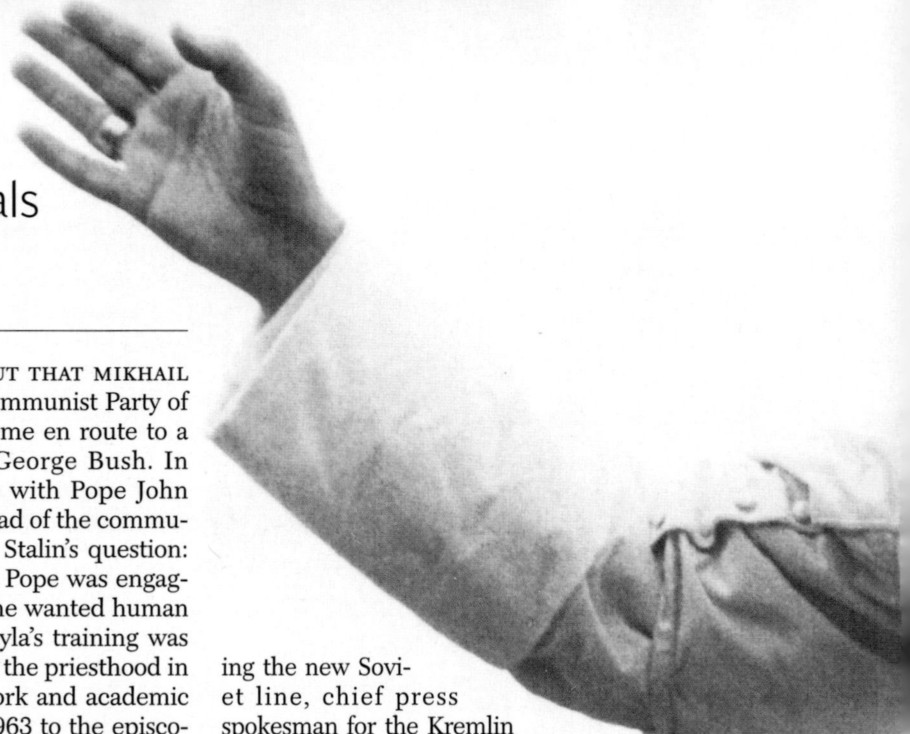

The most tireless moral
voice of a secular age,
he reminded humankind
of the worth of individuals
in the modern world

By **WILLIAM F. BUCKLEY JR.**

I N NOVEMBER 1989 WORD WENT OUT THAT MIKHAIL
Gorbachev, First Secretary of the Communist Party of
the Soviet Union, would stop in Rome en route to a
summit meeting with President George Bush. In
Rome he would have an audience with Pope John
Paul II. This was *glasnost*, 200 proof. The head of the communist world had bumped into the answer to Stalin's question:
How many divisions has the Pope? And the Pope was engag-
ing in spiritual geopolitics at summit level: he wanted human
rights for the faithful in Russia. Karol Wojtyla's training was
extensive, dating back to discreet studies for the priesthood in
Nazi-occupied Poland. After that, parish work and academic
studies under communist rule, leading in 1963 to the episco-
pacy in Cracow. Pity poor Gorbachev. Seventy-two years of
formal national commitment to atheism, backed by the
Gulag, and now, 1989, a street poll revealed that 40% of Soviet
citizens believed in God.

The Berlin Wall had come down a few weeks before, and
no one doubted any longer that the great Soviet enterprise was
headed for collapse. But for a while, Secretary Gorbachev
would be treated as you and I would be treated if we had dis-
posed of 40,000 nuclear missiles. And anyway, Gorbachev was
a polemical swinger right to the end. The ideological imagination was hardly dead. The following Sunday, no doubt expressing the new Sovi-
et line, chief press
spokesman for the Kremlin
Gennadi Gerasimov appeared with
Mike Wallace on *60 Minutes*. It's true,
he said, that communism is evolving, but so is Christianity.
Christian values and communist values—"especially early
Christian values"—are the same.

That was a subtle and learned line, and it is used in many
contexts to fondle the difficulties John Paul II has frequently
expressed about capitalism. In his long travails, Karol Wojtyla
has spoken critically about Western economic arrangements,
and it was this theme that caught the opportunistic eye of
Gerasimov. Didn't communism, like early Christianity, seek to

| **BORN** May 18, 1920, in Wadowice, Poland | 1946 Ordained as priest | 1958 Becomes auxiliary Bishop of Cracow | 1967 Named to the College of Cardinals | 1979 Makes papal visit to his homeland | 1998 Meets Castro and celebrates Mass in Cuba |
| --- | --- | --- | --- | --- | --- |
| 1920 | | 1956 Named professor of ethics at Lublin University | 1963 Appointed Archbishop | 1978 Elected Pope | 1981 Wounded by would-be assassin |

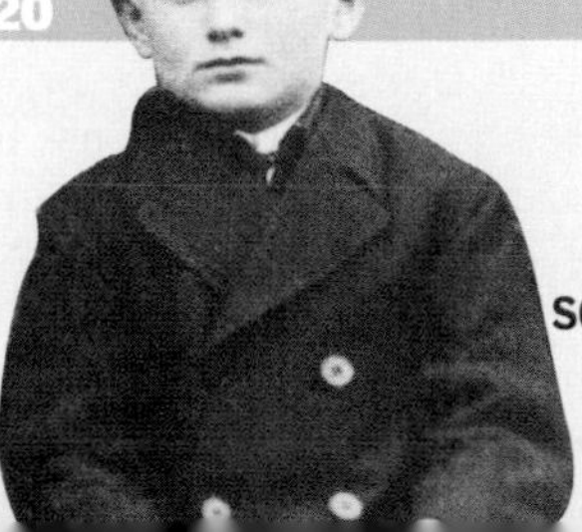

**SCHOOLBOY** Karol Wojtyla, c. 1930

eliminate poverty? Was not the communist ideal an expression of Christian concern for the communal ownership of property?

In Mexico, five months later, the Pope was speaking in Pancho Villa country and sounding very much like Pancho Villa. He wanted it made clear, he said, that in celebrating the collapse of communism, he had not meant to say capitalism had triumphed. The Pope told the great crowd that he had criticized communism not for its economic shortcomings but rather because it "violated or jeopardized the dignity of the person." That was the same papal language used in Canada in 1984 (and one hears traces of it today, most recently in Havana when the Pope met with Fidel Castro).

But then in 1991 *Centesimus annus* came in, a 25,000-word encyclical on the 100th anniversary of Leo XIII's *Rerum novarum*, the momentous condemnation of liberalism and materialism. Materialism meant then what it means today. By liberalism, Pope Leo had in mind contemporary movements that sought, in the name of "modernism," to free human beings from traditional ties to church and family.

In the centennial encyclical, Pope John Paul reiterated his frequent admonitions. The worker or manager who reports to duty at the shop every morning inflamed by the desire to make a better widget and sell more of it is one thing; quite another if he or she goes home listlessly unconcerned with human life and human attachments having to do with respect for the elderly, a love for one's family, the capacity to take joy from Christian perspectives. Papal prose is turgid, but here the Pope did say in almost as many words that socialism was an extravagant historical failure.

If, then, all one need do in evaluating capitalism is admonish against greed and abusive economic-political arrangements, the exorcism is quickly over, and Gerasimov is left as speechless as Gorbachev quickly became after losing his handle on the nuclear football.

John Paul II is by every measurement as cosmopolitan in experience and steeped in erudition as anyone who comes to mind. He speaks eight languages fluently; he is the author of scholarly books and dissertations and has traveled in virtually every country in the world. One supposes that, notwithstanding, he is not by personal

> **People repeat the Pope's words, and they know that he's their bulwark.**
>
> **WIKTOR KULERSKI, Solidarity activist, 1979**

**An ebullient Archbishop of Cracow enjoys a serenade**

experience familiar with the kind of thing one can pick up to read in urban kiosks or turn to view on late-night television. But you'd still deduce that Pope John Paul would not be surprised by anything he read or saw: he has been exposed at very close quarters to the ingenuity of God's creatures, no less creative in depravity than in goodness.

What does surprise is the near virginal conviction of this sophisticated Pole that Providence has kept a watchful eye on him. His recovery in 1981 from an assailant's bullet the Pope would probably not term miraculous—only because fastidious Catholic theology frowns on the use of that word, except when the theological department of weights and measures has been there with all its paraphernalia of skepticism and given an O.K. Still, he is known to believe that the good Lord had a hand in his survival, and he is said to believe that he is fated to be Pope right up through Jan. l, 2000, formally escorting the church into its third millennium. If this should prove so, if he is alive at that moment, there are probably a few medical observers who will be willing to use the word miraculous.

In any case, people will ask, What is it that Pope John Paul II uniquely brings to the millennium? Almost all who have experienced him at close quarters understand the special luminosity he radiates when surrounded in person by a million people. But the great historical backdrop of his splendor fades. He was the student and manual laborer from Wadowice in Poland who became the first non-Italian Pope in 450 years. His was the dominant spiritual presence in the final round of the great revolutionary challenge that began soon after the turn of the century and sought no less than to alter Western assumptions about human life. But that role is not really what the critics want to dwell upon. What's on their mind is the stands Pope John Paul has taken on—women. On their right to take Holy Orders, to abort a fetus, to frustrate insemination by artificial means. And they want to talk about the overexercise of papal authority, about the discipline he has exercised over dissident theologians.

The Rev. Richard P. McBrien is one of the most widely known U.S. theologians, a

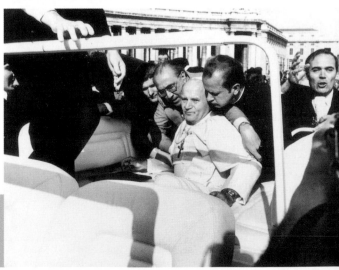

**John Paul lived to forgive the man who shot him in 1981**

professor at Notre Dame and the author of numerous books. The most recent of these is *Lives of the Popes.* At the end of the book, he undertakes a ranking. There is, first, "Outstanding Popes," followed by "Good or Above Average Popes." John Paul II makes neither of these categories. Father McBrien rates him as less than great because he did not flesh out Vatican II. But he rates him as "Historically Important," as Gorbachev would confirm.

That he is at least that is not questionable, even if one anticipates a millennium of wrangling about women's rights at the altar, the distribution of hierarchical power and allocutory nuance. But there are many thousands who will live well into the next century with photographic memories of John Paul II. The late-teenage boys and girls who gathered in great numbers to see him in Denver in 1993 will, many of them, be alive when John Paul II is dead in 50 years, and their recall will be sensual. I saw him in January, with the usual million people, including Fidel Castro. There was some

trepidation about the Pope's health at the Sunday Mass. The Pope was cautiously introduced by Havana's Jaime Cardinal Ortega. We heard then the voice of the Pope. Not very expressive, but the Spanish he spoke was well turned and clearly enunciated. In a matter of seconds he communicated his special, penetrating, transcendent warmth. Close-up we could see the ravages of his apparent affliction (Parkinson's), his age (77) and his gun wound (1981). The cumulative result of it all is a stoop and the listless expression on his face—the hangdog look. But then, intermittently, the great light within flashes, and one sees the most radiant face on the public scene, a presence so commanding as to have arrested a generation of humankind, who wonder gratefully whether the Lord Himself had a hand in shaping the special charisma of this servant of the servants of God. ∎

*William F. Buckley Jr. is editor-at-large of the* National Review *and the author of* Nearer, My God.

# Margaret Thatcher

## Champion of free minds and markets, she helped topple the welfare state and make the world safer for capitalism

**By PAUL JOHNSON**

SHE WAS THE CATALYST WHO SET IN MOTION A SERIES of interconnected events that gave a revolutionary twist to the century's last two decades and helped mankind end the millennium on a note of hope and confidence. The triumph of capitalism, the almost universal acceptance of the market as indispensable to prosperity, the collapse of Soviet imperialism, the downsizing of the state on nearly every continent and in almost every country in the world—Margaret Thatcher played a part in all those transformations, and it is not easy to see how any would have occurred without her.

Born in 1925, Margaret Hilda Roberts was an enormously industrious girl. The daughter of a Grantham shopkeeper, she studied on scholarship, worked her way to Oxford and took two degrees, in chemistry and law. Her fascination with politics led her into Parliament at age 34, when she argued her way into one of the best Tory seats in the country, Finchley in north London. Her quick mind (and faster mouth) led her up through the Tory ranks, and by age 44 she got settled into the "statutory woman's" place in the Cabinet as Education Minister that looked like the summit of her career.

But Thatcher was, and is, notoriously lucky. Her case is awesome testimony to the importance of sheer chance in history. In 1975 she challenged Edward Heath for the Tory leadership simply because the candidate of the Party's right wing abandoned the contest at the last minute. Thatcher stepped into the breach. When she went into Heath's office to tell him her decision, he did not even bother to look up. "You'll lose," he said. "Good day to you."

But as Victor Hugo put it, nothing is so powerful as "an idea whose time has come." And by the mid-'70s enough Tories were fed up with Heath and "the Ratchet Effect"—the way in which each statist advance was accepted by the Conservatives and then became a platform for a further statist advance.

She chose her issues carefully—and, it emerged, luckily. The legal duels she took on early in her tenure as Prime Minister sounded the themes that made her an enduring leader: open markets, vigorous debate and loyal alliances. Among her first fights: a struggle against Britain's out-of-control trade unions, which had destroyed three governments in succession. Thatcher turned the nation's anti-union feeling into a handsome parliamentary majority and a mandate to restrict union privileges by a series of laws that effectively ended Britain's trade-union problem once and for all. "Who governs Britain?" she famously asked as unions struggled for power. By 1980, everyone knew the answer: Thatcher governs.

Once the union citadel had been stormed, Thatcher quickly discovered that every area of the economy was open to judicious reform. Even as the rest of Europe toyed with socialism and state ownership, she set about privatizing the nationalized industries, which had been hitherto sacrosanct, no matter how inefficient. It worked. British Airways, an embarrassingly slovenly national carrier that very seldom showed a profit, was privatized and transformed into one of the world's best and most profitable airlines. British Steel, which lost more than £1 billion in its final years as a state concern, became the largest steel company in Europe.

By the mid-1980s, privatization was a new term in world

**BORN Oct. 13, 1925, in Grantham, England**

**1925**

**1979 Elected Britain's first female Prime Minister**

**1984 Survives terrorist assassination attempt**

**1992 Awarded title of Baroness Thatcher of Kesteven and takes seat in the House of Lords**

**1982 Recaptures the Falkland Islands from Argentina**

**1990 Resigns after losing support of the Conservative Party over differences on European Community policy**

**TORY TOT Margaret, age 4, with sister Muriel, 8**

government, and by the end of the decade more than 50 countries, on almost every continent, had set in motion privatization programs, floating loss-making public companies on the stock markets and in most cases transforming them into successful private-enterprise firms. Even left-oriented countries, which scorned the notion of privatization, began to reduce their public sector on the sly. Governments sent administrative and legal teams to Britain to study how it was done. It was perhaps Britain's biggest contribution to practical economics in the world since J.M. Keynes invented "Keynesianism," or even since Adam Smith published *The Wealth of Nations.*

But Thatcher became a world figure for more than just her politics. She combined a flamboyant willpower with evident femininity. It attracted universal attention, especially after she led Britain to a spectacular military victory over Argentina in 1982. She understood that politicians had to give military people clear orders about ends, then leave them to get on with the means. Still, she could not bear to lose men, ships or planes. "That's why we have extra ships and planes," the admirals had to tell her, "to make good the losses." Fidelity, like courage, loyalty and perseverance, were cardinal virtues to her, which she possessed in the highest degree. People

from all over the world began to look at her methods and achievements closely, and to seek to imitate them.

One of her earliest admirers was Ronald Reagan, who achieved power 18 months after she did. He too began to reverse the Ratchet Effect in the U.S. by effective deregulation, tax cutting and creating wider market opportunities for free enterprise. Reagan liked to listen to Thatcher's various lectures on the virtues of the market or the minimal state. "I'll remember that, Margaret," he would say. She listened carefully to his jokes, tried to get the point and laughed in the right places.

They turned their mutual affection into a potent foreign-policy partnership. With Reagan and Thatcher in power, the application of judicious pressure on the Soviet state to encourage it to reform or abolish itself, or to implode, became an admissible

With husband Denis during a Tory Party conference, 1978

policy. Thatcher warmly encouraged Reagan to rearm and thereby bring Russia to the negotiating table. She shared his view that Moscow ruled an "evil empire," and the sooner it was dismantled the better. Together with Reagan she pushed Mikhail Gorbachev to pursue his *perestroika* policy to its limits and so fatally to undermine the self-confidence of the Soviet élite. Historians will argue hotly about the precise role played by the various actors who brought about the end of Soviet communism. But it is already clear that Thatcher has an important place in this huge event.

It was the beginning of a new historical epoch. All the forces that had made the 20th century such a violent disappointment to idealists—totalitarianism, the gigantic state, the crushing of individual choice and initiative—were publicly and spectacularly defeated. Ascendant instead were the values that Thatcher had supported in the face of sometimes spectacular opposition: free markets and free minds. The world enters the 21st century and the 3rd millennium a wiser place, owing in no small part to the daughter of a shopkeeper, who proved that nothing is more effective than willpower allied to a few clear, simple and workable ideas. ∎

*British historian Paul Johnson's most recent work is* A History of the American People.

LABOUR ISN'T WORKING.

BRITAIN'S BETTER OFF WITH THE CONSERV

# Ayatullah Ruhollah
# Khomeini

Brazenly defying the West, he stirred Islam's faithful and authored a new form of religious government. The prescriptions were often chilling

By **MILTON VIORST**

TO WESTERNERS, HIS HOODED EYES AND SEVERE demeanor, his unkempt gray beard and his black turban and robes conveyed an avenger's wrath. The image is the man. Ayatullah Ruhollah Khomeini, the dour cleric who led an Islamic revolution in Iran, perceived himself above all as an avenger of the humiliations that the West had for more than a century inflicted on the Muslims of the Middle East.

He was among many Muslim autocrats in this century to embrace a mission designed as a corrective to the West. Kemal Ataturk, the most daring of them, introduced Turkey, after the fall of the Ottoman Empire in World War I, to Western-style secularism in order to toughen his society against Europe's imperial designs. In the 1950s, Egypt's Gamal Abdel Nasser, more intemperately, initiated a fierce campaign of Arab nationalism aimed at eradicating the vestiges of Western colonialism from the Arab world.

Khomeini took a different course. All three, at their apogee, were rulers of once great empires that had fallen into political and social disarray. But Ataturk and Nasser were committed to resurrection by beating the West at its own game of building strong secular states. Khomeini's strategy was to reject Western ways, keeping Iran close to its Islamic roots.

Some ask, focusing on this strategy, whether Khomeini was riding a popular wave in global affairs. In the late 20th century, Muslims were not alone in organizing to restore religious belief to government. Christians in America, Jews in Israel, even Hindus in India were promoting the same end. As a revolutionary, Khomeini sought to bring down not just the Shah's

Western-oriented state but also the secular Weltanschauung that stood behind it. Did Khomeini's triumph augur an intellectual shift of global magnitude?

While historians ponder this question, it is enough to say that Khomeini presided brilliantly over the overthrow of a wounded regime. He was merciless and cunning. His well-advertised piety complemented a prodigious skill in grasping and shaping Iran's complex politics. Most important, he knew how to exploit the feelings of nationalist resentment that characterized his time.

Ruhollah Khomeini—his given name means "inspired of God"—was born to a family of Shi'ite scholars in a village near Tehran in 1902. Shi'ism, a minority sect in Islam, is Iran's official religion. Like his father, he moved from theological studies to a career as an Islamic jurist. Throughout his life, he was acclaimed for the depth of his religious learning.

As a young seminary teacher, Khomeini was no activist. From the 1920s to the '40s, he watched passively as Reza

**BORN 1902 in Khomein, Iran**

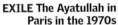
1902

**EXILE The Ayatullah in Paris in the 1970s**

# "Khomeini has offered us the opportunity to regain our frail religion... faith in the power of words."

**NORMAN MAILER, at a meeting of authors, New York City, February 1989**

Shah, a monarch who took Ataturk as his model, promoted secularization and narrowed clerical powers. Similarly, Khomeini was detached from the great crisis of the 1950s in which the new Shah, Reza Shah's son Mohammed Reza Pahlavi, turned to America to save himself from demonstrators on Tehran's streets who were clamoring for democratic reform. Khomeini was then the disciple of Iran's pre-eminent cleric, Ayatullah Mohammed Boroujerdi, a defender of the tradition of clerical deference to established power. But in 1962, after Boroujerdi's death, Khomeini revealed his long-hidden wrath and acquired a substantial following as a sharp-tongued antagonist of the young Shah's.

Khomeini was clearly at home with populist demagogy. He taunted the Shah for his ties with Israel, warning that the Jews were seeking to take over Iran. He denounced as non-Islamic a bill to grant the vote to women. He called a proposal to permit American servicemen based in Iran to be tried in U.S. military courts "a document for Iran's enslavement." In 1964 he was banished by the Shah to Turkey, then was permitted to relocate in the Shi'ite holy city of An Najaf in Iraq. But the Shah erred in thinking Khomeini would be forgotten. In An Najaf, he received Iranians of every station and sent home tape cassettes of sermons to be peddled in the bazaars. In exile, Khomeini became the acknowledged leader of the opposition.

**Khomeini's flock hails his return to Tehran in triumph in 1979**

In An Najaf, Khomeini also shaped a revolutionary doctrine. Shi'ism, historically, demanded of the state only that it keep itself open to clerical guidance. Though relations between clergy and state were often tense, they were rarely belligerent. Khomeini, condemning the Shah's servility to America and his secularism, deviated from accepted tenets to attack the regime's legitimacy, calling for a clerical state, which had no Islamic precedent.

In late 1978, huge street demonstrations calling for the Shah's abdication ignited the government's implosion. Students, the middle class, bazaar merchants, workers, the army—the pillars of society—successively abandoned the regime. The Shah had nowhere to turn for help but to the U.S. Yet the more he did so, the more isolated he became. In January 1979 he fled to the West. Two weeks later, Khomeini returned home in triumph.

Popularly acclaimed as leader, Khomeini set out to confirm his authority and lay the groundwork for a clerical state. With revolutionary fervor riding high, armed vigilante bands and kangaroo courts made bloody work of the Shah's last partisans. Khomeini canceled an experiment with parliamentarism and ordered an Assembly of Experts to draft an Islamic constitution. Overriding reservations from the Shi'ite hierarchy, the delegates designed a state that Khomeini would command and the clergy would run, enforcing religious law. In November, Khomeini partisans, with anti-American passions still rising, seized the U.S. embassy, took 52 hostages and then held most of them for 444 days.

OVER THE REMAINING DECADE OF HIS LIFE, KHOMEINI consolidated his rule. Proving himself as ruthless as the Shah had been, he had thousands killed while stamping out a rebellion of the secular left. He stacked the state bureaucracies with faithful clerics and drenched the schools and the media with his personal doctrines. After purging the military and security services, he rebuilt them to ensure their loyalty to the clerical state.

Khomeini also launched a campaign to "export"—the term was his—the revolution to surrounding Muslim countries. His provocations of Iraq in 1980 helped start a war that lasted eight years, at the cost of a million lives, and that ended only after America intervened to sink several Iranian warships in the Persian Gulf. Iranians asked whether God had revoked his blessing of the revolution. Khomeini described the defeat as "more deadly than taking poison."

To rally his demoralized supporters, he issued the celebrated fatwa condemning to death the writer Salman Rushdie for heresies contained in his novel *The Satanic Verses*. Though born a Muslim, Rushdie was not a Shi'ite; a British subject, he had no ties to Iran. The fatwa, an audacious claim of authority over Muslims everywhere, was the revolution's ultimate export. Khomeini died a few months later. But the fatwa lived on, a source of bitterness—as he intended it to be—between Iran and the West.

Beside the fatwa, what is Khomeini's legacy? The revolution, no longer at risk, still revels in having repeatedly, with impunity, defied the American Satan. The Islamic state was proof to the faithful—as the Soviet Union was to generations of communists—that the Western system need not be a universal model. Yet Khomeini rejected a parallel between his doctrines and the fundamentalism propounded by other Muslim dissidents. He never described himself as fundamentalist. He often said that Islam is not for 14 centuries ago in Arabia but for all time.

Since Khomeini's death, the popular appeal of an Islamic state—and of fundamentalism—has surely dimmed. Thinkers still debate and warriors kill, but no country seems prepared to emulate Iran. Perhaps revolutions happen only under majestic leaders, and no one like this modern-day prophet of militant Islam has since appeared. ∎

*Milton Viorst, a Middle East specialist, is the author of* In the Shadow of the Prophet.

| 1964-78 Is exiled to Iraq for criticizing the Shah and sparking riots; evicted by Saddam Hussein, he moves to a Paris suburb | 1979-81 His followers hold 52 Americans captive in the U.S. embassy in Tehran | 1989 In February, he demands the death of Salman Rushdie |
|---|---|---|
| | 1979 Returns to Iran, is acclaimed as leader of the Muslim revolution | 1989 In June, Khomeini dies in Tehran |

**1989**

Reagan groomed his image as a straight-shooting Westerner— and lassoed votes

# Ronald
# Reagan

## He brought Big Government to its knees and stared down the Soviet Union. And the audience loved it

**By PEGGY NOONAN**

CLARE BOOTHE LUCE FAMOUSLY SAID THAT EACH U.S. President is remembered for a sentence: "He freed the slaves"; "He made the Louisiana Purchase." You have to figure out your sentence, she used to tell John Kennedy, who would nod thoughtfully and then grouse when she left. Ronald Reagan knew, going in, the sentence he wanted, and he got it. He guided the American victory in the cold war. Under his leadership, a conflict that had absorbed a half-century of Western blood and treasure was ended—and the good guys finally won.

It is good to think of how he did it, because the gifts he brought to resolving the conflict reflected very much who he was as a man. He began with a common-sense conviction that the Soviets were not a people to be contained but a system to be defeated. This put him at odds with the long-held view of the foreign policy élites in the '60s, '70s and '80s, but Reagan had an old-fashioned sense that Americans could do any good thing if God blessed the effort. Removing expansionary communism from the world stage was a right and good thing, and why would God not smile upon it?

He was a historical romantic, his biographer Edmund Morris says, and that's about right. He was one tough romantic, though.

When Reagan first entered politics, in 1964, Khrushchev had already promised to bury the U.S., Sputnik had been launched and missiles placed in Cuba. It seemed reasonable to think the Soviets might someday overtake the West. By the time Reagan made a serious run for the presidency, in 1976, it was easy to think the Soviets might conquer America militarily.

But Reagan said no. When he became President, he did what he had promised for a decade to do: he said we were going to rearm, and we built up the U.S. military. He boosted defense spending to make it clear to the Soviets and the world—and to America—that the U.S. did not intend to lose.

As President, he kept pressure on the Soviets at a time when they were beginning to fail internally. He pushed for SDI, the strategic defense missile system that was rightly understood by the Soviets as both a financial challenge and an intimidating expression of the power of U.S. scientific innovation.

There are those who say it was all a bluff, that such a system could never have been and will never be successfully developed. Put that aside for a moment, and consider a more relevant fact: if it was a bluff, the Soviets didn't know it. And more to the point, Reagan as President had the credibility with the Soviets to make a serious threat. (And a particularly Reaganesque threat it was: he said not only would we build SDI, but we would also share it with them.)

Reagan's actions toward the Soviets were matched by his constant rhetorical pounding of communism. He kept it up, for eight years, from "the evil empire" to "Mr. Gorbachev, tear down this wall," a constant attempt to use words to educate and inspire. Margaret Thatcher said it best: Reagan took words and sent them out to fight for us. He never stopped trying to persuade, to win the world over, to help it think about the nature of democracy and the nature of communism, and to consider which system it was that threatened world peace.

**BORN**
Feb. 6, 1911, in Tampico, Ill.

**1911**

**PITCHMAN**
The star endorses cigarettes

CHESTERFIELD

**1947 Elected president of the Screen Actors Guild**

**1948 Divorced from Jane Wyman**

**1952 Marries Nancy Davis**

**1962 Changes from Democratic to Republican Party**

**1966 Elected California's Governor (re-elected 1970)**

**1980 Elected President of the U.S.**

**1981 Shot in attempted assassination**

**1984 Re-elected President**

# "When others demanded compromise, you preached conviction."

**MARGARET THATCHER, 1994 birthday gala for Reagan in Washington**

In doing all this—in insisting that, as the sign he kept on his desk in the Oval Office said, IT CAN BE DONE—he kept up the morale of the anticommunist West. And not only Americans. When Natan Sharansky was freed after nine years in the Gulag, he went to the White House and asked Reagan never to stop his hard-line speeches. Sharansky said news of those speeches was passed from prisoner to prisoner in the forced-labor camps.

After eight years of Reagan and his constant efforts, the Soviet Union collapsed. And Kremlin chieftains who had once promised to bury us were now asking for inclusion in NATO. That this is now a commonplace—ho-hum, the Berlin Wall fell—is proof of how quickly we absorb the astounding. An elderly woman I know was at lunch at a great resort one day before World War I began. Suddenly from the sky, one of those new flying machines, an aeroplane, which no one there had ever seen, zoomed in to land on the smooth, rolling lawn. Everyone ran out to look at this marvel and touch it. What, she was asked 70 years later, did you do after that? "We went inside and finished lunch."

That's what the world did after the Wall came down, and is doing now. We went inside and finished lunch. But it is

**Welcome to the "evil empire"! Reagan and Gorbachev kiss babies in Red Square, 1988**

good to remember: a marvel had visited, had come down and landed on the lawn, even though such things are impossible. And it's good to remember that though many people built and funded and sacrificed for the "plane," Ronald Reagan was its pilot.

Domestically, he was no less a smasher of the status quo, a leader for serious and "impossible" change. F.D.R., the great President of Reagan's young manhood and from whom he learned the sound and tone and tense of the presidency, convinced the country in the 1930s that only the bounty and power of the federal establishment could fully heal a wounded country. Reagan convinced (or reminded) the

country that the bounty came from us, the people, that the power was absorbed from us, the people, and that we the people would benefit from a good portion of their return. Reagan had a libertarian conviction, which is really an old American conviction, that power is best and most justly wielded from the individual to the community to the state and then the Federal Government—and not from the Federal Government on down. He thought, as Jefferson said, that that government governs best that governs least. He wanted to shrink the bloated monster; he wanted to cut very seriously the amount of money the monster took from the citizenry each year in taxes.

He was not afraid to speak on school prayer and abortion, though his aides warned him it hurt him in the polls. He cared about the polls but refused to let them silence him. Abortion is wrong, he said, because it both kills and coarsens.

In doing all this, in taking the actions he took at home and abroad, in using words and conviction and character to fight, he produced the biggest, most successful and most meaningful presidency since Franklin Roosevelt's. In fact, when you look at the great Presidents of this century, I think it comes down to two Roosevelts and a Reagan. Reagan kept Teddy's picture in his Cabinet Room, in part because he loved T.R.'s brio in tackling the big questions.

The result of Reagan's presidency? I asked him a few years after he left office what he thought his legacy was, how he would sum it up. It wasn't a very Reagan question: he didn't think much about his personal place in history, he thought about what was right and then tried to do it. But he told me he thought his eight years could be summed up this way: "He tried to expand the frontiers of human freedom in a world at peace with itself."

He came from nowhere, not from Hyannis Port or Greenwich but from nowhere. He was born above a store in Tampico, Ill., born in fact 16 years before Lucky Lindy landed in Paris. It is easy to romanticize the Midwest Reagan came from, but he didn't. "There was nothing in those towns," he told me when I asked, years ago, why he left. He wanted more, and got it, in Hollywood and beyond. But he was not just a lucky and blessed young man, a bright fellow smiled on by the gods. He had grit.

He showed one kind of grit by becoming a conservative in Hollywood in the '50s and '60s. Just when everyone else was going left, particularly everyone in Hollywood who could enhance his career, he was going right. But he held to his position. It is easier to have convictions when they are shared by everyone around you; it is easier to hold to those convictions when you are surrounded by like-minded people. He almost never was.

He could take it in the face and keep on walking. Reagan-

Always close, the Reagans—both Hollywood veterans—relax on a White House movie date in 1987

ites like to point to his 1976 run for the presidency, when he came within an inch of unseating Jerry Ford. When Reagan lost, he gave a valiant speech to his followers in which he spoke of the cause and signaled that he'd be back.

But I like to remember this: Reagan played Vegas. In 1954, when demand for his acting services was slowing, Reagan emceed a variety act to make money and keep his name in the air. He didn't like doing it. But it was what he had to do, so he did it. The point is, he knew what it was to be through, to have people not answer your calls. When I thought about this time in his life once, I thought, All the great ones have known failure, but only the greatest of the great use it. He always used his. It deepened him and sharpened him.

WHAT WAS IT THAT MADE HIM GREAT? YOU CAN argue that great moments call forth great leaders, that the '20s brought forth a Harding, but the dramatic and demanding '30s and '80s summoned an F.D.R. and a Reagan. In Reagan's case, there was also something else. It was that he didn't become President to reach some egocentric sense of personal destiny; he didn't need the presidency, and he didn't go for it because of some strange vanity, some weird desire to be loved or a need of power to fill the empty spaces within. He didn't want the presidency in order to be a big man. He wanted the presidency so that he could do big things.

I think as we look back we will see him as the last gentleman of American politics. He was as courtly and well mannered as Bill Clinton and Newt Gingrich are not. He was a person of dignity and weight, warmth and wit. The English say a gentleman is one who never insults another by accident, but Reagan took it a step further: he wouldn't insult another on purpose.

For all that, there was of course his famous detachment. I never understood it, and neither, from what I've seen, did anyone else. It is true that when you worked for him, whether for two years or 20, he didn't care that much about your feelings. His saving grace—and it is a big one, a key one to his nature—is that he didn't care much about his feelings either. The cause was all, the effort to make the world calmer and the country freer was all.

Reagan's achievements were adult achievements, but when I think of him now I think of the reaction he got from the young. It was as if some mutual sweetness were sensed on both sides. The man who ran speechwriting in the Reagan White House was Bently Elliott, and Ben's secretary was a woman in her early 20s named Donna. She adored Reagan. When he came back from long trips, when his helicopter landed on the White House lawn, the sound and whirr of the engine and blades would make our offices shake. We'd all stop and listen. Donna would call out, spoofing the mother in a '50s sitcom, "Daddy's home!" But you know, that's how I think a lot of people felt when Reagan was in the White House: Daddy's home. A wise and brave and responsible man is running things. And that's a good way to feel.

Another memory: Ben Elliott went with Reagan on his trip to China in 1984. Reagan spoke everywhere, as the ruling gerontocracy watched and weighed. The elders did not notice that the young of China were falling in love with the American President (that love was expressed in part in Beijing's great square during the pro-democracy movement of 1989). One day as Reagan spoke about the history of America and the nature of democracy, a young Chinese student, standing in the back and listening to the translation, turned to the American visitor, Ben Elliott. He didn't know much English, but he turned to Ben, pointed toward Reagan and said, eyes shining, "He is great Yankeeman."

One great Yankeeman is exactly what he was, and is. ■

*Peggy Noonan, author of* What I Saw at the Revolution, *was a special assistant and speechwriter for President Reagan.*

SŁUŻBOWY

SOLIDARNOSĆ

NSZZ

On the road to freedom: Walesa and Solidarity steered Poland away from communism

# Lech
# Walesa

## Poland's brash union organizer stood up to the Kremlin and dealt the Eastern bloc a fatal blow

**By TIMOTHY GARTON ASH**

LECH WALESA, THE FLY, FEISTY, MUSTACHIOED ELEC-trician from Gdansk, shaped the 20th century as the leader of the Solidarity movement that led the Poles out of communism. It is one of history's great ironies that the nearest thing we have ever seen to a genuine workers' revolution was directed against a so-called workers' state. Poland was again the icebreaker for the rest of Central Europe in the "velvet revolutions" of 1989. Walesa's contribution to the end of communism in Europe, and hence the end of

the cold war, stands beside those of his fellow Pole, Pope John Paul II, and the Soviet leader Mikhail Gorbachev.

Walesa's life, like those of Gorbachev and the Pope, was shaped by communism. Born to a family of peasant farmers in 1943, he came as a young man to work in the vast ship-yards that the communist state was developing on the Baltic coast, as did so many other peasant sons. A devout Roman Catholic, he was shocked by the repression of workers' protests in the 1970s and made contact with small opposition groups. Sacked from his job, he nonetheless climbed over the perimeter wall of the Lenin Shipyard in Gdansk in August 1980, at age 37, to join an occupation strike. With his electrifying personality, quick wit and gift of the gab, he was soon leading it. He moved the work-ers away from mere wage claims and toward a central, daringly political demand: free trade unions.

When the Polish communists made this concession, which was without precedent in the history of the communist world, the new union was christened Solidarnosc (Solidarity). Soon

> # "This prize won't change him one bit; there's not a living soul who could change him."
> **DANUTA WALESA, on her husband's 1983 Nobel Peace Prize**

it had 10 million members, and Walesa was its undisputed leader. For 16 months they struggled to find a way to coexist with the communist state, under the constant threat of Soviet invasion. Walesa—known to almost everyone simply as Lech—was foxy, unpredictable, often infuriating, but he had a natural genius for politics, a matchless ability for sensing popular moods, and great powers of swaying a crowd. Again and again, he used these powers for moderation. He jokingly described himself as a "fireman," dousing the flames of popular discontent. In the end, martial law was declared. Walesa was interned for 11 months and then released.

Yet Solidarity would not die, and Walesa remained its symbol. He was awarded the Nobel Peace Prize in 1983. With support from the Pope and the U.S., he and his colleagues in the underground leadership of Solidarity kept the flame alight, until the advent of Mikhail Gorbachev in the Kremlin brought new hope. In 1988 there was another occupation strike in the Lenin Shipyard, which Walesa again joined—though this time as the grand old man among younger workers. A few months later, the Polish communists entered into negotiations with Solidarity, at the first Round Table of 1989. Walesa and his colleagues secured semi-free elections in which Solidarity proceeded to triumph. In August, just nine years after he had climbed over the shipyard wall, Poland got its first noncommunist Prime Minister in more than 40 years. Where Poland led, the rest of Central Europe soon followed—and the Soviet Union was not far behind.

The next phase in Walesa's political career was more controversial. Angered by the fact that his former intellectual advisers were now running the country in cooperation with the former communists, he declared a "war at the top" of Solidarity. "I don't want to, but I must," he insisted. Fighting a populist campaign against his own former adviser, he was elected Poland's first noncommunist President, a post he held until 1995. Some people liked his stalwart, outspoken style. Others found him too undignified to be a head of state.

Brilliant as a people's tribune, he stumbled over long formal speeches. You never felt he was quite comfortable in the role. When he stayed with the British Queen at Windsor Castle, he quipped that the bed was so big, he couldn't find his wife.

Politically, he was also erratic. As Poland was struggling to be accepted into NATO, he suddenly proposed a NATO *bis*, a shadowy second NATO for those in waiting. Not for the first time, his colleagues put their heads in their hands. His closest adviser was his former chauffeur, with whom he played long games of table tennis. He developed close links with the military and security services. His critics accused him of being authoritarian, a "President with an ax." In another historical irony, he was defeated by a former communist, Aleksander Kwasniewski in 1995. Walesa went back to Gdansk, to his villa, his wife Danuta and their eight children. But at 54 he is still young, and he recently announced the formation of his own political party. Like Gorbachev, he finds it very difficult to accept that he has become a historical figure rather than a politician with serious chances.

**W**ALESA IS A PHENOMENON. STILL MUSTACHIOED but thickset now, he stands for many values that in the West might be thought conservative. Fierce patriotism ("nationalism," say his critics), strong Catholic views, the family. He's a fighter, of course. But he's also mercurial, unpredictable—and a consummate politician. He is an example of someone who was magnificent in the struggle for freedom but less so in more normal times, when freedom was won and the task was to consolidate a stable, law-abiding democracy. For all his presidential airs, he still retains something of the old Lech, the working-class wag and chancer whom his friends remember from the early days. But no one can deny him his place in history.

Without Walesa, the occupation strike in the Lenin Shipyard might never have taken off. Without him, Solidarity might never have been born. Without him, it might not have survived martial law and come back triumphantly to negotiate the transition from communism to democracy. And without the Polish icebreaking, Eastern Europe might still be frozen in a Soviet sphere of influence, and the world would be a very different place. With all Walesa's personal faults, his legacy is a huge gain in freedom, not just for the Poles. His services were, as an old Polish slogan has it, "for our freedom—and yours." ■

*Oxford historian and author Timothy Garton Ash is the author of* The Polish Revolution: Solidarity.

---

**BORN Sept. 29, 1943, in Popowo, Poland**

**1967 Starts as electrician at shipyard in Gdansk**

**1981 Arrested in government crackdown**

**1983 Awarded Nobel Peace Prize**

**1990 Elected President of Poland**

**1943**

**ON GUARD**
**As a loyal soldier in the 1960s**

**1980 Becomes leader of Solidarity**

**1982 Released from internment; martial law eased**

**1989 Solidarity legalized**

**1995 Defeated, he leaves office**

## Mikhail
# Gorbachev

By gently pushing open the gates of reform, he unleashed a democratic flood that deluged the Soviet universe and washed away the cold war

By **TATYANA TOLSTAYA**

IN 1985, WHEN THE FIRST RUMBLINGS OF MIKHAIL Gorbachev's thunder disturbed the moldy Soviet silence, the holy fools on the street—the people who always gather at flea markets and around churches—predicted that the new Czar would rule seven years. They assured anyone interested in listening that Gorbachev was "foretold in the Bible," that he was an apocalyptic figure: he had a mark on his forehead. Everyone had searched for signs in previous leaders as well, but Lenin's speech defect, Stalin's mustache, Brezhnev's eyebrows and Khrushchev's vast baldness were utterly human manifestations. The unusual birthmark on the new General Secretary's forehead, combined with his inexplicably radical actions, gave him a mystical aura. Writing about Gorbachev—who he was, where he came from, what he was after and what his personal stake was (there had to be one)—became just as intriguing as trying to figure out what Russia's future would be.

After he stepped down from his position as head of state, many people of course stopped thinking about him, and in Russian history, that in itself is extraordinary. How Gorbachev left power and what he has done since are unique episodes in Russian history, but he could have foreseen his own resignation: he prepared the ground and the atmosphere that made that resignation possible. Gorbachev is such an entirely political creature, and yet so charismatic, that it's hard to come to any conclusions about him as a person. Every attempt I know of has failed miserably. The phenomenon of Gorbachev has not yet been explained, and most of what I've read on the subject reminds me of how a biologist,

psychologist, lawyer or statistician might describe an angel.

Gorbachev has been discussed in human terms, the usual investigations have been made, his family tree has been studied, a former girlfriend has been unearthed (so what?), the spotlight has been turned on his wife. His completely ordinary education, colleagues, friends and past have all been gone over with a fine-tooth comb. By all accounts, Gorbachev shouldn't have been Gorbachev. Then the pundits study the politics of the Soviet Union, evoke the shadow of Ronald Reagan and Star Wars, drag out tables and graphs to show that the Soviet economy was doomed to self-destruct, that it already had, that the country couldn't have gone on that way any longer. But what was Reagan to us, when we had managed to overcome Hitler while living in the inhuman conditions of Stalinism? No single approach—and there have been many—can explain Gorbachev. Perhaps the holy fools with their metaphysical scenario were right when they whispered that he was marked and that seven years were given to him to transform Russia in the name of her as yet invisible but inevitable salvation and renaissance.

After the August 1991 coup, Gorbachev was deprived of power, cast out, laughed at and reproached with all the misfortunes, tragedies and lesser and greater catastrophes that took place during his rule. Society always reacts more painfully to individual deaths than it does to mass annihilation. The crackdowns in Georgia and Lithuania—the Gorbachev regime's clumsy attempts to preclude the country's collapse—led to the death of several dozen people. Their names are known, their photographs were published in the press, and one feels terribly

---

**BORN** March 2, 1931, in Privolnoye, a village in southern Russia

1931

**ROLE MODEL** Receiving a kerchief from a Young Pioneer, 1966

**1985** Elected General Secretary of the Communist Party of the Soviet Union

**1986** Initiates a period of political openness (*glasnost*) and transformation (*perestroika*) intended to modernize the U.S.S.R.

**1990** Awarded the Nobel Peace Prize

**1990-91** President of the Soviet Union until its dismantlement

sorry for them and their families. Boris Yeltsin's carnage in Chechnya, the bloody events in Tadjikistan, the establishment of feudal orders in the central Asian republics and the massive eradication of all human rights throughout the territory of the former Soviet Union are, however, regarded indifferently, as if they were in the order of things, as if they were not a direct consequence of the current regime's irresponsible policies.

Corruption did exist under Gorbachev; after Gorbachev it blossomed with new fervor. Oppressive poverty did exist under Gorbachev; after Gorbachev it reached the level of starvation. Under Gorbachev the system of residence permits did fetter the population; after Gorbachev hundreds up-

**Ending Kremlin isolation, Gorbachev mingles with the citizens of Orel in 1988**

on hundreds of thousands lost their property and the roofs over their heads and set off across the country seeking refuge from people as angry and hungry as they were.

No doubt Gorbachev made mistakes. No doubt his maneuvering between the Scylla of a totalitarian regime and the Charybdis of democratic ideas was far from irreproachable. No doubt he listened to and trusted the wrong people; no doubt his hearing and sight were dulled by the enormous pressure, and he made many crude, irreversible mistakes. But maybe not. In a country accustomed to the ruler's answering for everything, even burned stew and spilled milk are held against the Czar and never forgiven. Similarly, shamanism has always been a trait of the Russian national character: we cough and infect everyone around us, but when we all get sick, we throw stones at the shaman because his spells didn't work.

When Gorbachev was overthrown, for some reason everyone thought it was a good thing. The conservatives were pleased because in their eyes he was the cause of the regime's demise (they were absolutely right). The radicals were happy because in their opinion he was an obstacle to the republics' independence and too cautious in enacting economic reforms (they too were correct). This man with the stain on his forehead attempted simultaneously to contain

and transform the country, to destroy and reconstruct, right on the spot. One can be Hercules and clean the Augean stable. One can be Atlas and hold up the heavenly vault. But no one has ever succeeded in combining the two roles. Surgery was demanded of Gorbachev, but angry shouts broke out whenever he reached for the scalpel. He wasn't a Philippine healer who could remove a tumor without incisions or blood.

Strangely enough, no one ever thought Gorbachev particularly honest, fair or noble. But after he was gone, the country was overwhelmed by a flood of dishonesty, corruption, lies and outright banditry that no one expected. Those who reproached him for petty indulgences at government expense—for instance, every room of his government dacha had a television set—themselves stole billions; those who were indignant that he sought advice from his wife managed to set up their closest relatives with high-level, well-paid state jobs. All the pygmies of previous years, afraid to squeak in the pre-Gorbachev era, later, with no risk of response, felt justified in insulting him.

THE PETTINESS OF THE ACCUSATIONS speaks for itself. Gorbachev's Pizza Hut ads provoke particular ridicule, and while the idea is indeed amusing, they pay his rent. The scorn reminds me of how the Russian upper crust once castigated Peter the Great for being unafraid to roll up his sleeves and get his hands dirty. Amazingly, in our huge, multinational country, where the residents of St. Petersburg speak with a different accent from that in Moscow, Gorbachev's southern speech is held against him.

In the 1996 election, 1.5% of the electorate voted for him. That's about 1.5 million people. I think about those people; I wonder who they are. But I'll never know. The press hysteria before the election was extraordinary. Ordinary people no longer trusted or respected the moribund Yeltsin, but many were afraid of the communists and Gennadi Zyuganov, so the campaign was carried out under the slogans "The lesser of two evils" and "Better dead than red." All my friends either voted for Yeltsin, sighing and chanting the sacred phrases, or, overcome by apathy or revulsion, didn't vote at all. I asked everyone, "Why not vote for Gorbachev?" "He doesn't have a chance," was the answer. "I would, but others won't, and Zyuganov will be elected as a result," some said.

This, at least, was a pragmatic approach. But it turns out that there were 1.5 million dreamers, people who hadn't forgotten that bright if short period of time when the chains fell one after another, when every day brought greater freedom and hope, when life acquired meaning and prospects, when, it even seemed, people loved one another and felt that a general reconciliation was possible. ■

*The most recent book by Russian novelist and short-story writer Tatyana Tolstaya is* Sleepwalker in the Fog.

## Nelson
# Mandela

As the world's most famous prisoner and, now, his country's leader,
he exemplifies a moral integrity that shines far beyond South Africa

**By ANDRE BRINK**

**I**N A 1998 TELEVISION BROADCAST, BBC COMMENTATOR Brian Walden argued that Nelson Mandela, "perhaps the most generally admired figure of our age, falls short of the giants of the past." Mandela himself argues that "I was not a messiah, but an ordinary man who had become a leader because of extraordinary circumstances." Clearly, a changing world demands redefinition of old concepts. In the revolution led by Mandela to transform a model of racial division and oppression into an open democracy, he demonstrated that he didn't flinch from taking up arms, but his real qualities came to the fore after his time as an activist—during his 27 years in prison and in the years since his release, when he had to negotiate the challenge of turning a myth into a man.

Rolihlahla Mandela was born deep in the black homeland of Transkei on July 18, 1918. His first name could be interpreted, prophetically, as "troublemaker." The Nelson was added later, by a primary school teacher with delusions of imperial splendor. Mandela's boyhood was peaceful enough, spent on cattle herding and other rural pursuits, until the death of his father landed him in the care of a powerful relative, the acting regent of the Thembu people. But it was only after he left the missionary College of Fort Hare, where he had become involved in student protests against the white colonial rule of the institution, that he set out on the long walk toward personal and national liberation.

Having run away from his guardian to avoid an arranged marriage, he joined a law firm in Johannesburg as an appren-

tice. Years of daily exposure to the inhumanities of apartheid, where being black reduced one to the status of a nonperson, kindled in him a kind of absurd courage to change the world. It meant that instead of the easy life in a rural setting he'd been brought up for, or even a modest measure of success as a lawyer, his only certainties would be sacrifice and suffering, with little hope of success in a country in which centuries of colonial rule had concentrated all political and military power, all access to education and most of the wealth in the hands of the white minority. The classic conditions for a successful revolution were almost wholly absent: the great mass of have-nots had been humbled into docile collusion, the geographic expanse of the country hampered communication and mobility, and the prospects of a race war were not only unrealistic but also horrendous.

In these circumstances Mandela opted for nonviolence as a strategy. He joined the Youth League of the African National Congress and became involved in programs of passive resistance against the laws that forced blacks to carry passbooks and kept them in a position of permanent servility.

Exasperated, the government mounted a massive treason trial against its main opponents, Mandela among them. It dragged on for five years, until 1961, ending in the acquittal of all 156 accused. But by that time the country had been convulsed by the massacre of peaceful black demonstrators at Sharpeville in March 1960, and the government was intent on

> ## "We all see ourselves reflected in his glory. A glory that arises in his humility, his sense of forgiveness."
>
> **THABO MBEKI, A.N.C. leader, May 1994**

crushing all opposition. Most liberation movements, including the A.N.C., were banned. Earning a reputation as the Black Pimpernel, Mandela went underground for more than a year and traveled abroad to enlist support for the A.N.C.

Soon after his return, he was arrested and sentenced to imprisonment for five years on Robben Island; within months practically all the leaders of the A.N.C. were arrested. Mandela was hauled from prison to face with them an almost certain death sentence on charges of conspiracy. His statement from the dock was destined to smolder in the homes and servant quarters, the shacks and shebeens and huts and hovels of the oppressed, and to burn in the conscience of the world: "During my lifetime I have dedicated myself to the struggle of the African people. I have fought against white domination, and I have fought against black domination. I have cherished the ideal of a democratic and free society in which all persons live together in harmony and with equal opportunities. It is an ideal which I hope to live for and to achieve. But, if needs be, it is an ideal for which I am prepared to die."

Without any attempt to find a legal way out, Mandela assumed his full responsibility. This conferred a new status of moral dignity on his leadership, which became evident from the moment he was returned to Robben Island. Even on his first arrival, two years before, he had set an example by refusing to obey an order to jog from the harbor, where the ferry docked, to the prison gates. The warden in charge warned him bluntly that unless he started obeying, he might quite simply be killed and that no one on the mainland would ever be the wiser. Whereupon Mandela quietly retorted, "If you so much as lay a hand on me, I will take you to the highest court in the land, and when I finish with you, you will be as poor as a church mouse." Amazingly, the warden backed off. "Any man or institution that tries to rob me of my dignity will lose," Mandela later wrote in notes smuggled out by friends.

His major response to the indignities of the prison was a creative denial of victimhood, expressed most remarkably by a system of self-education, which earned the prison the appellation of "Island University." As the prisoners left their cells in the morning to toil in the extremes of summer and winter, buffeted by the merciless southeaster or broiled by the African sun (whose glare in the limestone quarry permanently impaired Mandela's vision), each team was assigned an instructor—in history, economics, politics, philosophy, whatever. Previously barren recreation hours were filled with cultural activities, and Mandela recalls with pride his acting in the role of Creon in Sophocles' *Antigone*.

After more than two decades in prison, confident that on some crucial issues a leader must make decisions on his own, Mandela decided on a new approach. And after painstaking preliminaries, the most famous prisoner in the world was escorted, in the greatest secrecy, to the State President's office to start negotiating not only his own release but also the nation's transition from apartheid to democracy. On Feb. 2, 1990, President F.W. de Klerk lifted the ban on the A.N.C. and announced Mandela's imminent release.

THEN BEGAN THE REAL TEST. EVERY INCH OF THE WAY, Mandela had to win the support of his own followers. More difficult still was the process of allaying white fears. But the patience, the wisdom, the visionary quality Mandela brought to his struggle, and above all the moral integrity with which he set about to unify a divided people, resulted in the country's first democratic elections and his selection as President.

The road since then has not been easy. Tormented by the scandals that pursued his wife Winnie, from whom he finally parted; plagued by corruption among his followers; dogged by worries about delivering on programs of job creation and housing in a country devastated by white greed, he has become a sadder, wiser man.

In the process he has undeniably made mistakes, arising from a stubborn belief in himself. Yet his stature and integrity remain such that these failings tend to enhance rather than diminish his humanity. Albert Camus once said one man's chains imply that we are all enslaved; Mandela proves through his own example that faith, hope and charity are qualities attainable by humanity as a whole. Through his willingness to walk the road of sacrifice, he has reaffirmed our common potential to move toward a new age.

And he is not deluded by the adulation of the world. Asked to comment on the BBC's unflattering verdict on his performance as a leader, Mandela said with a smile, "It helps to make you human." ∎

*André Brink, a professor at the University of Cape Town, is the author of* A Dry White Season *and other works.*

**BORN July 18, 1918, in the Transkei**

**1944 Joins the antiapartheid African National Congress**

**1962-90 Imprisoned because he advocated sabotage**

**1993 Shares the Nobel Peace Prize with F.W. de Klerk for dismantling apartheid**

1918

**PROTEST Burning his passbook, 1960**

**1956-61 Tried for treason and acquitted**

**1991 Becomes, one year after his release, president of the A.N.C.**

**1994 Elected South Africa's President**

# The Unknown Rebel

### With a single act of defiance, an anonymous Chinese hero revived the world's image of courage

**By PICO IYER**

**The power and the glory: Beijing, 1989**

ALMOST NOBODY KNEW HIS NAME. NOBODY OUTside his immediate neighborhood had read his words or heard him speak. Nobody knows what happened to him even one hour after his moment in the world's living rooms. But the man who stood before a column of tanks near Tiananmen Square—June 5, 1989—may have impressed his image on the global memory more vividly, more intimately than even Sun Yat-sen did. Almost certainly he was seen in his moment of self-transcendence by more people than ever laid eyes on Winston Churchill, Albert Einstein and James Joyce combined.

The meaning of his moment—it was no more than that—was instantly decipherable in any tongue, to any age: even the billions who cannot read and those who have never heard of Mao Zedong could follow what the "tank man" did. A small, unexceptional figure, carrying what looks to be his shopping, posts himself before an approaching tank, with a line of 17 more tanks behind it. The tank swerves right; he, to block it, moves left. The tank swerves left; he moves right. Then this anonymous bystander clambers up onto the vehicle of war and says something to its driver, which comes down to us as: "Why are you here? My city is in chaos because of you." One lone Everyman standing up to machinery, to force, to all the massed weight of the People's Republic—the largest nation in the world, comprising more than 1 billion people—while its all powerful leaders remain, as ever, in hiding somewhere within the bowels of the Great Hall of the People.

Occasionally, unexpectedly, history consents to disguise itself as allegory, and China, which traffics in grand impersonals, has often led the world in mass-producing symbols in block capitals. The man who defied the tank was standing on the Avenue of Eternal Peace, close by the Gate of Heavenly Peace, which leads into the Forbidden City. Nearby Tiananmen Square—the very heart of the Middle Kingdom, where students had demonstrated in 1919; where Mao had proclaimed a "People's Republic" in 1949; and where leaders inspect their People's Liberation Army troops—is a virtual monument to People Power in the abstract. Its western edge is taken up by the Great Hall of the People. Its eastern side is dominated by the Museum of Chinese Revolution. The Mao Zedong mausoleum swallows up its southern face.

For seven weeks, though, in the late spring of 1989—the modern year of revolutions—the Chinese people took back the square, first a few workers and students and teachers and soldiers, then more and more, until more than 1 million had assembled there. They set up, in the heart of the ancient nation, their own world within the world, complete with a daily newspaper, a broadcasting tent, even a 30-ft. plaster-covered statue they called the "Goddess of Democracy." Their "conference hall" was a Kentucky Fried Chicken parlor on the southwest corner of the square, and their spokesmen were 3,000 hunger strikers who spilled all over the central Monument to the People's Heroes. The unofficials even took over, and reversed, the formal symbolism of the government's ritual pageantry: when Mikhail Gorbachev came to

We knew that the purification of the republic could only be achieved by our sacrifice.

CHAI LING, student leader, hours after the massacre at Tiananmen

the Great Hall of the People for a state banquet during the demonstrations—the first visit by a Soviet leader in 30 years—he had to steal in by the back door.

Then, in the dark early hours of June 4, the government struck back, sending tanks from all directions toward Tiananmen Square and killing hundreds of workers and students and doctors and children, many later found shot in the back. In the unnatural quiet after the massacre, with the six-lane streets eerily empty and a burned-out bus along the road, it fell to the tank man to serve as the last great defender of the peace, an Unknown Soldier in the struggle for human rights.

As soon as the man had descended from the tank, anxious onlookers pulled him to safety, and the waters of anonymity closed around him once more. Some people said he was called Wang Weilin, was 19 years old and a student; others said not even that much could be confirmed. Some said he was a factory worker's son, others that he looked like a provincial just

arrived in the capital. When American newsmen asked Chinese leader Jiang Zemin a year later what had happened to the symbol of Chinese freedom—broadcast around the world—he replied, not very ringingly, "I think never killed."

In fact, the image of the man before the tank simplified—even distorted—many complex truths. The students leading the demonstrations notoriously bickered among themselves; many were moved by needs less lofty than pure freedom. At least seven retired generals had written to the *People's Daily* opposing the imposition of martial law, and many of the soldiers sent to put down the demonstrators were surely as young, as confused and as uncommitted to aggression as many of the students were. As one of the pro-democracy movement's leaders said, the heroes of the tank picture are two: the unknown figure who risked his life by standing in front of the juggernaut and the driver who rose to the moral challenge by refusing to mow down his compatriot.

> ## "We can in no way leave [rioters] unpunished and let them stage a comeback."
>
> **LI PENG, Prime Minister of China, June 19, 1989**

**U.S. students protest the Vietnam War in Washington, 1967**

Some nine years after the June 4 incident, moreover, it's unclear how much the agitators for democracy actually achieved. Li Peng, who oversaw the crackdown on them, is still near the top of China's hierarchy. Jiang, who proved his colors by coming down hard on demonstrators in Shanghai, is now the country's President. And on a bright winter morning, Tiananmen Square is still filled, as it was back then, with bird-faced kites and peasants from the countryside lining up to have their photos taken amid the monuments to Mao.

**Y**ET FOR ALL THE QUALIFICATIONS, THE MAN WHO stood before the tanks reminded us that the conviction of the young can generate a courage that their elders sometimes lack. And, like student rebels everywhere, he stood up against the very Great Man of History theory. In China in particular, a Celestial Empire that has often seemed to be ruled by committee, a "mandate of Heaven" consecrated to the might of the collective, the individual has sometimes been seen as hardly more than a work unit in some impersonal equation. A "small number" were killed, Mao once said of the death of 70,000, and in his Great Leap Forward, at least 20 million more were sacrificed to a leader's theories. In that context, the man before the tank seems almost a counter-Mao, daring to act as the common-man hero tirelessly promoted by propaganda and serving as a rebuke—or asterisk, at least—to the leaders and revolutionaries who share these pages.

More than a third of a century ago, before anyone had ever heard of the World Wide Web or CNN, Daniel Boorstin, in his uncannily prescient book *The Image*, described how, as we move deeper into what he called the Graphic Revolution, technology would threaten to diminish us. Ideas, even ideals, would be reduced to the level of images, and faith itself might be sim-

plified into credulity. "Two centuries ago, when a great man appeared," the historian wrote, "people looked for God's purpose in him; today we look for his press agent."

The hero—so ran Boorstin's prophecy—was being replaced by the celebrity, and where once our leaders seemed grander versions of ourselves, now they just looked like us on a giant screen. Nowadays, as we read about the purported telephone messages of a sitting President and listen to the future King of England whisper to his mistress, the power of technology not just to dehumanize but to demystify seems 30 times stronger than even Boorstin predicted.

But the man with the tank showed us another face, so to speak, of the camera and gave us an instance in which the image did not cut humanity down to size but elevated and affirmed it, serving as an instrument for democracy and justice. Instead of making the lofty trivial, as it so often seems to do, the image made the passing eternal and assisted in the resistance of an airbrushed history written by the winners. Technology, which can so often implement violence or oppression, can also give a nobody a voice and play havoc with power's vertical divisions by making a gesture speak a thousand words. The entire Tiananmen uprising, in fact, was a subversion underwritten by machines, which obey no government and observe no borders: the protesters got around official restrictions by communicating with friends abroad via fax; they followed their progress—unrecorded on Chinese TV—by watching themselves on foreigners' satellite sets in the Beijing Hotel; and in subsequent years they have used the Internet—and their Western training—to claim an economic freedom they could not get politically.

The second half of this century has been shadowed by one overwhelming, ungovernable thought: that the moods, even the whims, of a single individual, post-Oppenheimer, could destroy much of the globe in a moment. Yet the image of the man before the tank stands for the other side of that dark truth: that in a world ever more connected, the actions of a regular individual can light up the whole globe in an instant.

For centuries the walls of the grand palaces and castles of the Old World have been filled with ceremonial and often highly flattering pictures of noblemen and bewigged women looking out toward the posterity they hope to shape. But these days, in the video archives of the memory, playing in eternal rerun, are many new faces, unknown, that remind us how much history is made at the service entrance by people lopped out of the official photographs or working in obscurity to fashion our latest instruments and cures. In a century in which so many tried to impress their monogram on history, often in blood red, the man with the tank—Wang Weilin, or whoever—stands for the forces of the unnamed: the Unknown Soldier of a new Republic of the Image. ∎

*Pico Iyer is an essayist, novelist and travel writer. His most recent book is* Tropical Classical.

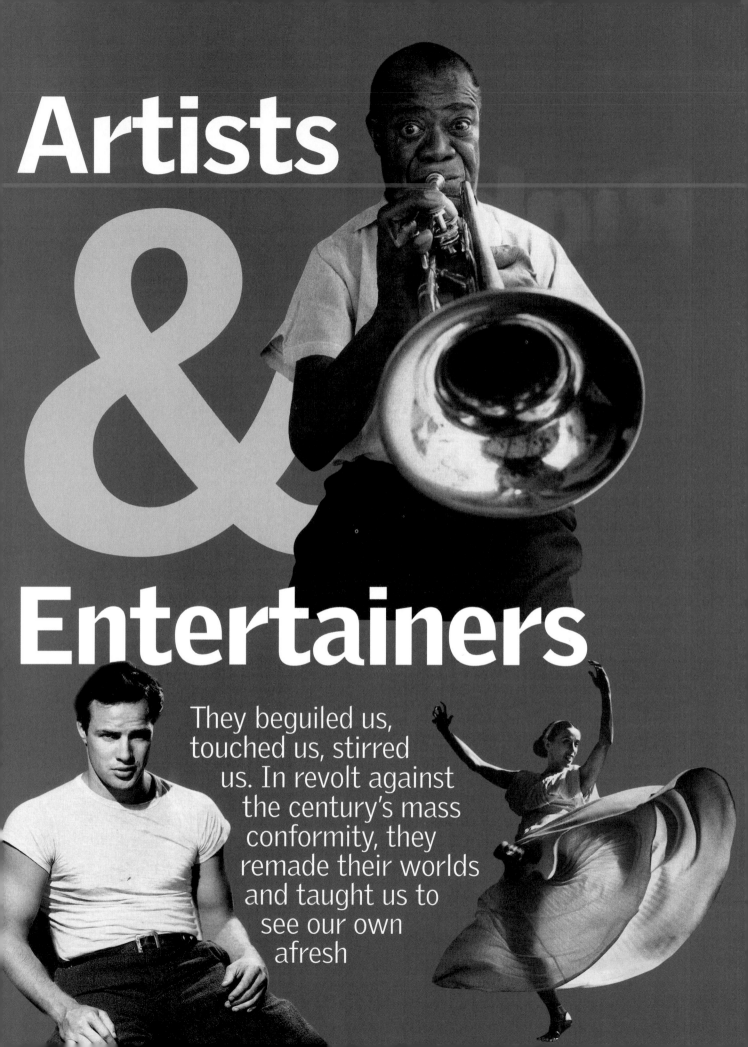

# Artists & Entertainers

They beguiled us, touched us, stirred us. In revolt against the century's mass conformity, they remade their worlds and taught us to see our own afresh

# Right
## Before
## Our Eyes

By CHRISTOPHER PORTERFIELD

**O**ur pell-mell 20th century wasted no time in first sounding its characteristic theme in the arts. That theme was—what else?—change. Radical, rapid, sweeping change. And more of it than had ever been seen before. Within the century's first two decades, Pablo Picasso, Igor Stravinsky and James Joyce— the advance squadron of modernism—created works that broke dramatically with the past, tearing apart traditional artistic structures and reassembling them in startling new ways. The convulsion of World War I only

**THE ARTIST**
Luba Lukova

reinforced the modernists' conviction that the West's moral and cultural heritage had collapsed. All that remained, in T.S. Eliot's vision, was a *Waste Land* crying out for creative renewal. To Virginia Woolf, what had happened was more fundamental even than geopolitics or culture. Looking back in 1924, she concluded that "on or about December, 1910, human character changed."

Yet where the arts were concerned, these pioneers still didn't know the half of it. Even as they shaped their dense, experimental innovations—sometimes deliberately designing them to flummox the bourgeoisie—change of a different order was taking place a few steps down the cultural and social scale. All kinds of exuberant, colorful and popular new art forms and media were springing to life—more new forms and media than had arisen in any previous century.

Already, in 1900, Guglielmo Marconi had worked out the essentials of radio. The phonograph was fast evolving into the basis for a recording industry. By 1912, 5 million Americans a day were attending a new entertainment called movies. New Orleans echoed with the sounds that were jumbling together gloriously as jazz. Denizens of Tin Pan Alley were polishing the wit and jaunty lyricism of the pop song and revamping European operetta into an original American theater form: the musical.

No previous century had seen such a potent interaction between the arts and technology. You have to go back to the invention of the printing press in the 1450s to find anything comparable. Now, seemingly overnight, machines and electronics were transforming virtually everything. Photography, an important 19th century invention, became almost a different medium in the 1920s and '30s with the combination of high-quality, handheld cameras, film on an advanceable roll, and the flashbulb. Photographers were free to roam the fields and streets. They could cover crimes and wars. Soft, pretty pictures gave way to a more spontaneous, realistic style.

Recording technology changed popular music from sheet music, performed in Victorian theaters and parlors, to disks that spread thousands or millions of copies of a given performance across the landscape (and across radio's airwaves). The original 78-r.p.m. record was just that—a passive record of a three- or four-minute song. In 1948 the l.p. accommodated longer pieces as well as the arrangement of various tracks according to a unifying theme. Soon, as with the Beatles' *Sgt. Pepper's Lonely Hearts Club Band,* an album became an electronic creation in its own right, impossible to duplicate in performance. These days, when voices and whole orchestras can be conjured out of a synthesizer, one wonders whether recording is even the word for it anymore.

But the most technological entertainment medium in history is movies, as anybody can surmise from seeing the small army of technicians on a sound stage or location. Technology gave the silents a voice in 1927 (though some of the great silent performers, such as Charlie Chaplin, took their time about speaking), but more important, it enabled film to refine its unique visual language.

What created the movies' vivid, fluent brand of illusion-

> After the 1960s, literature, theater and classical music lost the authority to set the cultural agenda. Today the influence, the action, the buzz is all pop.

ism—besides the talents of great filmmakers, of course—was the development of more mobile cameras, more expressive lighting, more sophisticated editing and, above all, more ingenious special effects that could bring to life prehistoric worlds of dinosaurs and future worlds of space travel. And let's not forget animated films, perhaps the purest cinema of all, in which technology allows the creation of an entire visual world unimpeded by such tiresome exigencies of the real world as sets, props and actors.

NEW TECHNOLOGIES MEANT NEW AUDIENCES—AND new relationships between artists and audiences. Movies were the century's first mass medium after print. But although millions of viewers could have the same experience at the movies, they experienced it a few hundred at a time, in individual theaters. Radio was the first entertainment medium to enable a mass audience to have the same experience instantaneously and simultaneously. Even more than movies, radio gave audiences an intensely communal feeling, a sense of being part of something national, as well as a special intimacy with its stars.

TV upped the ante by being as immediate as radio and as visual as the movies. Indeed, TV's mesmerizing hold is something unprecedented. A major TV event is overwhelmingly a shared national experience, and a TV star is a celebrity of a new order. When Lucy Ricardo has a baby, when *Seinfeld* goes off the air, it's not something that's happening out there—it's an event in our homes and in our lives.

And this is to say nothing of TV's power to bring us real-life events: a moon walk or the Olympics, an uprising in Tiananmen Square or Princess Diana's funeral. We conduct not only a lot of our fantasy lives on TV but also our political campaigns (and sometimes it's hard to tell which is which). From the Persian Gulf in 1991, we learned that global TV can even be a means of waging war.

The first two assumptions made about the advent of TV were dead wrong: that it would bury radio and that it would be a threat to movies. From the start, TV has provided a generous showcase for other arts—radio performances and movies included. Millions of people who, in earlier centuries or even earlier decades of this century, would never have seen world-class ballets, operas, concerts or museum works of art have seen them on TV. Not quite the same as live, perhaps, but considerably better than nothing.

The medium's own most distinctive format bears out a theory of its first prophet, Marshall McLuhan. TV discovered that on the whole, amid all its sitcoms and music and dramas, the most entertaining and sometimes the most gripping thing it can show us is people sitting and talking to one another, and to us. McLuhan argued that speech is the richest form of communication because it involves several of the senses—sight, sound, touch, etc.—and that speech on TV is the nearest facsimile yet to the face-to-face variety. Hence the ubiquitous talk show. Hence hosts with an uncanny ability to gaze into the camera and connect emotionally with viewers. And hence our feeling that we know Johnny Carson or Oprah Winfrey as we know a friend or a family member.

It's no accident that we tend to locate the defining artistic moments of recent decades in TV and other popular media, whereas in earlier decades we found them in, say, literature or painting. This stems from the other convulsion the century had in store for the arts in addition to World War I. (Oddly, it wasn't World War II. That conflict's primary impact came from the waves of European artists who fled Nazism for the U.S., enriching the country's homegrown arts and shifting the center of gravity in such fields as painting and classical music.)

The second major upheaval was the 1960s. Again, a rupture opened with the past; received standards and values were under siege, this time in the ferment of civil rights, the sexual revolution and Vietnam. In the arts the rumbling had started in the '50s, when Elvis Presley got everybody all shook up, when Jack Kerouac took to the road and Allen Ginsberg began to howl. In 1969, in a muddy field in New York's Catskill Mountains, more than 400,000 of their spiritual heirs gathered at the Woodstock Festival to stake their claim as a new generation and a new social and political force, complete with a language of their own—rock music.

From then on, youth and pop culture were in the ascendant. The rock sensibility permeated the other arts—painting, film, even TV. Blacks, women and others who had been jostling on the cultural fringe increasingly moved toward center stage.

And what about the heirs of Joyce and Stravinsky? Still doing brilliant work from time to time, to be sure. But broadly speaking, the energies of high modernism had played themselves out, and the ironic, self-conscious borrowings of postmodernism did not advance the cause much. Literature, the theater and classical music lost the authority to set the cultural agenda. Today the influence, the action, the buzz is all pop.

Here's another first for the 20th century: it's the first in

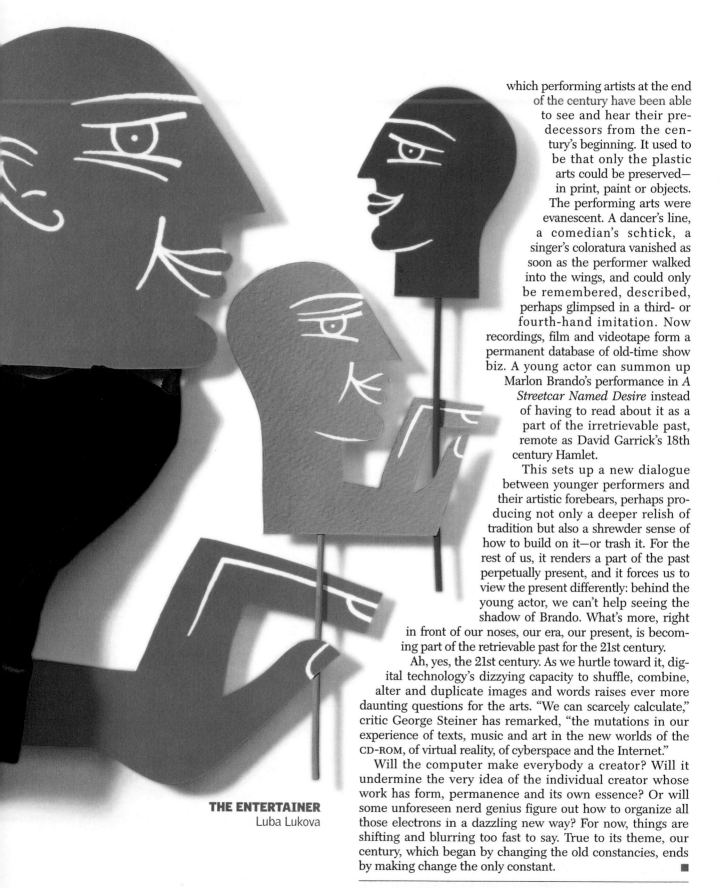

**THE ENTERTAINER**
Luba Lukova

which performing artists at the end of the century have been able to see and hear their predecessors from the century's beginning. It used to be that only the plastic arts could be preserved—in print, paint or objects. The performing arts were evanescent. A dancer's line, a comedian's schtick, a singer's coloratura vanished as soon as the performer walked into the wings, and could only be remembered, described, perhaps glimpsed in a third- or fourth-hand imitation. Now recordings, film and videotape form a permanent database of old-time show biz. A young actor can summon up Marlon Brando's performance in *A Streetcar Named Desire* instead of having to read about it as a part of the irretrievable past, remote as David Garrick's 18th century Hamlet.

This sets up a new dialogue between younger performers and their artistic forebears, perhaps producing not only a deeper relish of tradition but also a shrewder sense of how to build on it—or trash it. For the rest of us, it renders a part of the past perpetually present, and it forces us to view the present differently: behind the young actor, we can't help seeing the shadow of Brando. What's more, right in front of our noses, our era, our present, is becoming part of the retrievable past for the 21st century.

Ah, yes, the 21st century. As we hurtle toward it, digital technology's dizzying capacity to shuffle, combine, alter and duplicate images and words raises ever more daunting questions for the arts. "We can scarcely calculate," critic George Steiner has remarked, "the mutations in our experience of texts, music and art in the new worlds of the CD-ROM, of virtual reality, of cyberspace and the Internet."

Will the computer make everybody a creator? Will it undermine the very idea of the individual creator whose work has form, permanence and its own essence? Or will some unforeseen nerd genius figure out how to organize all those electrons in a dazzling new way? For now, things are shifting and blurring too fast to say. True to its theme, our century, which began by changing the old constancies, ends by making change the only constant. ∎

*Executive editor Christopher Porterfield has covered the arts and media for* TIME *for more than 30 years.*

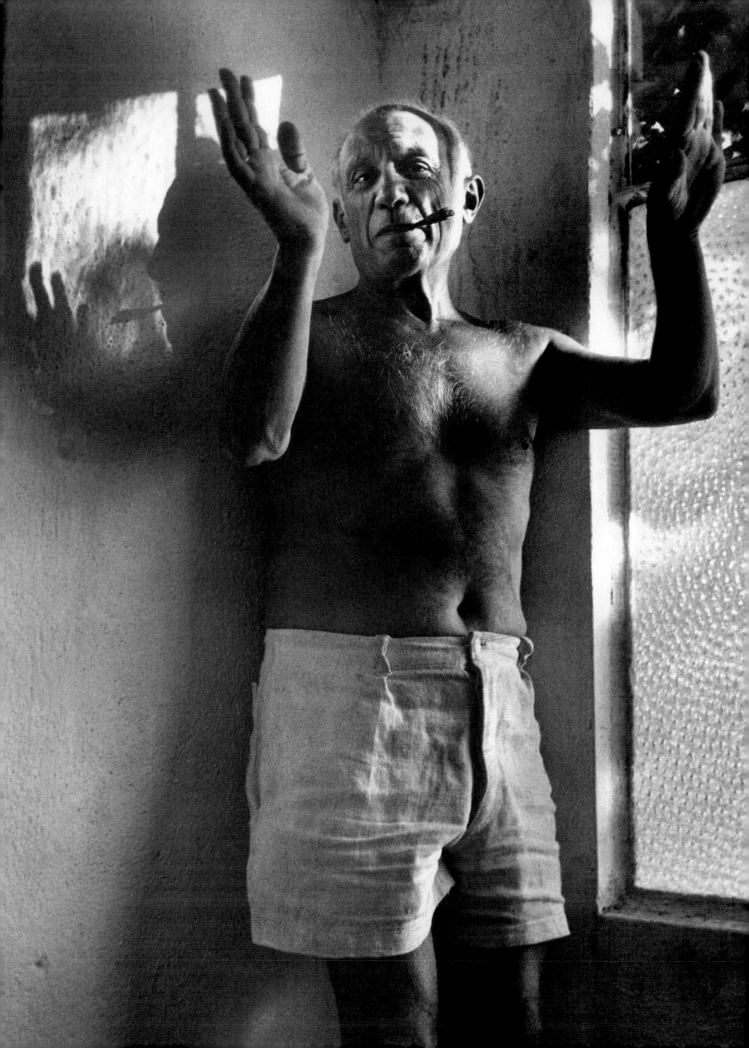

# Pablo Picasso

## Famous as no artist ever had been, he was a pioneer, a master and a protean monster, with a hand in every art movement of the century

**By ROBERT HUGHES**

TO SAY THAT PABLO PICASSO DOMINATED WESTERN art in the 20th century is, by now, the merest commonplace. Before his 50th birthday, the little Spaniard from Málaga had become the very prototype of the modern artist as public figure. No painter before him had had a mass audience in his own lifetime. The total public for Titian in the 16th century or Velázquez in the 17th was probably no more than a few thousand people—though that included most of the crowned heads, nobility and intelligentsia of Europe. Picasso's audience—meaning people who had heard of him and seen his work, at least in reproduction—was in the tens, possibly hundreds, of millions. He and his work were the subjects of unending analysis, gossip, dislike, adoration and rumor.

He was a superstitious, sarcastic man, sometimes rotten to his children, often beastly to his women. He had contempt for women artists. His famous remark about women being "goddesses or doormats" has rendered him odious to feminists, but women tended to walk into both roles open-eyed and eagerly, for his charm was legendary. Whole cultural industries derived from his much mythologized virility. He was the Minotaur in a canvas-and-paper labyrinth of his own construction.

Picasso's *Les Demoiselles d'Avignon,* 1907, jolted painting into modernity

He was also politically lucky. Though to Nazis his work was the epitome of "degenerate art," his fame protected him during the German occupation of Paris, where he lived; and after the war, when artists and writers were thought disgraced by the slightest affiliation with Nazism or fascism, Picasso gave enthusiastic endorsement to Joseph Stalin, a mass murderer on a scale far beyond Hitler's, and scarcely received a word of criticism for it, even in cold war America.

No painter or sculptor, not even the sainted Michelangelo, had been as famous as this in his own lifetime. And it is quite possible that none ever will be again, now that the mandate to set forth social meaning, to articulate myth and generate widely memorable images has been so largely transferred from painting and sculpture to other media: photography, movies, television. Though Marcel Duchamp, that cunning old fox of conceptual irony, has certainly had more influence on nominally vanguard art over the past 30 years, Picasso was the last great beneficiary of the belief that the language of painting and sculpture really mattered to people other than their devotees. And he was the first artist to enjoy the obsessive attention of mass media. Picasso stood at the intersection of these two worlds. If that had not been so, his restless changes of style, his constant pushing of the envelope, would

**BORN**
**Oct. 25, 1881, in Málaga, Spain**

**1904 Settles in Paris**

**1937 *Guernica* commemorates the Basque town bombed in the Spanish Civil War**

**1980 Exhibit filling New York City's Museum of Modern Art draws 1 million**

**1881**

**1973**

**EL NIÑO Paris would transform the young Spaniard**

**1910 Joins with Georges Braque to formulate Cubism**

**1962 Receives second Lenin Peace Prize from the Soviet Union**

**1973 Dies April 8 in France**

## He is the last artist in this century ... who will have been a real king during his lifetime.

**ROBERT MOTHERWELL, artist**

not have created such controversy—and thus such celebrity.

In today's art world, a place without living culture heroes, you can't even imagine such a protean monster arising. His output was vast. This is not a virtue in itself—only a few paintings by Vermeer survive, and fewer still by the brothers Van Eyck, but they are as firmly lodged in history as Picasso ever was or will be. Still, Picasso's oeuvre filled the world, and he left permanent marks on every discipline he entered. His work expanded fractally, one image breeding new clusters of others, right up to his death.

**In his Paris studio, 1915, where he explored Cubism with Braque**

Moreover, he was the artist with whom virtually every other artist had to reckon, and there was scarcely a 20th century movement that he didn't inspire, contribute to or—in the case of Cubism, which, in one of art history's great collaborations, he co-invented with Georges Braque—beget. The exception, since Picasso never painted an abstract picture in his life, was abstract art; but even there his handprints lay everywhere—one obvious example being his effect on the early work of American Abstract Expressionist painters Arshile Gorky, Jackson Pollock and Willem de Kooning, among others.

Much of the story of modern sculpture is bound up with welding and assembling images from sheet metal, rather than modeling in clay, casting in bronze or carving in wood; and

this tradition of the open constructed form rather than solid mass arose from one small guitar that Picasso snipped and joined out of tin in 1912. If collage—the gluing of previously unrelated things and images on a flat surface—became a basic mode of modern art, that too was due to Picasso's Cubist collaboration with Braque. He was never a member of the Surrealist group, but in the 1920s and '30s he produced some of the scariest distortions of the human body and the most violently irrational, erotic images of Eros and Thanatos ever committed to canvas. He was not a realist painter/reporter, still less anyone's official muralist, and yet *Guernica* remains the most powerful political image in modern art, rivaled only by some of the Mexican work of Diego Rivera.

Picasso was regarded as a boy genius, but if he had died before 1906, his 25th year, his mark on 20th century art would have been slight. The so-called Blue and Rose periods, with their wistful etiolated figures of beggars and circus folk, are not, despite their great popularity, much more than pendants to late 19th century Symbolism. It was the experience of modernity that created his modernism, and that happened in Paris. There, mass production and reproduction had come to the forefront of ordinary life: newspapers, printed labels, the overlay of posters on walls—the dizzily intense public life of signs, simultaneous, high-speed and layered. This was the cityscape of Cubism.

Picasso was not a philosopher or a mathematician (there is no "geometry" in Cubism), but the work he and Braque did between 1910 and 1918 was intuitively bound to the perceptions of thinkers like Einstein and Alfred North Whitehead: that reality is not figure and void, it is all relationships, a twinkling field of interdependent events. Long before any Pop artists were born, Picasso latched on to the magnetism of mass culture and how high art could refresh itself through common vernaculars. Cubism was hard to read, willfully ambiguous, and yet demotic too. It remains the most influential art dialect of the early 20th century. As if to distance himself from his imitators, Picasso then went to the opposite extreme of embracing the classical past, with his paintings of huge dropsical women dreaming Mediterranean dreams in homage to Corot and Ingres.

HIS "CLASSICAL" MODE, WHICH HE WOULD REVERT to for decades to come, can also be seen as a gesture of independence. After his collaboration with Braque ended with his comment that "Braque is my wife"—words that were as disparaging to women as to Braque—Picasso remained a loner for the rest of his career. But a loner with a court and *maîtresses en titre.* He didn't even form a friendship with Matisse until both artists were old. His close relationships tended to be with poets and writers.

Though the public saw him as the archetypal modernist, he was disconnected from much modern art. Some of the greatest modern painters—Kandinsky, for instance, or Mondrian—saw their work as an instrument of evolution and human development. But Picasso had no more of a Utopian streak than did his Spanish idol, Goya. The idea that art evolved, or had any kind of historical mission, struck him as ridiculous. "All I have ever made," he once said, "was made for the present and in the

**88**      T I M E   1 0 0

Women were "goddesses or doormats" the artist claimed, yet his charm attracted them

imposed on them a load of feeling, ranging from dreamy eroticism (as in some of his paintings of his mistress Marie-Thérèse Walter in the '30s) to a sardonic but frenzied hostility, that no Western artist had made them carry before. He did this through metamorphosis, recomposing the body as the shape of his fantasies of possession and of his sexual terrors. Now the hidden and comparatively decorous puns of Cubism (the sound holes of a mandolin, for instance, becoming the mask of Pierrot) came out of their closet. "To displace," as Picasso described the process, "to put eyes between the legs, or sex organs on the face. To contradict. Nature does many things the way I do, but she hides them! My painting is a series of cock-and-bull stories."

There seems little doubt that the greatest of Picasso's work came in the 30 years between *Les Demoiselles d'Avignon* (1907) and *Guernica* (1937). But of course he didn't decline into triviality. Consistently through the war years and the '50s, and even now and then in the '60s and '70s, he would produce paintings and prints of considerable power. Sometimes they would be folded into series of variations on the old masters and 19th century painters he needed to measure himself against, such as Velázquez and Goya, or Poussin, Delacroix, Manet and Courbet. In his last years particularly, his production took on a manic and obsessive quality, as though the creative act (however repetitious) could forestall death. Which it could not. His death left the public with a nostalgia for genius that no talent today, in the field of painting, can satisfy. ∎

TIME *art critic Robert Hughes is the author of* The Shock of the New, The Fatal Shore *and* American Visions.

hope that it will always remain in the present. When I have found something to express, I have done it without thinking of the past or the future." Interestingly, he also stood against the Expressionist belief that the work of art gains value by disclosing the truth, the inner being, of its author. "How can anyone enter into my dreams, my instincts, my desires, my thoughts … and above all grasp from them what I have been about—perhaps against my own will?" he exclaimed.

To make art was to achieve a tyrannous freedom from self-explanation. The artist's work was mediumistic ("Painting is stronger than me; it makes me do what it wants"), solipsistic even. To Picasso, the idea that painting did itself through him meant that it wasn't subject to cultural etiquette. None of the other fathers of Modernism felt it so strongly—not Matisse, not Mondrian, certainly not Braque.

In Picasso's work, everything is staked on sensation and desire. His aim was not to argue coherence but to go for the strongest level of feeling. He conveyed it with tremendous plastic force, making you feel the weight of forms and the tension of their relationships mainly by drawing and tonal structure. He was never a great colorist, like Matisse or Pierre Bonnard. But through metaphor, he crammed layers of meaning together to produce flashes of revelation. In the process, he reversed one of the currents of modern art. Modernism had rejected storytelling: what mattered was formal relationships. But Picasso brought it back in a disguised form, as a psychic narrative, told through metaphors, puns and equivalences.

The most powerful element in the story—at least after Cubism—was sex. The female nude was his obsessive subject. Everything in his pictorial universe, especially after 1920, seemed related to the naked bodies of women. Picasso

The enthusiast, mugging on the beach with son Claude in 1951

# Myriad Visions

The 20th century saw more restless experimentation with style and content in art than any other in history. Never before had there been so many ideas about what art could be or how it could be made; never had new art been the subject of such impassioned controversy or reached so large an audience. Museums, especially in the U.S., had to embrace newness or look retro. The century didn't see the birth of the avant-garde—that had happened earlier—but it did bring its death, after experiment and eccentricity became the norm. Inevitably, all that had seemed startling or threatening came to look normal, even classical, within a few decades. In the end, the new lost its power to shock. —By ROBERT HUGHES

## Nude Descending a Staircase, No. 2, 1912
Marcel Duchamp

Famously derided as "an explosion in a shingle factory," Duchamp's painting was one of the most controversial works featured in the celebrated Armory Show in New York City in 1913, the exhibit that first brought new art to the attention of the masses—who, predictably, were shocked and scandalized by what they saw. A brilliant provocateur, Duchamp is the father of conceptual art; his notorious 1917 work *Fountain*—a common urinal signed "R. Mutt"—argued the thesis that art was whatever the artist proclaimed it to be.

## Dance, 1909
Henri Matisse

In Matisse's flattened "primitivist" canvas, stately Mediterranean rhythms are translated into violent movement and hot color. The shock of this brilliant palette led art critic Louis Vauxcelles to describe Matisse and his fellow exhibitors at a 1905 show in Paris as *les fauves*—"the wild beasts." Fauvism had a short life-span, but Matisse had a gloriously long one, in which his creativity never flagged; toward the end of his life, in the 1940s and 1950s, he was creating powerful works in cutout colored paper.

## Autumn Rhythm, Number 30, 1950
### Jackson Pollock

Pollock's twisting, turbulent drip paintings brought a choked, blurting urgency to abstract art. With relentless energy, the painting explores one of the basic motifs of modernism: the process by which the work itself is made. TIME was slow to recognize the power and subtlety of Pollock's work, famously dubbing him "Jack the Dripper."

## One Hundred Cans, 1962
### Andy Warhol

Publicist, prankster and parvenu, Warhol was the avatar of Pop art, the realm where American art gave up its spiritual reach in exchange for the bounty of commerce. His assembly-line images of soup cans and celebrity icons register his vision that in our image-saturated society, the whole world has become product. In Warhol's wake, whole careers have been spun off from industrial knockoffs and images of calculated sensationalism.

## Monogram, 1955-59
### Robert Rauschenberg

Rauschenberg's talent—prancing, omnivorous and fecund—helped form a basic cultural assumption of the last half of the century: that a work of art could exist for any length of time, in any material (from paint to a patch of earth to a live human body), anywhere (in a gallery, onstage, on a video screen, on the street), for any purpose (invocation, threat, amusement, contemplation) and find any destination, from the museum to the trash can, and still remain art. Rauschenberg's assemblage of a stuffed Angora goat girdled with a tire remains funny, unsettling and provocative three decades after it first startled the public.

# Camera Ready

Photography not only provided this century with two of the things it likes best—greater realism and superior fantasies—but also showed how deeply entwined they can be. Circa 1900, ambitious photographers aspired to pictures that resembled paintings. Then came modernism, which taught them to rethink the characteristics of their own medium. Sharp focus, accidental arrangements and the just-the-facts stuff that cameras provide became a new path to the supreme fictions of art. Of the pleasures cameras give us, the transfiguration of plain reality is the most indispensable. It implies that the world is more than it seems—which, after all, it may well be. It's a paradox too lovely to ignore and too profound to solve. These are six great photographers who have pointed the way into its deepest parts. —By RICHARD LACAYO

## White Fence, 1916
## Paul Strand

When the century began, "art photography" meant the maidens and moonbeams of soft-focus "pictorialism," which mixed all-too-poetic subjects in a stew of darkroom retouching. Strand wiped the lens clean. While still in his 20s he recognized that sharper focus and straightforward subjects—some houses, a fence, the sky—could answer to both the ongoing yearning for the ineffable and the new era's demand for a crisper, more credible vision.

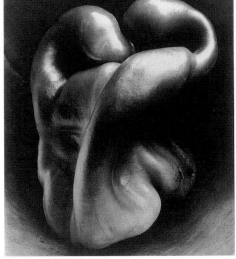

## Pepper #30, 1930
## Edward Weston

Weston's stated aim was the purest American transcendentalism: "To photograph a rock, have it look like a rock, but be more than a rock." Decades later, photographers, and not just nature photographers, would still be drawing on his notion that when an object is looked at steadily, even ferociously, substance gives way to spirit; that a cabbage, a pepper, a seashell, seen with every fold and gleam specified, can offer a sudden and sublime glimpse of heaven.

## Valencia, 1933
Henri Cartier-Bresson

Cartier-Bresson started as a painter in the early 1930s, when the art world was steeped in the dream logic of Surrealism. He soon brought that sensibility to photography. Roaming the streets of Paris or Madrid with a Leica, one of the earliest handheld 35-mm cameras, he jotted down the "decisive moments" when ordinary things crossed paths in surprising ways. He found the extraordinary around every corner. Because of him, later photographers knew where and how to look.

## Parade—Hoboken, N.J., 1955
Robert Frank

In the mid-1950s the Swiss-born Frank traveled across the U.S. with a small camera and a sober disposition. The photo book that resulted, *The Americans,* was a standing affront both to the conventions of photography (his pictures could be tilted, out of focus and dimly lit) and to the complacencies of the era. Frank advanced a disenchanted mood in photography and an emerging format—the personal documentary, as abrupt as a shout, as intimate as a diary, as intricate as a novel.

## Minamata, 1971
W. Eugene Smith

He didn't invent the photo essay. But more than any earlier photographer, Smith saw how it could offer a profound reckoning with the world. His grave narratives proceeded deeply into the lives of his subjects and the memory of his audience. He showed how pictures in a series—of a Spanish village fending off the 20th century or of a Japanese town struggling against mercury pollution that caused birth defects—could be stations on a path of understanding.

## Untitled Film Still, 1978
Cindy Sherman

Her invented movie stills were among the first ripe products of postmodernism, which turned a cold eye on things, like reality and identity, that we should not be too quick to think of as settled notions. Disguised in costumes and wigs, Sherman featured herself in strangely charged moments from imaginary movies. Her pictures were fictions about other fictions. But movies, after all, are the fictions by which we construct our memories, our self-images—our "truths."

"A machine for living in": the Villa Savoye in France

# Le Corbusier

## He was convinced that the bold new industrial age required an equally audacious style of architecture. And who better to design it than him?

By **WITOLD RYBCZYNSKI**

L E CORBUSIER LOVED MANHATTAN. HE LOVED ITS newness, he loved its Cartesian regularity, above all he loved its tall buildings. He had only one reservation, which he revealed on landing in New York City in 1935. The next day, a headline in the *Herald Tribune* declared that the celebrated architect FINDS AMERICAN SKYSCRAPERS MUCH TOO SMALL. Le Corbusier always thought big. He once proposed replacing a large part of the center of Paris with 18 sixty-story towers; that made headlines too.

He was born Charles-Edouard Jeanneret in Switzerland in 1887. When he was 29, he went to Paris, where he took his maternal grandfather's name, Le Corbusier, as his pseudonym. Jeanneret had been a small-town architect; Le Corbusier was a visionary. He believed that architecture had lost its way. Art Nouveau, all curves and sinuous decorations, had burned itself out in a brilliant burst of exuberance; the seductive Art Deco style promised to do the same. The Arts and Crafts movement, as the name implies, was hardly representative of an industrial age. Le Corbusier proclaimed that this new age deserved a brand-new architecture: "We must start again from zero."

The new architecture came to be known as the International Style. Of its many partisans—among them Ludwig Mies van der Rohe and Walter Gropius—none was better known than Le Corbusier. He was a tireless proselytizer, addressing the public in manifestos, pamphlets, exhibitions and his own magazine. He wrote books—dozens of them—on interior decoration, painting and architecture. They resembled instruction manuals. An example is his recipe for the International Style: raise the building on stilts, mix in a free-flowing floor plan, make the walls independent of the structure, add horizontal strip windows and top it off with a roof garden. But this makes him sound like a technician, and he was anything but. Although he dressed like a bureaucrat, in dark suits, bow ties and round horn-rimmed glasses, he was really an artist (he was an accomplished painter and sculptor). What is most memorable about the austere, white-walled villas that he built after World War I in and around Paris is their cool beauty and their airy sense of space. "A house is a machine for living in," he wrote. The machines he admired most were ocean liners, and his architecture spoke of sun and wind and the sea.

> # " I live like a monk and hate to show myself, but I have been called to all countries of the world to do battle. "
>
> ## LE CORBUSIER

By 1950 he had changed course, abandoning Purism, as he called it, for something more robust and sculptural. His spartan, lightweight architecture turned rustic, with heavy walls of brick and fieldstone and splashes of bright color. He discovered the potential of reinforced concrete and made it his own, leaving the material crudely unfinished, inside and out, the marks of wooden formwork plainly visible. Concrete allowed Le Corbusier to explore unusual shapes. The billowing roof of the chapel at Ronchamp, France, resembles a nun's wimple; the studios of the Carpenter Center for Visual Arts at Harvard push out of the building like huge cellos. For the state capital of Chandigarh in India, he created a temple precinct of heroic structures that appear prehistoric.

Le Corbusier was the most important architect of the 20th century. Frank Lloyd Wright was more prolific—Le Corbusier's built oeuvre comprises about 60 buildings—and many would argue he was more gifted. But Wright was a maverick; Le Corbusier dominated the architectural world, from that halcyon year of 1920, when he started publishing his magazine *L'Esprit Nouveau*, until his death in 1965. He inspired several generations of architects, not only in Europe but around the world. He was more than a mercurial innovator. Irascible, caustic, Calvinistic, Corbu was modern architecture's conscience.

He was also a city planner. "Modern town planning comes to birth with a new architecture," he wrote. "By this immense step in evolution, so brutal and so overwhelming, we burn our bridges and break with the past." He meant it. There were to be no more congested streets and sidewalks, no more bustling public squares, no more untidy neighborhoods. People would live in hygienic, regimented high-rise towers, set far apart in a parklike landscape. This rational city would be separated into discrete zones for working, living and leisure. Above all, everything should be done on a big scale—big buildings, big open spaces, big urban highways.

He called it La Ville Radieuse, the Radiant City. Despite the poetic title, his urban vision was authoritarian, inflexible and simplistic. Wherever it was tried—in Chandigarh by Le Corbusier himself or in Brasília by his followers—it failed. Standardization proved inhuman and disorienting. The open spaces were inhospitable; the bureaucratically imposed plan, socially destructive. In the U.S., the Radiant City took the form of vast urban-renewal schemes and regimented public housing projects that damaged the urban fabric beyond repair. Today these megaprojects are being dismantled, giving way to rows of houses fronting streets and sidewalks. Downtowns

**Corbu's bureaucratic demeanor masked the soul of an artist**

have discovered that combining, not separating, different activities is the key to success. So is the presence of lively residential neighborhoods, old as well as new. Cities have learned that preserving history makes a lot more sense than starting from zero. It has been an expensive lesson, and not one that Le Corbusier intended, but it too is part of his legacy. ∎

*Architect, author and educator Witold Rybczynski is writing a book on Frederick Law Olmsted.*

**BORN Oct. 6, 1887, in La Chaux-de-Fonds, Switzerland, as Charles-Edouard Jeanneret**

**1920 Adopts his maternal grandfather's name, Le Corbusier, as his *nom d'architecture***

**1951-55 Builds chapel at Ronchamp, France, at left**

**1887**                                                    **1965**

**1908 Works in Josef Hoffmann's Vienna studio**

**1923 Publishes *Towards a New Architecture***

**1965 Dies Aug. 27 in France**

**1950-51 Creates plan for city of Chandigarh, India**

# Five for the Ages

When does a building become more important than its purpose? Why do some buildings become such reference points that they may never be torn down? After all, many works of architectural merit and structural solidity have been destroyed in the name of war or progress (witness New York City's Pennsylvania Station). Some buildings, it seems, put down foundations in the psyche of their location; they may grow old but will never become dated. Le Corbusier's chapel at Ronchamp is a certain survivor. Here are five others likely to outlive us all. —By BELINDA LUSCOMBE

### Chrysler Building, 1930
#### William Van Alen
Manhattan's Roman-candle skyscraper, with a frieze of hubcaps and huge gargoyles resembling Chrysler radiator caps, is 1,048 ft. of shimmering charm. The building's signature is the marvelously inventive finial, a stack of seven groined vaults tapering to a steel spire, like the business end of a hypodermic needle, and pierced with windows that can be read as sunrays or as the spokes of a wheel. Finished in the first full year of the Great Depression, the building reflects the exuberance of the era when it was designed, the over-the-top 1920s. Rising like a blast of congealed and shining energy from the bedrock, it is a spectacle of Promethean ambition and daring.

### Fallingwater, 1937
#### Frank Lloyd Wright
Prolific, visionary, unorthodox, and ingenious, Wright built for a romantic America, a country with space and grace to spare. His deft synthesis of architecture and nature is perhaps best expressed in the private home Fallingwater, in Pennsylvania.

### Sydney Opera House, 1973
Joern Utzon

Is it all roof or all walls? As beloved now as it was controversial during construction, Utzon's visionary building is a blissful union of unique structure and breathtaking location. Sydneysiders who once derided it now fight over what buildings would be worthy to go next to it.

### Seagram Building, 1958
Ludwig Mies van der Rohe

The pioneering architect's glass obelisk firmly established the International Style as the template for skyscraper design when it first appeared among its stolid masonry-clad neighbors along New York City's Park Avenue. Soaring aloft on stilts, it includes a plaza, then a rarity in urban design, while its bronze-and-dark-glass skin gives it a classically refined stature.

### Guggenheim Bilbao, 1997
Frank Gehry

Shrouded in evanescent titanium that seems to change color with every dapple of sunlight, this massive gallery gleams like a voluptuous vision of the future that has suddenly appeared in an ancient Spanish town. The startlingly irregular building— the capstone of American architect Gehry's career—defies every convention of axiality, including the right angle. Just as Utzon's Sydney Opera House evokes the imagery of the great sailing ships that opened up Australia to the world, the Guggenheim Bilbao suggests a vast metal ship, full of compound curves, that has run aground— a sort of art-arc. Spectacular outside, it is equally gracious within, welcoming visitors with a soaring, ceremonial atrium.

# Martha Graham

## Her fierce choreography sometimes amazed and sometimes horrified, but in it she embodied modern dance—arrogantly and spectacularly

By TERRY TEACHOUT

THE FIRST THING YOU NOTICED WAS THE FACE, A dead-white mask of anguish with black holes for eyes, a curt slash of red for a mouth and cheekbones as high as the sky. Even if Martha Graham had done nothing else worth mentioning in her 96 years, she might be remembered for that face. But she also made dances to go with it—harsh, angular fantasies spun out of the strange proportions of her short-legged body and the pain and loneliness of her secret heart. If Graham ever gave birth, one critic quipped, it would be to a cube; instead, she became the mother of American dance.

Graham was far from the first dancer to rip off her toe shoes and break with the rigid conventions of 19th century ballet. America in the 1910s and '20s was full of young women (modern dance in the beginning was very much a women's movement) with similar notions. But it was her homegrown technique—the fierce pelvic contractions, the rugged "floor work" that startled those who took for granted that real dancers soared through the air—that caught on, becoming the cornerstone of postwar modern dance. Merce Cunningham, Paul Taylor, Twyla Tharp, Mark Morris—all are Graham's children and grandchildren. (Taylor and Cunningham even danced in her company, though they later repudiated her high-strung style.) Her methods are routinely taught today in studios the world over, but you need not have studied them or even have seen any of her dances to be influenced by them. They are part of the air every contemporary dancer breathes.

Born in 1894 in Allegheny, Pa., Graham moved with her family to California when she was 14. Three years later, she attended a Los Angeles recital by the dance pioneer Ruth St. Denis. It was the first dance performance of any kind that Graham had ever seen, and it overwhelmed her; in 1916 she joined Denishawn, the school and performing troupe that St. Denis co-led with her husband Ted Shawn. At 22, dangerously late for an aspiring dancer, Graham had found her destiny.

After seven years with Denishawn, Graham moved to New York City and struck out on her own, giving solo recitals and eventually launching her own company, in 1929. To raise funds, she danced at the opening of Radio City Music Hall, modeled furs and later gave classes in which she taught such actors as Bette Davis and Gregory Peck how to move. (Richard Boone claimed that to die onscreen, he simply did a one-count Graham fall.) But nothing could deflect her from what she believed to be her sacred mission: to "chart the graph of the heart" through movement. "That driving force of God that plunges through me is what I live for," she wrote, and believed every word of it. Others believed too, partly because of the hurricane-strength force of her personality—the Graham company would always bear an unsettling resemblance to a religious cult, with the choreographer as high priestess—but mainly because she delivered the goods.

Graham came decisively into her own in the '40s, turning out in rapid succession the decade-long series of angst-ridden dance dramas on which her reputation now chiefly rests. Enacted on symbol-strewn sets designed by the sculptor Isamu Noguchi, they were accompanied by scores commissioned from such noted composers as Aaron Copland and Samuel Barber.

**BORN May 11, 1894, in Allegheny, Pa.**

**1935 Establishes school of modern dance at Bennington College**

**1976 Receives the Presidential Medal of Freedom**

**1894**

**1991**

**1916 Joins the Denishawn dance troupe**

**1929 Launches her own company in New York City**

**1944 Choreographs** *Appalachian Spring*

**1968 Gives her final stage performance at age 74**

**1991 Dies on April 1 in New York City**

**RITES Exploring myths, 1920**

Graham continued to perform into her 70s, and her acolytes revered her as a high priestess of the dance until her death at 96

*Cave of the Heart* (1946), one of her many modern recastings of ancient Greek myth, contains a horrific solo in which the hate-crazed Medea gobbles her own entrails—perhaps Graham's most sensational coup de théâtre and one recalled with nightmarish clarity by all who saw her bring it off.

"How do you want to be remembered, as a dancer or as a choreographer?" Graham was once asked by choreographer Antony Tudor. "As a dancer, of course," she replied. "I pity you," Tudor said. His words proved prophetic. In her prime a performer of eye-scorching power, Graham insisted on dancing until 1968, long after her onstage appearances had degenerated into grisly self-caricature. Her unwillingness to let younger soloists take over led her to replace her signature pieces with new dances in which she substituted calculated effects for convincing movement. Adoring critics pretended nothing was wrong, but in fact she produced virtually no work of lasting interest from 1950 to her death 41 years later.

Her wishes notwithstanding, it is not likely that Graham will be remembered as a dancer, at least not very clearly: films of her performances are scarce and mostly primitive. Much of her choreography has failed to wear well, especially by comparison with the work of George Balanchine, the unrivaled master of neoclassical ballet, and Taylor and Cunningham, her apostate alumni. No more

Onstage at age 64 in 1958

than half a dozen of her dances, most notably *Cave of the Heart* and *Appalachian Spring* (1944), her radiant re-creation of a pioneer wedding, seem likely to stand the test of time. The rest are overwrought period pieces whose humorless, lapel-clutching intensity is less palatable now that their maker is no longer around to bring them to life.

Yet a theatrical legacy cannot always be measured by such seemingly objective yardsticks. Though there is no film of Nijinsky dancing, no one questions his place of honor in the history of 20th century ballet. Even if her beleaguered company should someday close its doors and her dances cease to be performed, Graham will doubtless be remembered in much the same way, for the shadow she cast was fully as long. Did she invent modern dance? No, but she came to embody it, arrogantly and spectacularly—and, it appears, permanently. "When the legend becomes fact," said the newspaper editor in John Ford's *The Man Who Shot Liberty Valance*, "print the legend." The legend of Martha Graham long ago became fact, just as her utterly personal technique has become part of the common vocabulary of dancers everywhere. "The center of the stage is where I am," she once said. It still is. ∎

TIME *contributing writer Terry Teachout covers dance for the New York* Daily News.

# Movers and Shakers

Gifted choreographers and stars jolted dance into brave
new forms that matched the century's accelerated pace

### Isadora Duncan

Though perhaps famous for her tempestuous personal life as much as for her choreography, Duncan was a pioneer whose "free dance"—often barefoot improvisations to the classics—anticipated modern dance.

### Fred Astaire

The great popular dancer's first partner was his sister Adele; in a string of classic movies it was Ginger Rogers—but even a vacuum cleaner, a hat rack or a drum set could set his feet flying. Astaire made elegance infectious.

### Mikhail Baryshnikov

In a century when Russian stars —Nijinsky, Makarova, Nureyev—dominated ballet, none found wider fame than the young Latvian. After defecting from the Soviet Union in 1974, he thrilled Western audiences with his athleticism and artistry.

### George Balanchine

Educated in the great Russian tradition, the young Georgian choreographed for Diaghilev's Ballets Russes, then came to America, where his neoclassical works for the New York City Ballet—elegant, alert, musical—stripped ballet of its flummery and propelled it to modernism's center stage.

# Coco
# Chanel

## She was shrewd, chic and on the cutting edge. The clothes she created changed the way women looked and how they looked at themselves

By INGRID SISCHY

COCO CHANEL WASN'T JUST AHEAD OF HER TIME. SHE was ahead of herself. If one looks at the work of contemporary fashion designers as different from one another as Tom Ford, Helmut Lang, Miuccia Prada, Jil Sander and Donatella Versace, one sees that many of their strategies echo what Chanel once did. Seventy-five years ago she mixed up the vocabulary of male and female clothes even as she created fashion that offered the wearer a feeling of hidden luxury rather than ostentation—just two examples of how her taste and sense of style overlap with today's fashion.

Chanel would not have defined herself as a feminist—in fact, she consistently spoke of femininity rather than of feminism—yet her work is unquestionably part of the liberation of women. She threw out a life jacket, as it were, to women not once but twice, during two distinct periods decades apart: the 1920s and the '50s. She not only appropriated styles, fabrics and articles of clothing that were worn by men but also, beginning with how she dressed herself, appropriated sports clothes as part of the language of fashion. One can see how her style evolved out of necessity and defiance. She couldn't afford the fashionable clothes of the period—so she rejected them and made her own, using, say, the sports jackets and ties that were everyday male attire around the racetrack, where she was climbing her first social ladders.

It's not by accident that she became associated with the modern movement that included Diaghilev, Picasso, Stravinsky and Cocteau. Like these artistic protagonists, she was determined to break the old formulas and invent a way of expressing herself. Cocteau once said of her that "she has, by a kind of miracle, worked in fashion according to rules that would seem to have value only for painters, musicians, poets."

By the late '60s, Chanel had become part of what she once rebelled against and hated—the Establishment. But if one looks at documentary footage of her from that period, one can still feel the spit and vinegar of the fiery peasant woman who began her fashion revolution against society by aiming at the head, with hats. Her boyish "flapper" creations were in stark contrast to the Belle Epoque millinery that was in vogue at the time, and about which she asked, "How can a brain function under those things?" Something that Chanel can never be accused of is not using her brain. Her sharp mind is apparent in everything she did, from her savvy use of logos to her deep understanding of the power of personality and packaging, even the importance of being copied. And she was always quotable: "Fashion is not simply a matter of clothes. Fashion is in the air, borne upon the wind. One intuits it. It is in the sky and on the road."

It is fitting, somehow, that Chanel was often photographed holding a cigarette or standing in front of her famous Art Deco wall of mirrors. Fashion tends to involve a good dose of smoke and mirrors, so it should come as no sur-

N°5
CHANEL
PERFUME

CHANEL INC
NEW YORK
N.Y. 10022
FL OZ

**BORN** Aug. 19, 1883, in French village of Saumur

**1910** Moves to Rue Cambon, where the House of Chanel remains

**STYLIN'** Coco in a Chanel suit and hat, 1929

**1939** Closes her fashion house when France declares war on Germany

**1954** Launches successful comeback

1883 ——————————————————————————————— 1971

**1909** Opens first shop, a millinery, in Paris

**1923** Debuts Chanel No. 5

**1945** Exiled to Switzerland for her love affair with a Nazi officer

**1971** Dies Jan. 10 in Paris

Smoke and mirrors: Chanel in 1957, savoring her "second coming"

Her hands betrayed Chanel's age in the 1950s—but her sense of style was timeless

prise that Gabrielle Chanel's version of her life involved a multitude of lies, inventions, cover-ups and revisions. But as Prada said to me: "She was really a genius. It's hard to pin down exactly why, but it has something to do with her wanting to be different and wanting to be independent."

CERTAINLY CHANEL'S LIFE WAS UNPREDICTABLE. EVEN her death—in 1971, at age 87 in her private quarters at the Ritz Hotel—was a plush ending that probably would not have been predicted for Chanel by the nuns in the Aubazine orphanage, where she spent time as a ward of the state after her mother died and her father ran off. No doubt the sisters at the convent in Moulins, who took her in when she was 17, raised their eyebrows when the young woman left the seamstress job they had helped her get to try for a career as a cabaret singer. This stint as a performer—she was apparently charming but no Piaf—led her to take up with the local swells and become the backup mistress of Etienne Balsan, a playboy who would finance her move to Paris and the opening of her first hat business. That arrangement gave way to a bigger and better deal when she moved on to his friend, Arthur ("Boy") Capel, who is said to have been the love of her life and who backed her expansion from hats to clothes and from Paris to the coastal resorts of Deauville and Biarritz. One of her first successes was the loose-fitting sweater, which she belted and teamed with a skirt. These early victories were similar to the clothes she had been making for herself—women's clothes made out of Everyman materials such as jersey, usually associated with men's undergarments.

Throughout the '20s, Chanel's social, sexual and professional progress continued, and her eminence grew to the status of legend. By the early '30s she'd been courted by Hollywood, gone and come back. She had almost married one of the richest men in Europe, the Duke of Westminster; when she didn't, her explanation was, "There have been several Duchesses of Westminster. There is only one Chanel." In fact, there were many Coco Chanels, just as her work had many

Chanel's return to the fashion world has been variously attributed to falling perfume sales, disgust at what she was seeing in the fashion of the day or simple boredom. All these explanations seem plausible, and so does Karl Lagerfeld's theory of why, this time around, the Chanel suit met with such phenomenal success. Lagerfeld—who designs Chanel today and who has turned the company into an even bigger, more tuned-in business than it was before—points out, "By the '50s she had the benefit of distance, and so could truly distill the Chanel look. Time and culture had caught up with her."

In Europe, her return to fashion was deemed an utter flop at first, but Americans couldn't buy her suits fast enough. Yet again Chanel had put herself into the yolk of the zeitgeist. By the time Katharine Hepburn played her on Broadway in 1969, Chanel had achieved first-name recognition and was simply Coco. ■

*Ingrid Sischy is editor in chief of* Interview *and a contributing editor to* Vanity Fair.

**Pure Coco: a sleeveless suit over long-sleeved blouse, 1954**

phases and many styles, including Gypsy skirts, over-the-top fake jewelry and glittering evening wear—made of crystal and jet beads laid over black and white georgette crepe—not just the plainer jersey suits and "little black dresses" that made her famous. But probably the single element that most ensured Chanel's being remembered, even when it would have been easier to write her off, is not a piece of clothing but a form of liquid gold—Chanel No. 5, in its Art Deco bottle, which was launched in 1923. It was the first perfume to bear a designer's name.

One could say perfume helped keep Chanel's name pretty throughout the period when her reputation got ugly: World War II. This is when her anti-Semitism, homophobia (even though she dabbled in bisexuality) and other base inclinations emerged. She responded to the war by shutting down her fashion business and hooking up with Hans Gunther von Dincklage, a Nazi officer whose favors included permission to reside in her beloved Ritz Hotel. Years later, in 1954, when she decided to make a comeback, her name still had "disgraced" attached to it.

# James Joyce

His *Ulysses* befuddled readers and challenged aspiring writers; it also revolutionized 20th century fiction

By PAUL GRAY

Joyce with Sylvia Beach, who first published *Ulysses* in 1922

JAMES JOYCE ONCE TOLD A FRIEND, "ONE OF THE things I could never get accustomed to in my youth was the difference I found between life and literature." All serious young readers notice this difference. Joyce dedicated his career to erasing it and in the process revolutionized 20th century fiction.

The life he would put into his literature was chiefly his own. Born near Dublin in 1882, James Augustine Aloysius was the oldest of the 10 surviving children of John and Mary Jane Joyce. His father was irascible, witty, hard drinking and ruinously improvident; his mother, a devout Roman Catholic, helplessly watched her family slide into near poverty and hoped for a happier life in the hereafter. James' entire education came at the hands of the Jesuits, who did a better job with him than they may have intended. By the time Joyce graduated from University College, Dublin, in 1902, he decided he had learned enough to reject his religion and all his obligations to family, homeland and the British who ruled there. Literature would be his vocation and his bid for immortality.

He fled Ireland into self-imposed exile late in 1904, taking with him Nora Barnacle, a young woman from Galway who was working as a hotel chambermaid in Dublin when Joyce met her earlier that year. He departed Dublin with nearly all the narratives he would ever need already stored in his memory. What remained for him to do was transform this cache into art that could measure up to his own expectations.

As he and Nora and then their two children moved among and around European cities—Pula, Trieste, Zurich, Rome, Paris—Joyce found clerical and teaching jobs that provided subsistence to his family and his writing. His first published book of fiction, *Dubliners* (1914), contained 15 stories short on conventional plots but long on evocative atmosphere and language. *A Portrait of the Artist as a Young Man* (1916) provided a remarkably objective and linguistically complex account of Stephen Dedalus, i.e., James Joyce, from his birth to his decision to leave Dublin in pursuit of his art.

*Portrait* did not sell well enough to relieve Joyce's chronic financial worries, but his work by then had attracted the attention of a number of influential avant-gardists, most notably the expatriate American poet Ezra Pound, who believed a new century demanded new art, poetry, fiction, music—everything. Such supporters rallied to promote Joyce and his experimental writings, and he did not disappoint them.

He began *Ulysses* in 1914; portions of it in progress appeared in the *Egoist* in England and the *Little Review* in America, until the U.S. Post Office, on grounds of alleged obscenity, confiscated three issues containing Joyce's excerpts and fined the editors $100. The censorship flap only heightened curiosity about Joyce's forthcoming book. Even

**BORN**
Feb. 2, 1882, in a Dublin suburb

**1882**

**1888 In a sailor suit at age 6½**

**1904 Falls in love with Nora Barnacle, flees with her to the Continent**

**1916 *A Portrait of the Artist as a Young Man* published**

**1914 *Dubliners* published**

**1922 *Ulysses* published on 40th birthday**

**1919 The U.S. Post Office seizes magazines carrying portions of *Ulysses* on grounds of obscenity**

**1939 Some 17 years in the writing, *Finnegans Wake* appears**

**1941**

**1941 Dies Jan. 13 in Zurich**

> *Ulysses*... I rather wish I had never read it. It gives me an inferiority complex. When I read a book like this... I feel like a eunuch.
>
> **GEORGE ORWELL, in a letter to Brenda Salkeld in 1934**

before *Ulysses* was published, critics were comparing Joyce's breakthroughs to those of Einstein and Freud.

Joyce received the first copy of *Ulysses* on his 40th birthday, in 1922. It was his most exhaustive attempt yet to collapse the distinction between literature and life. First of all, he tossed out most of the narrative techniques found in 19th century fiction. *Ulysses* has no discernible plot, no series of obstacles that a hero or heroine must surmount on the way to a happy ending. The book offers no all-knowing narrator, à la Dickens or Tolstoy, to guide the reader, describe the characters and settings, provide background information, summarize events and explain, from time to time, the story's moral significance.

With so many traditional methods of narrative abandoned, what was left? Perhaps the clearest and most concise description of Joyce's technique came from the critic Edmund Wilson: "Joyce has attempted in *Ulysses* to render as exhaustively, as precisely and as directly as it is possible in words to do, what our participation in life is like—or rather, what it seems to us like as from moment to moment we live."

A first reading of *Ulysses* can thus be a baffling experience, although no book more generously rewards patience and fortitude. Stephen Dedalus reappears, still stuck in Dublin, dreaming of escape. Then we meet Leopold Bloom, or rather we meet his thoughts as he prepares breakfast for his wife Molly. (We experience her thoughts as she drifts off to sleep at the end of the book.)

*Ulysses* is the account of one day in Dublin—June 16, 1904, Joyce's private tribute to Nora, since that was the date on which they first went out together. The book follows the movements of not only Dedalus and Bloom but also hundreds of other Dubliners as they walk the streets, meet and talk, then talk some more in restaurants and pubs. All this activity seems random, a record of urban happenstance.

**B**UT NOTHING IN *ULYSSES* IS TRULY RANDOM. BENEATH the surface realism of the novel, its apparently artless transcription of life's flow, lurks a complicated plan. Friends who were in on the secret of *Ulysses* urged Joyce to share it, to make things easier for his readers. He resisted at first: "I've put in so many enigmas and puzzles that it will keep the professors busy for centuries arguing over what I meant, and that's the only way of ensuring one's immortality."

Joyce later relented, and so the world learned that *Ulysses* was, among many other things, a modern retelling of Homer's *Odyssey*, with Bloom as the wandering hero, Stephen as Telemachus and Molly as a Penelope decidedly less faithful than the original. T.S. Eliot, who recognized the novel's underpinnings, wrote that Joyce's use of classical myth as a method of ordering modern experience had "the importance of a scientific discovery."

*Ulysses* made Joyce famous, if not always in a manner to his liking. When a fan approached him and asked, "May I kiss the hand that wrote *Ulysses*?" Joyce said, "No, it did lots of other things too." But more important, *Ulysses* became a source book for 20th century literature. It expanded the domain of permissible subjects in fiction, following Bloom not only into his secret erotic fantasies but his outdoor privy as well.

Its multiple narrative voices and extravagant wordplay made *Ulysses* a virtual thesaurus of styles for writers wrestling with the problem of rendering contemporary life. Aspects of Joyce's accomplishment in *Ulysses* can be seen in the works of William Faulkner, Albert Camus, Samuel Beckett, Saul Bellow, Gabriel García Márquez and Toni Morrison, all of whom, unlike Joyce, won the Nobel Prize for Literature.

But the only author who tried to surpass the encyclopedic scope of *Ulysses* was Joyce himself. He spent 17 years working on *Finnegans Wake*, a book intended to portray Dublin's sleeping life as thoroughly as *Ulysses* had explored the wide-awake city. This task, Joyce decided, required the invention of a new language that would mime the experience of dreaming, crammed with multilingual puns and *Jabberwocky*-like sentences. Even Joyce's champions expressed doubts. To Pound's complaint about obscurity, Joyce replied, "The action of my new work takes place at night. It's natural things should not be so clear at night, isn't it now?" Today, only dedicated Joyceans regularly attend the *Wake*. A century from now, his readers may catch up with him. ∎

**With his grandson Stephen—named after *Portrait's* narrator**

TIME *senior writer Paul Gray wrote his Ph.D. dissertation on James Joyce's short fiction.*

# Fiction Turns Inward

The encroachments of mass media and the march toward subjectivity prompted by Freud drove 20th century writers inward toward personal visions. The greatest authors managed to make their art heard and remembered amid the clamor

## Franz Kafka

People who have never read his books recognize his last name as an adjective: Kafkaesque, a signature form of 20th century dread. During his brief life in Prague, he wrote about webs of inexplicable predicaments, as in *The Metamorphosis* (1915). What do you do when you wake up as an insect?

## Virginia Woolf

Her life span coincided with that of Joyce, and her interest in creating a new 20th century fiction was as strong as his. But her innovative novels, most notably *Mrs. Dalloway* (1925) and *To the Lighthouse* (1927), put women at the center of a changing world and offered a vocabulary of feminism to women and men alike.

## Ernest Hemingway

His spare prose, particularly in his novels *The Sun Also Rises* (1926) and *A Farewell to Arms* (1929), inspired acolytes and parodists. But his writings also redefined the notion of individual heroism after the indiscriminate carnage of World War I. His lonely protagonists were existentialists before their time.

## Ralph Ellison

His novel *Invisible Man* (1952) began with the sentence "I am an invisible man" and concluded, "Who knows but that, on the lower frequencies, I speak for you?" The words in between brought African-American experiences vividly into the literary mainstream and spurred a renaissance that continues to this day.

## Gabriel García Márquez

The Colombian's phantasmagoric *One Hundred Years of Solitude*, published in 1967 and translated into English in 1970, delighted readers worldwide and introduced "magic realism" into the critical lexicon. His Nobel Prize in 1982 only ratified his stature as the foremost Latin American writer of his era.

# T. S. Eliot

## Fiction was threatening to eclipse serious poetry. He provided the stark salvation of *The Waste Land*

**By HELEN VENDLER**

IN 1670 ANDREW ELIOT LEFT EAST COKER IN SOMERSET, England, for Boston. Two hundred and eighteen years later, his direct descendant, Thomas Stearns Eliot—who would become the most celebrated English-language poet of the century—was born in St. Louis, Mo., to a businessman and a poet, Henry and Charlotte Eliot. Although young Tom was brilliantly educated in English and European literature and in Eastern and Western philosophy and religion, he fled—in his mid-20s—the career in philosophy awaiting him at Harvard, and moved to England. There he married (disastrously), met the entrepreneurial Ezra Pound and, while working at Lloyds Bank, brought out *Prufrock and Other Observations.* Five years later, after a nervous breakdown and a stay in a Swiss sanatorium, he published *The Waste Land.* Modern poetry had struck its note.

Not everyone was impressed. Dorothy Wellesley, writing to W.B. Yeats, said petulantly, "But Eliot, that man isn't modern. He wrings the past dry and pours the juice down the throats of those who are either too busy, or too creative to read as much as he does." "The juice of the past" isn't a bad description of the lifeblood of *The Waste Land;* but it was a past so disarranged—with the Buddha next to St. Augustine, and Ovid next to Wagner—that a reader felt thrust into a time machine of disorienting simultaneity. And the poem had an unsettling habit of saying, out of the blue, "Oed' und leer das Meer," or something even more peculiar. It ended, in fact, with a cascade of lines in different languages—English,

Italian, Latin, French, Sanskrit. Still, readers felt the desperate spiritual quest behind the poem—and were seduced by the unerring musicality of its free-verse lines.

*The Waste Land* was a deeply unoptimistic, un-Christian and therefore un-American poem, prefaced by the suicidal words of the Cumaean Sibyl, "I want to die." It is, we could say, the first Euro-poem. In its desolation at the breakup of the Judeo-Christian past, the poem turns for salvation to the Buddha and his three ethical commandments: Give, Sympathize, Control. But on the way to its ritually religious close ("Shantih, shantih, shantih"), it films a succession of loveless or violent or failed sexual unions—among the educated ("My nerves are bad tonight") and the uneducated ("He, the young man carbuncular, arrives"), and in the poet's own life ("your heart would have responded/ Gaily"). It speaks of an absent God and of a dead father; Eliot's recently dead father had left capital outright to the other children, but permitted his wayward son only the interest on his portion.

It annoyed Eliot that *The Waste Land* was interpreted as a prophetic statement: he referred to it (somewhat disingenu-

**Eliot's mother, center, and sister visit him in England, 1921**

**BORN Sept. 26, 1888, in St. Louis, Mo.**

**1888**

**AT 30 Eliot in 1918, a year after *Prufrock***

**1914 Moves to England; meets Ezra Pound**

**1917 Publishes *Prufrock and Other Observations***

**1922 Publishes *The Waste Land***

**1927 Is confirmed in the Church of England and becomes a British subject**

**1948 Awarded the Nobel Prize for Literature and the British Order of Merit**

**1965**

**1965 Dies Jan. 4**

**1981 *Cats* opens in London**

Old Possum confers with his muse: after his death, Eliot won pop culture fame as the versifier of *Cats*

# Eliot has thought of things I had not thought of, and I'm damned if many of the others have done so.

**EZRA POUND, poet**

ously) as "just a piece of rhythmical grumbling." Yet World War I had intervened between the writing of most of the poems included in *Prufrock* and the composition of *The Waste Land;* and in a 1915 letter to Conrad Aiken, Eliot had said, "The War suffocates me." Whether or not Eliot had written down the Armageddon of the West, he had showed up the lightweight poetry dominating American magazines. Nothing could have been further from either bland escapism or Imagist stylization than the music-hall syncopation ("O O O O that Shakespeherian Rag") and the pub vulgarity ("What you get married for if you don't want children") of *The Waste Land.* Eliot's poem went off like a bomb in a genteel drawing-room, as he intended it to.

HOW COULD *THE WASTE LAND*—AND THE SAD POEMS, almost as peculiar, that followed it (from *The Hollow Men* to *Little Gidding*)—succeed to such an extent that by 1956 the University of Minnesota needed to stage his lecture there in a basketball arena? The astonishing growth of literacy between 1910 and 1940 certainly helps to explain the rise of an audience for modernist writing. But it was an audience chiefly of fiction readers. Fiction had claimed "real life," and in 1910 poetry was subsisting, for the most part, on vague appeals to nature and to God. Though from 1897 on, Edwin Arlington Robinson had been writing his grim, intelligent poetry of American failures (*Miniver Cheevy* among them), he was not a popular American poet: Joyce Kilmer and Edgar Guest were the poets who sold.

Lovers of poetry in the premodernist era had been surviving on a thin diet of either Platonic idealism or a post-'90s "decadence," and it was felt that barbaric and businesslike America could not equal the sophistication of England. Eliot's vignettes of modern life (some sardonic, some elegiac), and his meditation on consciousness and its aridities, reclaimed for American poetry a terrain of close observation and complex intelligence that had seemed lost. The heartbreak under the poised irony of Eliot's work was not lost on his audience, who suddenly felt that in understanding Eliot, they understood themselves.

The discontinuous and "impersonal" Eliot of course provoked rebellion in some poets. John Berryman wrote, "Let's have narrative, and at least one dominant personality, and no fragmentation! In short, let us have something spectacularly NOT *The Waste Land.*" But other younger poets disagreed. Charles Wright, 1998's Pulitzer Prize poet, first read the *Four Quartets* (Eliot's World War II poem) in the Army-base library in Verona, Italy. "I loved the music; I loved the investigation of the past," he says. "The sound of it was so beautiful to me." The voice of the *Quartets*—meditative, grave, sorrowful, but also dry, experienced and harsh—has been important to poets from Wright to John Ashbery, because it allowed the conversational tone of everyday life to enter into the discussion of the deepest subjects.

After Eliot's unhappy marriage and separation (Vivienne Eliot died in a mental hospital), he was baptized in the Anglican church, and his poetry became more orthodox. Eventually, he could no longer summon the intense concentration of

heart, mind and imagination necessary to produce significant poetry, and he subsided into the versifier of *Old Possum's Book of Practical Cats*—ironically, the work by which he is now most widely known in the U.S., thanks to its popularization in the musical *Cats.* He was a formidably intelligent critic of literature and culture, though he did not escape—any more than we can ourselves—the limitations and prejudices of his time and his upbringing. He sent the stock of the 17th century poets soaring while arguing against the romantic notion of "self-expression" in favor of a poetry that was severe and classical.

Eliot died in 1965. He chose to be buried in East Coker with his ancestors, remaining the unrepentant exile whose Americanness—his Protestant New England, his St. Louis, his Mississippi River—can be seen better by hindsight than it could when he was alive. ∎

*Helen Vendler teaches at Harvard. Her most recent book is* The Art of Shakespeare's Sonnets.

**A convivial Eliot with second wife Valerie Fletcher, circa 1959**

# Other Voices

The 20th century perfected the hard sells of propaganda and advertising, but talented people still worked to counter the debased language of politics and business with the exhilaration and consolation of memorable speech, of poetry, of words striving to be true to themselves

## William Butler Yeats

He was temperamentally a Romantic, eager for seclusion: "I will arise and go now, and go to Innisfree." But public life would not let him. Whatever his subject, he turned current events into lasting art. In the aftermath of World War I, he pronounced a memorable verdict: "Things fall apart; the center cannot hold;/ Mere anarchy is loosed upon the world."

## Robert Frost

His invitation to read at John F. Kennedy's 1961 Inauguration only confirmed his status as America's most widely recognized poet. That popularity stemmed largely from his readability; his poetry seemed to speak plainly, in rhyme. But his surfaces concealed depths. The simple line "And miles to go before I sleep" suggests a trip toward death.

## W.H. Auden

The most technically adroit poet of his era, he dazzled readers when his works first appeared in the late 1920s. Striking a distinctive postwar note, his landscapes bristled with rusting machinery and ominous border crossings. He shied away from definitive statements, hedging even his love poems: "Lay your sleeping head, my love,/ Human on my faithless arm."

## Sylvia Plath

The searing poems she wrote just before her suicide in 1963 made her a feminist martyr; mentor Robert Lowell described her work as "playing Russian roulette with six cartridges in the cylinder." Plath's poem to her long-dead father redefined confessional writing: "Every woman adores a Fascist,/ The boot in the face, the brute/ Brute heart of a brute like you."

## Allen Ginsberg

In the 1950s he emerged as a bardic reincarnation of Walt Whitman. His incantatory, long-lined verses were styled not for parlor reading or classroom study but for public performances, featuring himself. He provided the music for the Beat movement and a vision of modern malaise: "I saw the best minds of my generation destroyed by madness."

Always on the outside: as the Tramp in 1925's *The Gold Rush*

# Charlie
# Chaplin

The endearing figure of his Little Tramp
was instantly recognizable around the
globe and brought laughter to millions.
Still is. Still does. And always will

By ANN DOUGLAS

EVERY FEW WEEKS, OUTSIDE THE MOVIE THEATER IN VIRTUALLY ANY American town in the late 1910s, appeared the life-size cardboard figure of a small tramp—outfitted in tattered, baggy pants, a cutaway coat and vest, impossibly large, worn-out shoes and a battered derby hat—bearing the inscription I AM HERE TODAY. An advertisement for a Charlie Chaplin film was a promise of happiness, of that precious, almost shocking moment when art delivers what life cannot, when experience and delight become synonymous, and our investments yield the fabulous, unmerited bonanza we never get past expecting.

Eighty years later, Chaplin is still here. In a 1995 worldwide survey of film critics, Chaplin was voted the greatest actor in movie history. He was the first, and to date the last, person to control every aspect of the film-making process—founding his own studio, United Artists, with Douglas Fairbanks, Mary Pickford and D.W. Griffith, and producing, casting, directing, writing, scoring and editing the movies he starred in.

In the first decades of the 20th century, when weekly moviegoing was a national habit, Chaplin more or less invented global recognizability and helped turn an industry into an art. In 1916, his third year in films, his salary of $10,000 a week made him the highest-paid actor—possibly the highest-paid person—in the world. By 1920, "Chaplinitis," accompanied by a flood of Chaplin dances, songs, dolls, comic books and cocktails, was rampant. Filmmaker Mack Sennett thought him "just the greatest artist who ever lived." Other early admirers included George Bernard Shaw, Marcel Proust and Sigmund Freud. Later, in the 1950s, Chaplin was one of the icons of the Beat Generation. Jack Kerouac went on the road because he too wanted to be a hobo. From 1981 to 1987, IBM used the Tramp to advertise its venture into personal computers.

Born in London in 1889, Chaplin spent his childhood in shabby furnished rooms, state poorhouses and an orphanage. He was never sure who his real father was; his mother Hannah's husband Charles Chaplin, a singer, deserted the family early and died of alcoholism in 1901. Hannah, a small-time actress, was in and out of mental hospitals. Though he pursued learning passionately in later years, Charlie left school at 10 to work as a mime and roustabout on the British vaudeville circuit. The poverty of his life then inspired the Tramp's trademark costume, a creative travesty of formal dinner dress suggesting the authoritative adult reimagined by a clear-eyed child, the

Spoofing Hitler as Adenoid Hynkel in *The Great Dictator*, 1940

silent films, *The Kid* (1921), *The Gold Rush* (1925), *The Circus* (1928) and *City Lights* (1931).

The terrifyingly comic Adenoid Hynkel (a takeoff on Hitler), whom Chaplin played in *The Great Dictator,* or Verdoux, the sardonic mass murderer of middle-aged women, may seem drastic departures from the "little fellow," but the Tramp is always ambivalent and many-sided. Funniest when he is most afraid, mincing and smirking as he attempts to placate those immune to pacification, constantly susceptible to reprogramming by nearby bodies or machines, skidding around a corner or sliding seamlessly from a pat to a shove while desire and doubt chase each other across his face, the Tramp is never unself-conscious, never free of calculation, never anything but a hard-pressed if often divinely light-hearted member of an endangered species, entitled to any means of defense he can devise. Faced with a frequently malign universe, he can never quite bring himself to choose between his pleasure in the improvisatory shifts of strategic retreat and his impulse to love some creature palpably weaker and more threatened than himself.

When a character in *Monsieur Verdoux* remarks that if the unborn knew of the approach of life, they would dread it as much as the living do death, Chaplin was simply spelling out what we've known all along. The Tramp, it seemed, was mute not by necessity but by choice. He'd tried to protect us from his thoughts, but if the times insisted that he tell what he saw as well as what he was, he could only reveal that the innocent chaos of comedy depends on a mania for control, that the cruelest of ironies attend the most heartfelt invocations of pathos. Speech is the language of hatred as silence is that of love.

ON CHAPLIN'S FIRST NIGHT IN NEW YORK IN 1910, HE walked around the theater district, dazzled by its lights and movement. "This is it!" he told himself. "This is where I belong!" Yet he never became a U.S. citizen. An internationalist by temperament and fame, he considered patriotism "the greatest insanity that the world has ever suffered." As the Depression gave way to World War II and the cold war, the increasingly politicized message of his films, his expressed sympathies with pacifists, communists and Soviet supporters, became suspect. It didn't help that Chaplin, a bafflingly complex and private man, had a weakness for young girls. His first two wives were 16 when he married them; his last, Oona O'Neill, daughter of Eugene O'Neill, was 18. In 1943 he was the defendant in a public pater-

guilty class reinvented in the image of the innocent one. His "little fellow" was the expression of a wildly sentimental, deeply felt allegiance to rags over riches by the star of the century's most conspicuous Horatio Alger scenario.

From the start, his extraordinary athleticism, expressive grace, impeccable timing, endless inventiveness and genius for hard work set Chaplin apart. In 1910 he made his first trip to America, with Fred Karno's Speechless Comedians. In 1913 he joined Sennett's Keystone Studios in New York City. Although his first film, *Making a Living* (1914), brought him nationwide praise, he was unhappy with the slapstick speed, cop chases and bathing-beauty escapades that were Sennett's specialty. The advent of movies in the late 1890s had brought full visibility to the human personality, to the corporeal self that print, the dominant medium before film, could only describe and abstract. In a Sennett comedy, speechlessness raised itself to a racket, but Chaplin instinctively understood that visibility needs leisure as well as silence to work its most intimate magic.

The actor, not the camera, did the acting in his films. Never a formal innovator, Chaplin found his persona and plot early and never totally abandoned them. For 13 years, he resisted talking pictures, launched with *The Jazz Singer* in 1927. Even then, the talkies he made, among them the masterpieces *The Great Dictator* (1940), *Monsieur Verdoux* (1947) and *Limelight* (1952), were daringly far-flung variations on his greatest

**BORN April 16, 1889, in London**

**1889**

**ICON Vamping as the Tramp**

**1913 Accepts job with Mack Sennett's Keystone Studios**

**1915 *The Tramp* debuts**

**1919 Forms United Artists with Pickford, Fairbanks and Griffith**

**Chaplin/the Tramp enjoys a sylvan idyll, complete with nymphs, in 1919's *Sunnyside***

nity suit. Denouncing his "leering, sneering attitude" toward the U.S. and his "unsavory" morals, public officials, citizens' groups and gossip columnists led a boycott of his pictures.

J. Edgar Hoover's FBI put together a dossier on Chaplin that reached almost 2,000 pages. Wrongly identifying him as "Israel Thonstein," a Jew passing for a Gentile, the FBI found no evidence that he had ever belonged to the Communist Party or engaged in treasonous activity. In 1952, however, two days after Chaplin sailed for England to promote *Limelight*, Attorney General James McGranery revoked his re-entry permit. Loathing the witch-hunts and "moral pomposity" of the cold war U.S., and believing he had "lost the affections" of the American public, Chaplin settled with Oona and their family in Switzerland (where he died in 1977).

With the advent of the '60s and the Vietnam War, Chaplin's American fortunes turned. He orchestrated a festival of his films in New York in 1963. Amid the loudest and longest ovation in its history, he accepted a special Oscar from the Academy of Motion Picture Arts and Sciences in 1972. Chaplin, then 83, said he'd long ago given up radical politics, a welcome remark in a nation where popular favor has often been synonymous with depoliticization. But the ravishing charm and brilliance of his films are inseparable from his convictions.

At the end of *City Lights*, when the heroine at last sees the man who has delivered her from blindness, we watch her romantic dreams die. "You?" she asks, incredulous. "Yes," the Tramp nods, his face, caught in extreme close-up, a map of pride, shame and devotion. It's the oldest story in show business—the last shall yet be, if not first, at least recognized, and perhaps even loved. ∎

*Ann Douglas is the author of* Terrible Honesty: Mongrel Manhattan in the 1920s.

**Chaplin finally found happiness in his marriage to Oona O'Neill**

**1952 Denied re-entry into U.S.; settles in Switzerland**

**1975 Knighted by Queen Elizabeth II**

**1977**

**1940 First talkie: *The Great Dictator***

**1972 Returns to U.S. to accept a special Oscar**

**1977 Dies on Dec. 25**

# Steven
# Spielberg

No director or producer has ever put together a more popular body of work. That's why the movies we're now seeing are made in his image

By ROGER EBERT

TEVEN SPIELBERG'S FIRST FILMS were made at a time when directors were the most important people in Hollywood, and his more recent ones at a time when marketing controls the industry. That he has remained the most powerful filmmaker in the world during both periods says something for his talent and his flexibility. No one else has put together a more popular body of work, yet within the entertainer there is also an artist capable of *The Color Purple*, *Schindler's List* and *Saving Private Ryan*. When entertainer and artist came fully together, the result was *E.T., the Extra-Terrestrial*, a remarkable fusion of mass appeal and stylistic mastery.

Spielberg's most important contribution to modern movies is his insight that there was an enormous audience to be created if old-style B-movie stories were made with A-level craftsmanship and enhanced with the latest developments in special effects. Consider such titles as *Raiders of the Lost Ark* and the other Indiana Jones movies, *Close Encounters of the Third Kind*, *E.T.* and *Jurassic Park*. Look also at the films he produced but didn't direct,

like the *Back to the Future* series, *Gremlins*, *Who Framed Roger Rabbit* and *Twister*. The story lines were the stuff of Saturday serials, but the filmmaking was cutting edge and delivered what films have always promised: they showed us something amazing that we hadn't seen before.

Directors talk about their master images, the images that occur in more than one film because they express something fundamental about the way the filmmakers see things. Spielberg once told me that his master image was the light flooding in through the doorway in *Close Encounters*, suggesting, simultaneously, a brightness and a mystery outside. This strong backlighting turns up in many of his films: E.T.'s spaceship door is filled with light, Indy Jones often uses strong beams from powerful flashlights, and the aliens walk out of light in *Close Encounters*.

In Spielberg, the light source conceals mystery, whereas for many other directors it is darkness that conceals mystery. The difference is that for Spielberg, mystery offers promise instead of threat. That orientation apparently developed when he was growing

**BORN** Dec. 18, 1946, in Cincinnati, Ohio

1946

**ACTION! Directing home movies as a boy**

**1969 With *Amblin'*,** makes professional debut at Atlanta Film Festival

**1974 Directs first feature, *The Sugarland Express*,** with Goldie Hawn

**1975 Directs *Jaws***

**1982 Makes *E.T.***

**1994 *Schindler's List* wins** Oscar for Best Director and Best Picture; forms Dream-Works SKG with two partners

**1998 *Saving Private Ryan* is hailed as a masterwork**

up in Phoenix, Ariz. One day we sat and talked about his childhood, and he told me of a formative experience.

"My dad took me out to see a meteor shower when I was a little kid," he said, "and it was scary for me because he woke me up in the middle of the night. My heart was beating; I didn't know what he wanted to do. He wouldn't tell me, and he put me in the car and we went off, and I saw all these people lying on blankets, looking up at the sky. And my dad spread out a blanket. We lay down and looked at the sky, and I saw for the first time all these meteors. What scared me was being awakened in the middle of the night and taken somewhere without being told where. But what didn't scare me, but was very soothing, was watching this cosmic meteor shower. And I think from that moment on, I never looked at the sky and thought it was a bad place."

There are two important elements there: the sense of wonder and hope, and the identification with a child's point of view. Spielberg's best characters are like elaborations of the heroes from old *Boy's Life* serials, plucky kids who aren't afraid to get in over their head. Even Oskar Schindler has something of that in his makeup—the boy's delight in pulling off a daring scheme and getting away with it.

Spielberg heroes don't often find themselves in complex emotional entanglements (Celie in *The Color Purple* is an exception). One of his rare failures was

*Always*, with its story of a ghost watching his girl fall in love with another man. The typical Spielberg hero is drawn to discovery, and the key shot in many of his films is the revelation of the wonder he has discovered. Remember the spellbinding initial glimpse of the living dinosaurs in *Jurassic Park*?

SPIELBERG'S FIRST IMPORTANT THEATRICAL film was *The Sugarland Express*, made in 1974, a time when gifted auteurs like Scorsese, Altman, Coppola, De Palma and Malick ruled Hollywood. Their god was Orson Welles, who made the masterpiece *Citizen Kane* entirely without studio interference, and they too wanted to make the Great American Movie. But a year later, with *Jaws*, Spielberg changed the course of modern Hollywood history. *Jaws* was a hit of vast proportions, inspiring executives to go for the home run instead of the base hit. And it came out in the summer, a season the major studios had generally ceded to cheaper exploitation films. Within a few years, the *Jaws* model would inspire an industry in which budgets ran wild because the rewards seemed limitless, in which summer action pictures dominated the industry and in which the hottest young directors wanted to make the Great American Blockbuster.

Spielberg can't be blamed for that seismic shift in the industry. *Jaws* only happened to inaugurate it. If the shark had sunk for good (as it threatened to during the troubled filming), another picture would have ushered in the age of the movie best sellers—maybe *Star Wars*, in 1977. And no one is more aware than Spielberg of his own weaknesses. When I asked him once to make the case against his films, he grinned and started the list: "They say, 'Oh, he cuts too fast; his edits are too quick; he uses wide-angle lenses; he doesn't photograph women very well; he's tricky; he likes to dig a hole in the ground and put the camera in the hole and shoot up at people; he's too gimmicky; he's more in love with the camera than he is with the story.'"

All true. But you could make a longer list of his strengths, including his direct line to our subconscious. Spielberg has always maintained obsessive quality control, and when his films work, they work on every level that a film can reach. I remember seeing *E.T.* at the Cannes Film Festival, where it played before the most sophisticated filmgoers in the world and reduced them to tears and cheers.

In the history of the last third of 20th century cinema, Spielberg is the most influential figure, for better and worse. In his lesser films he relied too much on shallow stories and special effects for their own sake. (Will anyone treasure *The Lost World: Jurassic Park* a century from now?) In his best films he tapped into dreams fashioned by our better natures. ∎

*Roger Ebert is the film critic of the Chicago* Sun-Times *and co-host of TV's* Siskel & Ebert.

**Left, Spielberg's master image in *Close Encounters*: a child faces a mysteriously compelling flood of light. Right, directing his 1998 hit *Saving Private Ryan***

# Auteurs Who Made Milestones

Three of them turned out Hollywood hits, the others were film critics' darlings, but each of these directors created films that have left an indelible impression on our collective cultural memory

### D.W. Griffith

"He gave us the grammar of film-making," said Lillian Gish of the contribution of pioneer Hollywood director Griffith. He found cinema stagey and theatrical; by jamming his camera into the action, by rapid cross-cutting, by building shots into sequences and sequences into narratives, Griffith made the movies *move*. In such masterworks as *Birth of a Nation* (1915), he used close-ups, long-shots in panorama and poetic fade-ins and fade-outs to ratchet up both the technology and the art of the cinema.

### Preston Sturges

He had an ear for the American vernacular, an eye for American eccentricity and a soul attuned to American dreaming. He wrote and directed his seven great comedies, including *The Lady Eve,* in four years, then fell out of orbit. But thanks to celluloid, his gift continues to delight new generations of fans.

### Alfred Hitchcock

In cliché, the great British director was the master of suspense. In reality, he was the quaking poet-victim of anxieties and obsessions that almost everyone shares. Which is why Hitchcock's best work—*Shadow of a Doubt, Notorious, Vertigo*—clings so undismissably to our imagination.

## Akira Kurosawa

He worked the streets of modern Tokyo and the byways of feudal Japan, seeing and forging the connection between the Hollywood western and the samurai epic. Kurosawa is perhaps the most eclectic director who has ever lived, which is another way of saying he's also a great universalist, an artist who has always sought the common emotional thread in all our cultural costumes.

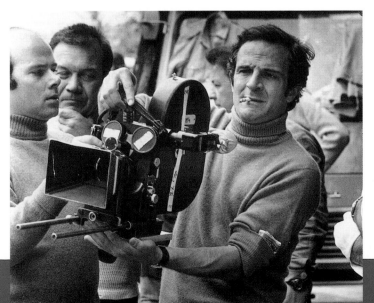

## Ingmar Bergman

Childhood is another name for claustrophobia, marriage is a torture chamber, and God is probably a deaf-mute. Bergman's is the cinema of suffocation, redeemed only by the unblinking intensity of his gaze, the austere power of his technique, the passion of his dispassion.

## François Truffaut

He was the first exuberant surfer of the New Wave, happily hanging 10 as it crashed on formalism's beach. But in films like *The 400 Blows* and *Jules and Jim*, he was a good-natured revolutionary; from the start, his fervor was tempered by a humanistic romanticism both rueful and rollicking.

# Igor
# Stravinsky

His *Rite of Spring* heralded the century. After that, he
never stopped reinventing himself—or modern music

**By PHILIP GLASS**

> ## He was so lighthearted, so funny, so playful. He loved games. He had childlike enthusiasms.
>
> GEORGE BALANCHINE

PARIS' THÉÂTRE DES CHAMPS-ÉLYSÉES, ON MAY 29, 1913, was the setting of the most notorious event in the musical history of this century—the world premiere of *The Rite of Spring*. Trouble began with the playing of the first notes, in the ultrahigh register of the bassoon, as the renowned composer Camille Saint-Saëns conspicuously walked out, complaining loudly of the misuse of the instrument. Soon other protests became so loud that the dancers could barely hear their cues. Fights broke out in the audience. Thus Modernism arrived in music, its calling card delivered by the 30-year-old Russian composer Igor Stravinsky.

Born in 1882 in Oranienbaum, Russia, a city southwest of St. Petersburg, Stravinsky was rooted in the nationalistic school that drew inspiration from Russia's beautifully expressive folk music. His father was an opera singer who performed in Kiev and St. Petersburg, but the young composer's greatest musical influence was his teacher, Nikolay Rimsky-Korsakov. The colorful, fantastic orchestration that Stravinsky brought to his folk song–inspired melodies was clearly derived from Rimsky-Korsakov. But the primitive, offbeat rhythmic drive he added was entirely his own. The result was a music never before heard in a theater or concert hall.

In 1910 Serge Diaghilev, then director of the world-famous Ballets Russes, invited Stravinsky to compose works for his company's upcoming season at the Paris Opera. *The Firebird*, the first to appear, was a sensation. *Petrushka* and *The Rite of Spring* quickly followed. Soon Stravinsky's audaciously innovative works confirmed his status as the leading composer of the day, a position he hardly relinquished until his death nearly 60 years later.

After leaving Russia, Stravinsky lived for a while in Switzerland and then moved to Paris. In 1939 he fled the war in Europe for the U.S., settling in Hollywood. In 1969 he left California for New York City. (The story goes that when asked why he made such a move at his advanced age, he replied, "To mutate faster.") Over the years, Stravinsky experimented with virtually every technique of 20th century music: tonal, polytonal and

With Balanchine, top left, and dancers

12-tone serialism. He reinvented and personalized each form while adapting the melodic styles of earlier eras to the new times. In the end, his own musical voice always prevailed.

In 1947 Stravinsky befriended Robert Craft, a 23-year-old conductor who was to become his chronicler, interpreter and, oddly, his mentor in some ways. Craft persuaded him to take a more sympathetic view of Arnold Schoenberg's 12-tone school, which led to Stravinsky's last great stylistic development.

In his long career, there was scarcely a musical form that Stravinsky did not turn his hand to. He regularly produced symphonies, concertos, oratorios and an almost bewildering variety of choral works. For me, however, Stravinsky was at his most sublime when he wrote for the theater. There were operas, including *The Rake's Progress*, composed for a libretto by W.H. Auden and one of a handful of 20th century operas that have found a secure place in the repertory. The ballets also continued; the last of his masterpieces, *Agon*, composed for another Russian, choreographer George Balanchine, came in 1957.

I heard him conduct only once, during a program in his honor in 1959 at New York City's Town Hall. What an event that was! Stravinsky led a performance of *Les Noces*, a vocal/theater work accompanied by four pianos—played by Samuel Barber, Aaron Copland, Lukas Foss and Roger Sessions. Each brought his own charisma to the event, but all seemed to be in awe of Stravinsky—as if he appeared before them with one foot on earth and the other planted firmly on Olympus.

He was electrifying for me too. He conducted with an energy and vividness that completely conveyed his every musical intention. Seeing him at that moment, embodying his work in demeanor and gestures, is one of my most treasured musical memories. Here was Stravinsky, a musical revolutionary whose own evolution never stopped. There is not a composer who lived during his time or is alive today who was not touched, and sometimes transformed, by his work. ∎

*Composer-performer Philip Glass has written many works of opera and musical theater.*

BORN June 17, 1882, in Oranienbaum, Russia

1907 Becomes Rimsky-Korsakov's student

1910 Produces ballet *The Firebird* with Diaghilev

1913 Premiere of ballet *The Rite of Spring* causes a riot in Paris

1882

THE DANCE With Nijinksy, in costume as Petrushka

1939 Settles in Hollywood

1951 Composes opera *The Rake's Progress* using a libretto by W.H. Auden

1957 Creates his final ballet masterpiece, *Agon*, with Balanchine

1971 Dies April 6; buried in Venice near Diaghilev

1971

# Louis
# Armstrong

With dazzling virtuosity on the trumpet
and an innovative singing style,
Satchmo was the fountainhead of a
thoroughly original American sound

By STANLEY CROUCH

OPS. SWEET PAPA DIP. SATCHMO. HE HAD PERFECT pitch and perfect rhythm. His improvised melodies and singing could be as lofty as a moon flight or as low-down as the blood drops of a street thug dying in the gutter. Like most of the great innovators in jazz, he was a small man. But the extent of his influence across jazz, across American music and around the world has such continuing stature that he is one of the few who can easily be mentioned with Stravinsky, Picasso and Joyce. His life was the embodiment of one who moves from rags to riches, from anonymity to internationally imitated innovator. Louis Daniel Armstrong supplied revolutionary language that took on such pervasiveness that it became commonplace, like the light bulb, the airplane, the telephone.

That is why Armstrong remains a deep force in our American expression. Not only do we hear him in those trumpet players who represent the present renaissance in jazz— Wynton Marsalis, Wallace Roney, Terence Blanchard, Roy Hargrove, Nicholas Payton—we can also detect his influence in certain rhythms that sweep from country-and-western music all the way over to the chanted doggerel of rap.

For many years it was thought that Armstrong was born in New Orleans on July 4, 1900, a perfect day for the man who wrote the musical Declaration of Independence for Americans of this century. But the estimable writer Gary Giddins discovered the birth certificate that proves Armstrong was born Aug. 4, 1901. He grew up at the bottom, hustling and hustling, trying to bring something home to eat, sometimes searching garbage cans for food that might still be suitable for supper.

The spirit of Armstrong's world, however, was not dominated by the deprivation of poverty and the dangers of wild living. What struck him most, as his memoir, *Satchmo: My Life in New Orleans*, attests, was the ceremonial vigor of the people. Ranging from almost European pale to jet black, the Negroes of New Orleans had many social clubs, parades and picnics. With rags, blues, snippets from opera, church music and whatever else, a wide breadth of rhythm and tune was created to accompany or stimulate every kind of human involvement. Before becoming an instrumentalist, Armstrong the child was either dancing for pennies or singing for his supper with a strolling quartet of other kids who wandered New Orleans freshening up the subtropical evening with some sweetly harmonized notes.

He had some knucklehead in his soul too. While a genial fountain of joy, Armstrong was a street boy, and he had a dirty mouth. It was his shooting off a pistol on New Year's Eve that got him thrown into the Colored Waifs' Home, an institution bent on refining ruffians. It was there that young Louis first put his lips to the mouthpiece of a cornet. Like any American boy, no matter his point of social origin, he had his dreams. At night he used to lie in bed, hearing the masterly Freddie Keppard out in the streets blowing that golden horn, and hope that he too would someday have command of a clarion sound.

The sound developed very quickly, and he was soon known around New Orleans as formidable. The places he played and the people he knew were sweet and innocent at one end of the spectrum and rough at the other. He played picnics for young Negro girls, Mississippi riverboats on which the white people had never seen Negroes in tuxedos before, and dives where the customers cut and shot one another. One time he witnessed two women fighting to the death with knives. Out of those experiences, everything from pomp to humor to erotic charisma to grief to majesty to the profoundly gruesome and monumentally spiritual worked its way into his tone. He became a beacon of American feeling.

Musicians then were wont to have "cutting sessions"—battles of imagination and stamina. From 1920 on, young Louis was hell on two feet if somebody was in the mood to challenge him. Fairly soon, he was left alone. He also did a little pimping but got out of the game when one of his girls stabbed him. With a trout sandwich among his effects, Armstrong took a train to Chicago in 1922, where he joined his mentor Joe ("King") Oliver, and the revolution took place in full form. King Oliver and his Creole Jazz Band, featuring the dark young powerhouse with the large mouth, brought out the people and all the musicians, black and white, who wanted to know how it was truly done. The most impressive white musician of his time, Bix Beiderbecke, jumped up and went glassy-eyed the first time he heard Armstrong.

When he was called to New York City in 1924 by the bigtime bandleader Fletcher Henderson, Armstrong looked exactly like what he was, a young man who was not to be fooled around with and might slap the taste out of your mouth if you went too far. His improvisations set the city on its head. The stiff rhythms of the time were slashed away by his combination of the percussive and the soaring. He soon returned to Chicago, perfected what he was doing and made one record after another that reordered American music, such as *Potato Head Blues* and *I'm a Ding Dong Daddy*.

**BORN Aug. 4, 1901, in New Orleans**

**1922 Joins Joe ("King") Oliver's band in Chicago**

**1932 Visits Europe; plays for the King of England**

**1956 Shines in MGM musical *High Society***

**1964 His recording of *Hello, Dolly!* hits No. 1**

**1901**

**1971**

**1915 Gets first cornet at the Colored Waifs' Home**

**1925 Begins recording with the Hot Five**

**1956 Hailed by crowds during African tour**

**1971 Dies July 6 in New York City**

**"** How can you help loving a guy that makes the world a happy place like Louis does? If he couldn't blow a note, he'd still be worth his weight in laughs. **"** MUGGSY SPANIER, cornetist

Now you has jazz: Satchmo wows Grace Kelly and Bing Crosby on the set of *High Society*

fashion plate. His slang was the lingua franca. Oh, he was something.

Louis Armstrong was so much, in fact, that the big bands sounded like him, their featured improvisers took direction from him, and every school of jazz since has had to address how he interpreted the basics of the idiom—swing, blues, ballads and Afro-Hispanic rhythms. While every jazz instrumentalist owes him an enormous debt, singers as different as Bing Crosby, Billie Holiday, Ella Fitzgerald, Sarah Vaughan, Frank Sinatra, Elvis Presley and Marvin Gaye have Armstrong in common as well. His freedom, his wit, his discipline, his bawdiness, his majesty and his irrepressible willingness to do battle with deep sorrow and the wages of death give his music a perpetual position in the wave of the future that is the station of all great art.

Armstrong traveled the world constantly. One example of his charming brashness revealed itself when he concertized before the King of England in 1932 and introduced a number by saying, "This one's for you, Rex: *I'll Be Glad When You're Dead, You Rascal You.*" He had a great love for children, was always willing to help out fellow musicians and passed out laxatives to royalty and heads of state. However well he was received in Europe, the large public celebrations with which West Africans welcomed him during a tour in the '50s were far more appropriate for this sequoia of 20th century music.

He usually accepted human life as it came, and he shaped it his way. But he didn't accept everything. By the middle '50s, Armstrong had been dismissed by younger Negro musicians as some sort of minstrel figure, an embarrassment, too jovial and hot in a time when cool disdain was the new order. He was, they said, holding Negroes back because he smiled too much and wasn't demanding a certain level of respect from white folks. But when Armstrong called out President Eisenhower for not standing behind those black children as school integration began in Little Rock, Ark., 40 years ago, there was not a peep heard from anyone else in the jazz world. His heroism remained singular. Such is the way of the truly great: they do what they do in conjunction or all by themselves. They get the job done. Louis Daniel Armstrong was that kind. ■

Needing more space for his improvised line, Armstrong rejected the contrapuntal New Orleans front line of clarinet, trumpet and trombone in favor of the single, featured horn, which soon became the convention. His combination of virtuosity, strength and passion was unprecedented. No one in Western music—not even Bach—has ever set the innovative pace on an instrument, then stood up to sing and converted the vocalists. Pops. Sweet Papa Dip. Satchmo.

THE MELODIC AND RHYTHMIC VISTAS ARMSTRONG opened up solved the mind-body problem as the world witnessed how the brain and the muscles could work in perfect coordination on the aesthetic spot. Apollo and Dionysus met in the sweating container of a genius from New Orleans whose sensitivity and passion were epic in completely new terms. In his radical reinterpretations, Armstrong bent and twisted popular songs with his horn and his voice until they were shorn of sentimentality and elevated to serious art. He brought the change agent of swing to the world, the most revolutionary rhythm of his century. He learned how to dress and became a

*Essayist Stanley Crouch's latest book is* Always in Pursuit: Fresh American Perspectives.

# Cool Cats and All That Jazz

Propelled by masters of improvisation, jazz absorbs, transforms, discards, but always replenishes itself.

### Duke Ellington

With such classics as *Black, Brown and Beige,* the master composer's big band was jazz's gold standard from the '30s to the '50s. Duke's compositions—timelessly elegant and invested with rich textures and emotional fullness—helped push jazz to unparalleled heights. And he could swing, as in his 1956 album *Ellington at Newport.*

### Ella Fitzgerald

From her days fronting a big band in the '30s to swinging and scatting with bebopster Dizzy Gillespie in the '40s to her classic '50s series of "songbook" albums, Ella's voice glistened with a bell-like—yet swinging—clarity.

### Charlie Parker

The musical quantum leap known as bebop shook the jazz world in the mid-1940s. Its prime energy source was sax man Parker. Unhinging improvisation from song melody, jumping into dissonances and spinning out complex lines, Parker dominated postwar jazz.

### Miles Davis

*Kind of Blue,* Davis' landmark 1959 recording with John Coltrane and Cannonball Adderley, was the apotheosis of Cool Jazz. Distilling the music to bare essence, Davis and arranger Gil Evans created a lean, sensuous sound that broke with the intensity of bebop and attracted millions of new listeners to jazz.

# Frank Sinatra

He loved, he brawled, he had style, he had guts, he could even act. And, oh yeah, he defined American pop music

BY BRUCE HANDY

RANK SINATRA HAS RECEIVED FAR TOO MANY TRIBUTES already. Even before his death in May 1998, there was the 80th-birthday hoopla in 1995, followed by the flock of books circling,vulture-like, in clear anticipation of his passing. At this point any recounting of his accomplishments—his unassailable greatness as a singer, his somewhat more assailable greatness as an actor, his impeccable taste as a curator of the great American songbook, his ancillary talents as both philanthropist and thug, his status as a totem of midcentury masculinity—inevitably takes on a dutiful, ritualistic air. So what better way to breathe a little life into the process than with an insult?

"George Steinbrenner with a voice" was the epithet coined by a colleague of mine—born in the baby boom's dead center, it should be noted—who objects to the bad-hair Republican bluster of Sinatra's later years, his belting out of all those anthems of middle-aged self-assertion. He did it his way. He can make it anywhere. He picks himself up and gets back in the race—that's life, or Sinatra's blowhard version of it anyway. It is the artfully projected world view of a casino entertainer, a glorified greeter, whose job it was to make old guys with bum tickers and second wives feel good about themselves.

On one hand, my colleague's view of Sinatra as scourge of baby boomers— the anti–Judy Collins, if you will—is a crude caricature of a complex artist, as reductive as any neo swinger's fetishistic prattling about the man's way with a pocket handkerchief. On the other hand, it is a caricature I too used to believe in.

Should anyone even care what people like my colleague and me think of Sinatra? My own higher notions about music were incubated while listening to Jethro

The easy stance belies his hard-won mastery: recording in 1954

" Underneath it all, I think, Frank was just a very old-fashioned Italian man. "

NANCY REAGAN

Tull albums (whoa—a flute!). Sinatra's body of work, meanwhile, stretches back to the 1930s and is nothing less than "the final statement on pre-rock pop," as Will Friedwald, the invaluable Sinatra scholar, recently wrote of the *Songs for Swingin' Lovers!* album, released in 1956 and generally considered Sinatra's finest LP. "Something radically different just had to come next," Friedwald continues, "because nothing in the realm of Tin Pan Alley could top this bravura celebration of grown-up love." You can't sum up Sinatra's achievement more succinctly than that.

But he had nearly 40 years of performing left ahead of him in 1956; more than two-thirds of his professional life was spent in the rock era, much of it reacting to rhythms and attitudes he found alien. "The most brutal, ugly, degenerate, vicious form of expression it has been my displeasure to hear," Sinatra wrote of rock 'n' roll at the time of Elvis Presley's pre-eminence, no doubt hoping to turn back the Mongols. It didn't quite work, and in efforts to maintain his commercial viability, Sinatra would eventually record Presley's hit *Love Me Tender* as well as works by Paul Simon (*Mrs. Robinson*), George Harrison (*Something*) and Joni Mitchell (*Both Sides Now*). The results were often awkward—this is the Sinatra people like me used to make fun of. But listen with more knowing ears: when Sinatra sings "You stick around, Jack, it might show" on *Something*, you get the feeling not that he's hoking it up Vegas-style so much as he's rooting around for rhythmic complexity in a beautiful if simple song; he's a muscle car idling on a leafy suburban cul-de-sac.

Sinatra—this is both his gift and, on occasion, his downfall—is always Sinatra. Beyond his technical prowess as a jazz-influenced pop singer, building on the innovations of Louis Armstrong, Bing Crosby and Billie Holiday, there is the sheer force of conviction, feeling, the weight of personal history in his voice. In this, only Holiday is his rival—perhaps even his better. Both exemplify what people in my generation like to tell ourselves is unique to rock 'n' roll and its offshoots: the immediacy, the idiosyncrasy, the genuineness of expression. Sinatra is the century's musical equipoise, the pivot between the carefully crafted pop of its beginning and the looser, fiercer sounds of its end.

These are not original observations; people who had the fortune to grow up with Sinatra already knew. I first caught on when, while listening to a Sinatra greatest-hits album I had bought for a girlfriend as an ironic courtship gesture—I was young, it was the '80s—the song *Strangers in the Night*

"Rat Pack" shenanigans with Davis, Martin and Bishop, 1960

caught my ear. It's an admittedly queer place to start amid the glories of the Sinatra canon, a chintzy little hit from 1966 with a dopey pop-rock arrangement; the singer himself gives it the brush-off with his famous dooby-dooby-doo coda during the fade-out. But even here Sinatra manages to invest the ticky-tacky lyrics—"Strangers in the night/ Exchanging glances/ Wondering in the night/ What were the chances"—with a palpable yearning that transcends, maybe even exalts, its surroundings. I was hooked.

This, really, is my point: masterpieces—like *Songs for Swingin' Lovers!*—are easy to love. They are what we remember artists for, but they aren't always as illuminating, or as cherishable, as the failures and throwaways. More often than not, even Sinatra's crud speaks his virtues. You can't ask much more of a performer than that. ∎

*Bruce Handy is a senior writer at* TIME *and the proprietor of the Spectator column in the magazine's Arts & Media section.*

**BORN**
**Dec. 12, 1915, in Hoboken, N.J.**

**1940 Joins Tommy Dorsey band**

**1954 Wins Oscar for** *From Here to Eternity*

**1985 Awarded Presidential Medal of Freedom**

1915

1998

**1935 Wins radio talent show**

**1944 Solo concerts at New York's Paramount Theater cause bobby-soxer riots**

**1960 Makes first Rat Pack movie,** *Ocean's Eleven*

**1998 Dies May 14 in Los Angeles**

Rodgers, left, and Hammerstein: driven to innovate, they flopped only when they aimed too high

ing and writing amateur routines. It was after the Saturday matinee of a college varsity revue that he first met Rodgers, whose older brother had brought him to the show. Years later, remembering this meeting, Hammerstein wrote, "Behind the sometimes too serious face of an extraordinarily talented composer ... I see a dark-eyed little boy."

Like Rodgers, Hammerstein was keen to push the boundaries of the musical, which was only slightly more sophisticated than a vaudeville revue. In the program of his 1924 Broadway show *Rose-Marie*, for instance, he and the other authors wrote that the musical numbers were too integral to the book to list separately. Three years later, with Jerome Kern, he had his biggest success with *Show Boat*, the musical he adapted from Edna Ferber's novel of the same name with the express intention of weaving songs seamlessly into a narrative about addictive gambling, alcoholism and miscegenation. Years later, Hammerstein dealt with racial issues again in *South Pacific*.

That summer they had sold a song to producer Lew Fields for a show called *A Lonely Romeo*. (Extraordinarily, some of Rodgers' songs, to his own lyrics, appeared on Broadway even earlier, when he was 16.)

But it wasn't until 1925 that Rodgers and Hart had a major hit. They wrote the songs for a lighthearted revue called *The Garrick Gaieties*. Its *Manhattan* was an overnight success, and the legendary partnership was flying at last. Such songs as *The Lady Is a Tramp*, *Dancing on the Ceiling*, *My Heart Stood Still* and *Blue Moon* etched the duo a permanent place in theater history.

R ODGERS WAS ALWAYS KEEN ON BREAKING new ground. Many believe *Pal Joey* (1940), the story of the emcee of a sleazy nightclub, to be a landmark musical. With its unscrupulous leading character and bitingly realistic view of life, the show moved the musical-comedy format into more serious territory. But even as Rodgers and Hart were taking the musical to new levels, their partnership was becoming increasingly strained. Hart was a serious drinker, and by the time of his last collaboration with Rodgers, *By Jupiter* in 1942, he was virtually an alcoholic. Rodgers was desperate. No one was more forthcoming with help than his old friend Oscar Hammerstein II.

Hammerstein was born in New York City on July 12, 1895. His father William was a theatrical manager; his grandfather Oscar I, a legendary impresario who took on the Metropolitan Opera by building his own opera house. The young Oscar was stagestruck from childhood, and by the time he attended Columbia University, he was perform-

Critics said *Oklahoma!* would bomb—but it revolutionized musical comedy

By the time Rodgers and Hammerstein were discussing the Hart crisis, the 46-year-old Hammerstein was considered something of a has-been. He had a string of flops to his name. (Famously, after the successful debut of *Oklahoma!* he took an advertisement in *Variety* listing all his recent catastrophes with the punch line: "I've done it before and I can do it again!")

The announcement that Rodgers and Hammerstein were to collaborate on *Oklahoma!*—the Theatre Guild production based on Lynn Riggs' novel *Green Grow the Lilacs*—was initially greeted with skepticism. The financial backing for *Away We Go!* (as the show was then called) proved very difficult to raise. MGM, which owned the dramatic rights, refused to make a $69,000 investment for half the profits. The word on the tryout in New Haven, Conn., was awful. One of Walter Winchell's informants wired the columnist: "No girls, no legs, no jokes, no chance."

**B**UT ON MARCH 31, 1943, *OKLAHOMA!* OPENED IN triumph on Broadway. A show that began with a lone woman churning butter onstage to the strains of an offstage voice singing *Oh, What a Beautiful Mornin'* captivated its first-night audience. This revolutionary, naturalistic musical also changed the mainstream of the genre forever.

Rodgers and Hammerstein wrote nine musicals together. Five are legendary hits: *Oklahoma!, Carousel, South Pacific, The King and I* and *The Sound of Music.* (*Flower Drum Song* was a success, but not in the same league as the golden five.) They wrote one film musical, *State Fair,* and the TV special *Cinderella,* starring Lesley Ann Warren. They were also hugely canny producers. Irving Berlin's *Annie Get Your Gun* was but one of the works they produced that was not their own. Their flops—*Allegro, Me and Juliet* and *Pipe Dream*—were probably a result, as much as anything, of their trying too consciously to be innovative.

What sets the great Rodgers and Hammerstein musicals apart for me is their directness and their awareness of the importance of construction in musical theater. Years ago, I played through the piano score of *South Pacific.* It is staggering how skillfully reprises are used as scene-change music that sets up a following number or underlines a previous point. It could only be the product of a hugely close relationship in which each partner sensed organically where the other, and the show, was going.

After Hammerstein's death from cancer in 1960, Rodgers valiantly plowed on. He worked with Stephen Sondheim on a musical, *Do I Hear a Waltz?* An attempt at a collaboration with Alan Jay Lerner, lyricist of *My Fair Lady,* came to nothing. I can vouch for Alan's never having had the almost puritanical discipline that Rodgers found so satisfactory in Hammerstein. Sadly, too, with one or two exceptions, the post-Hammerstein melodies paled against Rodgers' former output. Who can say why? Perhaps it was simply the lack of the right partner to provide inspiration and bring out the best in him. Musical partnerships are, after all, like marriages—built on a chemistry that is intangible, perhaps not even definable. Nearly 40 years later, the partnership of Rodgers and Hammerstein has not yet been equaled. It probably never will be. ■

*Composer Andrew Lloyd Webber's hits include* Phantom of the Opera *and* Cats. *His new musical is* Whistle Down the Wind.

**Jerome Robbins choreographed the enchanting dances for *The King and I***

**_The Sound of Music_ was their final collaboration**

# Landmarks Of the Stage

Its role as the people's storyteller usurped by the upstart technologies of cinema and television, the theater groped to find new ways to astonish, to provoke, to entertain. Each of these powerful plays helped the theater find a new vocabulary— and ensured its continuing vitality

## Six Characters in Search of an Author (1921) Luigi Pirandello

In his dark drama about a group of people who interrupt a play rehearsal claiming to be a playwright's unfinished fictional creations, Luigi Pirandello compelled audiences to reconsider their notions of truth and illusion.

## Waiting for Godot (1953)
### Samuel Beckett

Two tramps anxiously pass the time expecting Godot. Why? Who is he? We're never told. Nobel-prizewinner Samuel Beckett's unsettling absurdist play captured the postwar mood of alienation and disorientation and has inspired dramatists from Harold Pinter to David Mamet.

## A Raisin in the Sun (1959)
### Lorraine Hansberry

Lorraine Hansberry's warm-hearted story of a struggling middle-class black family had audiences—white as well as black—now weeping, now roaring with pleasure. Its commercial success opened the stage door at last to African-American playwrights.

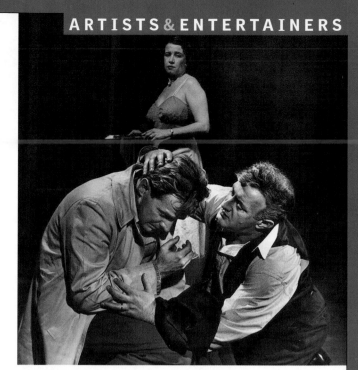

## A Streetcar Named Desire (1947)
### Tennessee Williams

Drenching the stage in the Southern-gothic sensibility of novelist William Faulkner, Tennessee Williams yoked poetic imagery to gritty naturalism—and breathed life into two of the century's great roles: Blanche DuBois and Stanley Kowalski.

## Death of a Salesman (1949)
### Arthur Miller

With tender regard, Arthur Miller fashioned an elegy to Willy Loman, a materialistic, worn-out drummer who has succumbed to the "wrong" American Dream. Miller proved that tragic drama could be rooted in the world of the average man.

## Who's Afraid of Virginia Woolf?
### (1962) Edward Albee

The language was both savage and witty, the emotion raw and intense, the denouement thrilling and unexpected. Shocked audiences had never experienced anything like the domestic hell that Edward Albee evoked so theatrically. After this, no topic, no means of expression could be taboo for playwrights.

## The Boys in the Band (1968)
### Mart Crowley

In Mart Crowley's validating comedy about a gay birthday party, fiercely funny turns into poignantly revealing. The mainstream success of the groundbreaking work emboldened a generation of homosexual playwrights to treat their lives and concerns with unblinking, unashamed honesty.

# The
# Beatles

Irrepressible and irresistible, they were—and remain
—the world's most astonishing rock-'n'-roll band

By **KURT LODER**

**B**OOMERS CAN BE TIRESOME WHEN they natter on too long about the fun-swollen fabulousness of the 1960s. I mean, I was there: "Flower power"? Patchouli oil? Peter Max posters? Please. But even the mistiest of such geezers is likely to be right about the rock and soul music of that decade: Who could overstate its distinctive exuberance, its heady inventiveness, or the thrill of its sheer abundance? And who could overcelebrate those most emblematic of '60s pop phenomena, the Beatles? For the Beatles were then, and remain to this day, the world's most astonishing rock-'n'-roll band.

I use the adjective advisedly. Unrelenting astonishment is what I clearly recall feeling, as a teenager myself back in the winter of 1964, when "Beatlemania," an obscure hysteria that had erupted in Britain the year before, suddenly jumped the Atlantic and took instant root here. First, in January, came the spine-tingling arrival of *I Want to Hold Your Hand*—a great, convulsive rock-'n'-roll record that, to the bafflement of many a teen garage band across the land, actually had more than three chords (five more, to be exact—incredible). Then one week later, *She Loves You* careened onto the charts—wooo! The week after that came the headlong rush of *Please Please Me*, and by April, the top five singles in the country were all Beatles records. By year's end they had logged a head-spinning 29 hits on the U.S. charts. It is hard—no, it is impossible—to imagine any of the gazillion or so carefully marketed little bands of today replicating a quarter of that feat. (Even a contemporary English group such as Oasis, which baldly appropriates the superficialities of the Beatles' style, entirely misses the still magical heart of their music.)

Ed Sullivan, the poker-faced TV variety-show host, having spotted the effervescent moptops in mid–mob scene at London's Heathrow Airport the previous October ("Who the hell are the Beatles?" he'd asked excitedly), brought them over to play his show early on, in February 1964, and 70 million people tuned in. A congratulatory telegram from Elvis Presley, the great, lost god of rockabilly, was read at the beginning of the show, in what might have been seen as torch-passing fashion, and Americans—or American youth, at any rate—promptly fell in love. ("I give them a year," said Sullivan's musical director.)

It is a commonplace of pop-music commentary to point out that at the time of the Beatles' first appearance on the Sullivan show, the U.S. was a country uniquely in need of some cheering up. The assassination of a young and charismatic President little more than two months earlier had cast a pall on the national mood, and of course there were rumors of war. Certainly the moment was propitious for the four lads from Liverpool.

Looking back, though, it seems likely that the Beatles—with their buoyant spirits, their bottomless charm, their unaccustomed and irrepressible wit—could probably have boosted the mirth quotient at a clown convention. Their overflowing gifts for songcraft, harmony and instrumental excitement, their spiffy suits and nifty haircuts, their bright quips and ready smiles, made them appear almost otherworldly, as if they had just beamed down from some distant and far happier planet.

Actually, of course, they hailed from Liverpool, a semi-grim seaport on the northwestern coast of England. John Lennon, born there in 1940, never knew the seagoing father who had deserted his mother; mainly a doting aunt

The moptops are coming! The Fab Four in the first concert of their first U.S. tour, Feb. 11, 1964, in Washington, D.C.

raised the boy. He grew up arty and angry—and musical, it turned out, after his mother bought him the traditional cheap kid guitar (the label inside said GUARANTEED NOT TO SPLIT), and he quickly worked out the chords to the Buddy Holly hit *That'll Be the Day.*

Paul McCartney, born in 1942 and destined to become Lennon's songwriting soul mate, seemed a sunnier type: well mannered, level-headed, all that. But he had weathered trauma of his own, losing his mother to breast cancer in his early teens. McCartney met Lennon in the logical way, given the times and the two boys' musical interests: on the skiffle scene.

Skiffle music—a sort of jugband clatter ideally suited to inexpensive and homemade instruments—was all the rage, and in 1957 Lennon formed a band called the Quarrymen. By the following year, the group had been joined by McCartney and his school friend George Harrison, then just 14. In 1960, calling themselves the Silver Beatles, and with drummer

**Songwriters Lennon and McCartney get in tune, 1963**

Pete Best in tow, they sailed to Germany to play the riotous red-light-district bars of Hamburg, drink Herculean quantities of beer and gulp down handfuls of illicitly energizing pills to keep them stage ready seven nights a week.

In 1962 Best was replaced by another drummer, basset-eyed Ringo Starr (born Richard Starkey in 1940). After passing an audition that their manager, Brian Epstein, had arranged with EMI's Parlophone label, the group cut its first single, *Love Me Do,* a moderate hit. In January 1963 a second single, *Please Please Me,* went to No. 1, and Beatlemania hit Britain.

It is commonly thought that by the time the Beatles arrived in the U.S., rock-'n'-roll music, an uproarious sound

forged by such pioneers as Chuck Berry, Little Richard and Elvis Presley, had all but died out, leaving the charts littered with such unconvincing rock-lite commodities as Frankie Avalon, Bobby Rydell and Chubby Checker. This is not entirely true. Although Presley had been drafted into the Army in 1958 (and was never quite the same after he got out), and Buddy Holly had been killed in a plane crash in 1959, and Berry, Little Richard and Jerry Lee Lewis were all otherwise sidelined, there was no gaping lack of good music around. In 1963—the year before the Beatles broke Stateside—the charts were filled with great records by the Drifters, the Beach Boys, Roy Orbison, Sam Cooke, Motown's Miracles and Martha and the Vandellas, and celebrated Phil Spector girl groups such as the Crystals and the Ronettes.

What set the Beatles apart, amid all those fabled acts, was their dazzling interpersonal chemistry (showcased to irresistible effect in the 1964 feature film *A Hard Day's Night,* which critic Andrew Sarris called "the *Citizen Kane* of jukebox movies"), their novel sound (produced on offbeat—to most Americans—Gretsch, Rickenbacker and Hofner guitars and cranked out through snarly little Vox amplifiers brought over from England) and of course their awesome facility for making ravishing hit records.

By 1965 even the nonfab world had been forced to take notice of this all-conquering cultural force. The Beatles had become such a huge British export that they were given a royal award: the Member of the Order of the British Empire, or M.B.E. (They took this about as seriously as anyone might have expected, all four of them firing up a joint in a Buckingham

**1957**
**Lennon meets McCartney at church picnic near Liverpool**

**1964 Arrival in America;** *I Want to Hold Your Hand* **tops charts, first of their 20 No. 1 hits; seen by 70 million on** *Ed Sullivan Show*

**1970 Band breaks up amid infighting**

When the Music Died

John Lennon

**1957**

**1959 George, John and Paul as the Quarrymen**

**1962 With Ringo and George, first recording session as the Beatles**

**1967** *Sgt. Pepper* **is released**

**1980**

**1980 Lennon is killed, ending reunion hopes**

After this concert in San Francisco's Candlestick Park in August, 1966, the Beatles gave up touring to concentrate on making albums

Palace washroom before the ceremony, and Ringo commenting on his M.B.E., "I'll keep it to dust when I'm old.")

Having scored a breakthrough with their chart-topping 1965 album *Rubber Soul*—the record whose elegant lyrics and luminous melodies lifted them forever out of the world of simple teen idols and into the realm of art—the Beatles, exhausted, decided to stop touring. After a final concert in San Francisco in 1966, they would come together again as a group only in recording studios. But there they spun out ever more elaborate masterpieces: the tripped-out psychedelic special *Revolver* in 1966; the breathtaking concept epic *Sgt. Pepper's Lonely Hearts Club Band* in 1967; the strangely alienated,

every-man-for-himself *White Album* (officially called *The Beatles*) in 1968; and the gorgeous *Abbey Road* in 1969.

For millions of fans worldwide, these albums mapped a path through the puzzling and sometimes scary '60s. The paths of Lennon and McCartney, however, were diverging drastically. Each took a wife (John married Japanese avant-garde artist Yoko Ono, and Paul wed American rock photographer Linda Eastman) and drifted even farther apart, Lennon growing bitter, McCartney adopting the air of the contented family man.

By 1969 Lennon was ready to quit the group. McCartney is said to have talked him out of going public with this desire; but then in April 1970 McCartney himself announced that the group was disbanding. In December he filed suit to have the partnership dissolved and a receiver appointed to handle its affairs. When the other three Beatles dropped their appeal of this action in 1971, the most fabulously successful band of all time (with more than 100 million records sold to date) came to an end.

And so it was over. McCartney and his wife formed a new band. Harrison followed his Indo-mystical inclinations until fans lost interest. Ringo made occasional records, movies and TV commercials. And Lennon moved to New York City, where he had always wanted to be, and ironically became that most English of figures, the reclusive eccentric. He was shot down in 1980, and the Beatles were nevermore. Except for their music, which is eternal. ∎

In 1967 the band posed with Maharishi Mahesh Yogi; the infatuation was brief

*Kurt Loder, a former editor at* Rolling Stone *magazine, is the anchorman for* MTV *News.*

# Rock of Ages

Roaring out of the honky-tonks and juke joints along the Mississippi River, rock 'n' roll's ecstatic holler and irrepressible beat percolated around the globe, lifting spirits—and filling dance floors—from Memphis to Kingston to Moscow

## Elvis Presley

The young Mississippian's synthesis of black, country and gospel music helped him create a simple, raw performing style; his onstage gyrations made "the Pelvis" a hit with '50s kids—and anathema to their parents. Ironically, Presley didn't write his own songs and wasn't a proficient guitarist. Nor was he adept at handling his career and business. But he had a wonderful magic: everyone copied his look, his gestures, his clothes, his cool-yet-sultry attitude. Elvis remains rock's most influential solo artist.

## Chuck Berry

For most kids in the '50s, rock 'n' roll began when Elvis Presley checked into the Heartbreak Hotel. But the hipper kids then knew what we all know now: rock's real daddy was the man who sang "Hail, hail, rock 'n' roll/ Deliver me from the days of old." That was Berry, a duck-walking, roll-over-Beethovening firebrand from St. Louis who unreeled a string of hits—from *Johnny B. Goode* to *School Days*—that defined rock 'n' roll's music, moods, moves and malevolence.

## Bob Marley

The Jamaican's jagged, pulsing songs challenged the conscience, soothed the spirit and stirred up the soul all at once. The first superstar from the Third World, he popularized, even personified, the rhythm of reggae and its roots in the pitiless poverty and mystical spiritualism of the black Jamaican underclass. An outspoken voice for racial equality, Marley was also a tireless promoter of Rastafarianism, the pro-African sect whose dread-locked followers smoke ganja—marijuana—as a religious rite.

## Bruce Springsteen

In the 1970s, when rock 'n' roll's primal passions had become ossified into self-satisfied "art rock," the New Jerseyan's gleeful performances, primal riffs and gritty, fresh-from-the-streets story songs recharged the music. "The night's busted open/ These two lanes can take us anywhere," he promised, reminding hosts of fans (and imitators) that rock was music of the people, by the people and for the people.

## Madonna

Sexy and spirited, the Material Girl spawned a generation of "wannabes" in the 1980s, as preteen girls aped her carefully constructed harlot-on-a-bender persona. A leading proponent of the Andy Warhol school of pop music, she stressed style over substance and mastered the music-video form that came of age with her. Her exuberant dancing, showmanship and theatrical flair made her live shows special events that delighted fans worldwide.

# Bob
# Dylan

## Master poet and caustic social critic, he is the guiding spirit of the counterculture generation

**By JAY COCKS**

H E WAS BORN WITH A SNAKE IN BOTH HIS FISTS WHILE a hurricane was blowing. You must know that. Know the fact, or the music, or the truth inside the mythology, spun from roots by his rough magic into cloth of gold, into songs that are the shifting, stormy center of American popular music in the second part of the very century when the music was invented.

Bob Dylan couldn't wait for the music to change. He couldn't be only part of the change. He was the change itself. The snake and the hurricane.

And you do know that. If you've been listening only in passing, you know, among other things, that the answer's blowin' in the wind, the times they are a-changin', everybody must get stoned, they're selling postcards of the hanging, and that to live outside the law you must be honest. Later, listening more closely, you found out that we're goin' all the way till the wheels fall off and burn, that dignity's never been photographed, and that no one plays the blues like Blind Willie McTell.

Those are legends and home truths, passed along in song, that became part of a cultural vocabulary and an ongoing American myth. Hundreds of songs; more than 500 and counting. Forty-three albums; more than 57 million copies sold. A series of dreams about America as it once and never was. It was folk music, deep within its core, from the mountains and the delta and the blacktop of Highway 61. Rhythm

and blues too, and juke-joint rock 'n' roll, and hymns from backwoods churches and gospel shouts from riverside baptisms. He put all that together, and found words to match it.

Before him there was only Bobby Vinton. Well, no, not really. But at the time Dylan first arrived in New York City from the Midwest, rock music had lost its leader—Elvis—to a series of movie musicals. Chuck Berry, Little Richard, Johnny Cash, Carl Perkins, Sam Cooke, Jackie Wilson—all those pioneers Dylan had loved and emulated in high school rock-'n'-roll bands—had been superseded by a series of well-scrubbed teen idols who had as much edge as a corsage.

It was a bland-out all across the bandwidth, a kind of musical hangover from the Eisenhower era. Rock 'n' roll had erupted dead in the heart of Ike's easeful America. In the Kennedy years, when the world started to shake and rattle, the music suddenly turned as thick and sweet as a malted. Jazz had the power, but jazz was for grownups, and its impact was largely instrumental. Anyone who wanted to listen to a song, and take something away from it that would last a little longer than a good-night kiss, turned on to folk.

So Bob Dylan, a rock-'n'-roll American kid who first heard Woody Guthrie while enrolled for a few months at the University of Minnesota, took up folk. Got a ride to New York. Settled in Greenwich Village. Took any gig he could get. Within two years—tops—turned folk inside out.

And then abandoned it. Subsumed it, really, inside the raucous, unyielding, cataclysmic rock 'n' roll that he let loose on an audience that didn't like to be reminded how hidebound it was. What had been music of comment and protest became songs of unprecedented personal testament, delivered with a literal and savage electricity. Dylan got booed when he showed up with rock musicians behind him, and the booing didn't let up until his great songs like *Desolation Row* and *Like a Rolling Stone* pierced the consciousness of a whole new generation, making everyone realize that rock music could be as direct, as personal and as vital as a novel or a poem. That popular music could be expression as well as recreation.

Dylan was suddenly a singer no longer. He was a shaman. A lot of people called him a prophet. In a way, it must have been scarier than being booed. Everything he sang, said, did or even wore took on a specific gravity that made it harder and harder for him to move. The music became so important to so many people, took on such awesome proportions, that Dylan could respond only with the ultimate sanity: silence.

After a motorcycle accident in 1966, he used the recovery

**BORN** May 24, 1941, in Duluth, Minn., as Robert Allan Zimmerman

**1963** Writes protest classic *Blowin' in the Wind*

**1965** Goes electric at Newport Folk Fest

**BORN AGAIN** Explores Christianity on 1979's *Slow Train Coming*

SLOW TRAIN COMING
BOB DYLAN

**1998** *Time Out of Mind* wins Grammy for Album of the Year

**1941**

**1961** Moves to New York City's Greenwich Village

**1964-66** The folk of *The Times They Are A-Changin'* becomes the raw rock of *Blonde on Blonde*

**1989** Inducted into Rock and Roll Hall of Fame

## "He's always on to the next thing. It's as though it's a compulsion, and in a sense, it serves him. It serves his art."

**JOAN BAEZ**

**Playing folk songs for civil rights activists in Mississippi, 1962**

was greeted as a masterpiece, his greatest work since *Blood on the Tracks* more than 20 years before. In fact, it was much of a piece with the extraordinary albums he's been making for most of this decade, including *Oh, Mercy*, a kind of prelude and companion piece released in 1989, and two subsequent albums of folk music that seem to have been made in some secret, mysterious place where the past never stops.

Dylan had a brush with mortality just before the last album was released, and spent some serious time in the hospital, which brought everyone up short. It was a warning that time was passing, everywhere but in his music. So *Time Out of Mind* brought Dylan safely back home again to the hot center. It was as if everyone suddenly woke up and figured it was Dylan who had been asleep all these years. In fact, as always, he was the only one with his eyes open. To know that, all you had to do—still, and ever—is listen. And ask yourself the same question he flung at us.

How does it feel? ∎

*Jay Cocks, a former cinema and music reviewer for* TIME, *is a screenwriter whose films include* The Age of Innocence.

**Dylan with poet Allen Ginsberg at Jack Kerouac's grave, 1975**

time to retreat and cook up some new music that was mystical and playful, and so deliberately rough-edged that it seemed almost spontaneous. It wasn't, of course, but the music of those years—much of it heard in the song cycle that's known informally as the *Basement Tapes*—charted a more inward course. It was music that deflected any easy response.

A dizzying number of changes followed—from born-again Christian testifying to deep blues—but Dylan has been consistent only in one thing: he has never stopped making great music, or being cagey about it. And funny, when he feels like it. And hip, without peer or precedent. Accepting a Grammy Award for Lifetime Achievement in 1991, he leaned into the mike and delivered himself of this reflection: "Well, my daddy, he didn't leave me much, you know he was a very simple man, but what he did tell me was this, he did say, 'Son,' he said, he say, 'you know it's possible to become so defiled in this world that your own father and mother will abandon you, and if that happens, God will always believe in your ability to mend your ways.'" Say amen, somebody. He gave us a great record in 1997. The album, *Time Out of Mind*,

# Voices To Heal the Spirit

From gospel to the blues to soul, black artists transformed pain into songs of passion and pride

### Robert Johnson

His brooding, anguished voice and ringing guitar— and his death by poisoning at age 27—made Johnson a legend. His 42 surviving takes from the mid-'30s set the stage for rhythm-and-blues, rock and soul.

### Bessie Smith

A protégé of blues pioneer "Ma" Rainey, Smith was the first black woman superstar, attracting huge audiences—and record sales. She was one of the first artists to express social protest in song.

### Mahalia Jackson

"Blues are the songs of despair," Jackson liked to say. "Gospel songs are the songs of hope." The grand-daughter of slaves brought spirituals swinging into the mainstream with her creamy contralto and her ebullient style: whacking her hands together, shaking her head, raising the roof—and the heart.

### Ray Charles

Defying categorization, the blind singer/pianist first gained fame when black musicians were confined to the rhythm-and-blues genre, then imbued idioms as divergent as country, rock and pop with his soulful shout.

# Aretha Franklin

## The Queen of Soul reigns supreme with a heavenly voice and terrestrial passion

**By CHRISTOPHER JOHN FARLEY**

the Rev. C.L. Franklin, said, "Truth is, Aretha hasn't ever left the church!"

Never left!

*Truth is, songs are her ministry. Her voice is her temple. Truth is, her light is shining!*

That's right! That's right!

*Can I get a witness?*

American music, like America itself, seems too democratic for any title to endure. Ask almost any rapper or alternative rocker if Elvis is the King of Rock, and all you'll get is a sneer. Michael Jackson likes to call himself the King of Pop, but we all know the true king of pop is whoever has the No. 1 album in a given week. All told, there's only one monarch in music whose title has never rung false and still holds up—and that's Aretha Franklin, the Queen of Soul.

Her reign has been long. Born in 1942 in Memphis, Tenn., she started recording when she was just 14. Since then, she has had 20 No. 1 R.-and-B. hits and won 17 Grammys. Her breakthrough album, *I Never Loved a Man the Way I Love You* (1967), was a Top 40 smash. Three decades later, after disco, after the Macarena, after innumerable musical trendlets and one-hit wonders, Franklin's critically acclaimed 1998 album *A Rose Is Still a Rose* was another Top 40 smash. Although her output has sometimes been tagged (unfairly, for the most part) as erratic, she has had a major album in every decade of her career, including *Amazing Grace* (1972) and *Who's Zoomin' Who?* (1985).

Her reign has been storied. She sang at Martin Luther King's funeral and at William Jefferson Clinton's Inaugural gala. She has worked with Carole King and Puff Daddy. The Michigan legislature once declared her voice to be one of the state's natural resources.

But this isn't about accolades; this is about soul. This is about that glorious mezzo-soprano, the gospel growls, the throaty howls, the girlish vocal tickles, the swoops, the dives, the blue-sky high notes, the blue-sea low notes. Female vocalists don't get the credit as innovators that male instrumentalists do. They should. Franklin has mastered her instrument as surely as John Coltrane mastered his sax; her vocal technique has been studied and copied by those who came after her, including Chaka Khan in the '70s and Whitney Houston in the '80s.

And Franklin's influence has only grown in the '90s. The dominant divas of this decade—Mariah Carey, Mary J. Blige,

*S*ISTERS AND BROTHERS, THE SUBJECT OF TODAY'S *sermon is that light of our lives, the Queen of Soul, sister Aretha Franklin.* Preach, Reverend! *Now in the Scriptures,* Luke 11: 33, *we are taught, "No one lights a lamp and puts it in a place where it will be hidden." Now, y'all know the queen got her start singing in the New Bethel Baptist Church in Detroit. People say she left the sacred for the secular, forsook gospel for pop. But, truth is, as her father,*

Toni Braxton—are all, musically speaking, Sunday-school students of Aretha's. The queen still rules: early in 1998 Franklin co-starred in *Divas Live*, a benefit concert on the cable channel VH-1, with some of the most popular young female singers of the '90s, including Carey and Celine Dion. The younger stars were blown offstage by the force of Franklin's talent.

Like Ray Charles, Sam Cooke and Marvin Gaye, Franklin helped bring spiritual passion into pop music. In 1961 she signed with Columbia, which tried to turn her into a singer of jazzy pop. In 1966 she switched to Atlantic, delved into soul and began to flourish. Unlike many of her performing peers, Franklin took a strong hand in creating her own sound. Her guiding principle with producers, she says, is "if you're here to record me, then let's record me—and not you."

From the moment she sang *Respect*—that still famous call for recognition and appreciation—Franklin helped complete the task begun by Billie Holiday and others, converting American pop from a patriarchal monologue into a coed dialogue. Women were no longer just going to stand around and sing about broken hearts; they were going to demand respect, and even spell it out for you if there was some part of that word you didn't understand. As Franklin declares on *Do Right Woman—Do Right Man:* "A woman's ... not just a plaything/ She's flesh and blood just like a man."

But to hear Franklin's voice is to hear many voices: she sings not just for black women but for all women. Her pop hit *Sisters Are Doin' It for Themselves* (1985) was a duet, notably, with a white singer, Annie Lennox. Franklin sings not just about the female condition but about the human one. *I Say a Little Prayer* (1968) and *Love Pang* (1998) are existential soul, capturing heartache juxtaposed with workaday life—brushing your teeth, drinking morning coffee. By singing of such things, she exalts the mundane, giving a voice, a powerful one, to everyday folks and events.

Franklin is not simply the Queen of Soul; she is royalty in the fields of gospel, blues, rock and pop as well. A sharp, rhythmically fierce pianist, she was the first female inductee into the Rock and Roll Hall of Fame. Though she wrote a number of her hits, including the sexually brazen *Dr. Feelgood*, she also displayed brilliance in making other people's songs her own, such as Curtis Mayfield's pop gem *Something He Can Feel.* Or listen

The queen upstages a pretender: Mariah Carey and Franklin on *Divas Live*

to her 1971 gospel-charged take on the Simon and Garfunkel classic *Bridge over Troubled Water.* That water's a good deal more troubled when Franklin sings the song; even the bridge seems sturdier.

In person, Franklin is sly and funny, but has melancholy, magic-drained eyes. The twice-divorced diva's life has sometimes had the hard, sad stomp of a blues song: in 1979 her father was shot by burglars, fell into a coma and died. Producer Jerry Wexler once wrote, "I think of Aretha as Our Lady of Mysterious Sorrows ... anguish surrounds Aretha as surely as the glory of her musical aura."

As social critic Derrick Bell writes in his book *Gospel Choirs*, one of black music's earliest functions was to get people through hard times. During slavery, spirituals would sometimes be encoded with secret messages, directions on how to get North to freedom. Franklin's cryptic hurt serves a similar function; it draws us in, it commands empathy, and it ultimately points us north. Listen to her voice on the prayerful *Wholy Holy*, spiraling away, taking us away. North out of heartbreak, north out of oppression, north toward where we want to go.

*Preach, Reverend!*

Can I get a witness?                                    ∎

TIME *music critic Christopher John Farley is the author of the novel* My Favorite War.

**BORN March 25, 1942, in Memphis, Tenn.**

**1954 Emerges as singing prodigy in church choir at age 12**

**1966 Switches to Atlantic Records; hits start coming**

**1987 First woman inducted into the Rock and Roll Hall of Fame**

**1942**

**1944 Moves to Detroit with father, pastor of the New Bethel Baptist Church**

**1961 Signs with Columbia Records, which fails to make her a star**

**1967 *Respect* hits No. 1; she wins her first Grammy**

**R-E-S-P-E-C-T The renowned singer is also a fine pianist**

# Lucille
# Ball

## The first lady of comedy brought us laughter and emotional truth. No wonder everybody loved Lucy

**By RICHARD ZOGLIN**

Antics aside, *I Love Lucy* was grounded in emotional honesty

**I**T HAPPENED SOMEWHERE BETWEEN THE CLUNKY premier episode (Lucy Thinks Ricky Is Trying to Murder Her) and her first truly classic routine, the Vitameatavegamin commercial, in which Lucy gets steadily soused as she keeps downing spoonfuls of the alcohol-laced potion she's trying to hawk on TV. (Watch the spasm that jolts her face when she gets her first taste of the foul brew; it could serve as a textbook for comics well into the next millennium.) *I Love Lucy* debuted on CBS in October 1951, but at first it looked little different from other domestic comedies that were starting to make the move from radio to TV, like *My Favorite Husband*, the radio show Ball had co-starred in for three years. Lucy Ricardo was, in those early *I Love Lucy* episodes, just a generic daffy housewife. Ethel (Vivian Vance), her neighbor and landlady, was a stock busybody. Desi Arnaz, as bandleader Ricky Ricardo, hadn't yet become one of the finest straight men in TV history. William Frawley, as Fred Mertz, seemed a Hollywood has-been in search of work, which he was.

Then magic struck. Guided by Ball's comic brilliance, the show developed the shape and depth of great comedy. Lucy's quirks and foibles—her craving to be in show biz, her crazy schemes that always backfired, the constant fights with the Mertzes—became as particularized and familiar as the face across the dinner table. For four out of its six seasons (only six!), *I Love Lucy* was the No. 1–rated show on television; at its peak, in 1952-53, it averaged an incredible 67.3 rating,

meaning that on a typical Monday night, more than two-thirds of all homes with TV sets were tuned to *Lucy*.

Ball's dizzy redhead with the elastic face and saucer eyes was the model for scores of comic TV females to follow. She and her show, moreover, helped define a still nascent medium. Before *I Love Lucy*, TV was feeling its way, adapting forms from other media. Live TV drama was an outgrowth of Broadway theater; game shows were transplanted from radio; variety shows and early comedy stars like Milton Berle came out of vaudeville. *I Love Lucy* was unmistakably a television show, and Ball the perfect star for the small screen. "I look like everybody's idea of an actress," she once said, "but I feel like a housewife." Sid Caesar and Jackie Gleason were big men with larger-than-life personas; Lucy was one of us.

She grew up in Jamestown, N.Y., where her father, an

**Partner in crime: Longtime sidekick Vivian Vance, left, outdoes Lucy on the candy line**

**Lucy clowns with Buster Keaton at a birthday bash, circa 1944**

electrician, died when she was just three. At 15 she began making forays to New York City to try to break into show business. She had little luck as an actress but worked as a model before moving to Hollywood in 1933 for a part in the chorus of *Roman Scandals*. Strikingly pretty, with chestnut hair dyed blond (until MGM hairdressers, seeking a more distinctive look, turned it red in 1942), she landed bit parts in B movies and moved up to classy fare like *Stage Door*, in which she held her own with Katharine Hepburn and Ginger Rogers.

Buster Keaton, the great silent clown working as a consultant at MGM, recognized her comic gifts and worked with her on stunts. She got a few chances to show off her talent in films like *DuBarry Was a Lady* (with Red Skelton) and *Fancy Pants* (with Bob Hope) but never broke through to the top. By the end of the 1940s, with Ball approaching 40, her movie career was all but finished.

It was her husband Desi—a Cuban bandleader she married shortly after they met on the set of *Too Many Girls* in 1940—who urged her to try television. CBS was interested in Ball, but not in the fellow with the pronounced Spanish accent she wanted to play her husband. To prove that the audience would accept them as a couple, Lucy and Desi cooked up a vaudeville act and took it on tour. It got rave reviews ("a sock new act," said *Variety*), and CBS relented.

But there were other haggles. Lucy and Desi wanted to shoot the show in Hollywood, rather than in New York City, where most TV was then being done. And for better quality, they insisted on shooting on film, rather than doing it live and recording on kinescope. CBS balked at the extra cost; the couple agreed to take a salary cut in return for full ownership of the program. It was a shrewd business decision: *I Love Lucy* was the launching pad for Desilu Productions, which (with other shows, like *Our Miss Brooks* and *The Untouchables*) became one of TV's most successful independent producers, before Paramount bought it in 1967.

# Anybody alive who had TV felt Lucy was part of the family. I don't know if that ever will be duplicated.

CAROL BURNETT, at the time of Ball's death in 1989

Today *I Love Lucy*, with its farcical plots, broad physical humor and unliberated picture of marriage, is sometimes dismissed as a relic. Yet the show has the timeless perfection of a crystal goblet. For all its comic hyperbole, *Lucy* explored universal themes: the tensions of married life, the clash between career and home, the meaning of loyalty and friendship. The series also reflected most of the decade's important social trends. The Ricardos made their contribution to the baby boom in January 1953—TV's Little Ricky was born on the same day that Ball gave birth, by caesarean, to her second child, Desi Jr. (A daughter, Lucie, had been born in 1951.) They traveled to California just as the nation was turning west, in a hilarious series of shows that epitomized our conception of—and obsession with—Hollywood glamour. And when the nation began moving to the suburbs, so too, in their last season, did the Ricardos.

Ball was a lithe and inventive physical comedian, and her famous slapstick bits—trying to keep up with a candy assembly line, stomping grapes in an Italian wine vat—were justly celebrated. But she was far more than a clown. Her mobile face could register a whole dictionary of emotions; her comic timing was unmatched; her devotion to the truth of her character never flagged. She was a tireless perfectionist. For one scene in which she needed to pop a paper bag, she spent three hours testing bags to make sure she got the right size and sound.

MOST OF ALL, *I LOVE LUCY* WAS GROUNDED IN emotional honesty. Though the couple had a tempestuous marriage offscreen (Desi was an unrepentant philanderer), the Ricardos' kisses showed the spark of real attraction. In the episode where Lucy finds out she is pregnant, she can't break the news to Ricky because he is too busy. Finally, she takes a table at his nightclub show and passes him an anonymous note asking that he sing a song, *We're Having a Baby*, to the father-to-be. As Ricky roams the room looking for the happy couple, he spies Lucy and moves on. Then he does a heartrending double take, glides to his knees and asks, voice cracking, if it's true. Finishing the scene together onstage, the couple are overcome by the real emotion of their own impending baby. Director William Asher, dismayed by the unplanned tears, even shot a second, more upbeat take. Luckily he used the first one; it's the most touching moment in sitcom history.

Tired of the grind of a weekly series, Lucy and Desi ended *I Love Lucy* in 1957, when it was still No. 1. For three more years, they did hourlong specials, then broke up the act for good when they divorced in 1960. Ball returned to TV with two other popular (if less satisfying) TV series, *The Lucy Show* and *Here's Lucy*; made a few more movies (starring in *Mame* in 1974); and attempted a final comeback in the 1986 ABC sitcom *Life with Lucy*, which lasted an ignominious eight weeks. But *I Love Lucy* lives on in reruns around the world, an endless loop of laughter and a reminder of the woman who helped make TV a habit, and an art. ■

*TIME senior writer Richard Zoglin still watches* I Love Lucy *reruns each day at 9 a.m.*

**A first taste of classic Lucy Ricardo: Oversampling the elixir**

**Brilliant troupers, the Arnazes were also savvy TV producers**

# Jim Henson

## Hundreds of millions of kids—and adults— have been entranced by the Muppetmaster

### By JAMES COLLINS

**J**IM HENSON CAN BE CREDITED with many accomplishments: he had the most profound influence on children of any entertainer of his time; he adapted the ancient art of puppetry to the most modern of mediums, television, transforming both; he created a TV show that was one of the most popular on earth. But Henson's greatest achievement was broader than any of these. Through his work, he helped sustain the qualities of fancifulness, warmth and consideration that have been so threatened by our coarse, cynical age.

Born in 1936, Henson grew up in the small town of Leland, Miss., where his father worked as an agronomist for the Federal Government. When Henson was in fifth grade, his father took a job in Washington, and the family moved to a suburb in Maryland. There, in high school, Henson became fascinated by television. "I loved the idea," he once said, "that what you saw was taking place somewhere else at the same time." In the summer of 1954, just before he entered the University of Maryland, he learned that a local station needed someone to perform with puppets on a children's show. Henson wasn't particularly interested in puppets, but he did want to get into TV, so he and a friend made a couple—one was called Pierre the French Rat—and they were hired.

The job didn't last long, but within a few months, Henson was back on TV, puppeteering for another station, the local NBC affiliate. Soon he had his own five-minute program, called *Sam and Friends.* It aired live twice a day, once before the network news with Chet Huntley and David Brinkley and later preceding the *Tonight* show, which at that time starred Steve Allen. Remaining in college, where he studied art and theater design, Henson produced *Sam and Friends* for six years. Assisting him was a fellow student named Jane Nebel, whom he married in 1959.

Puppets have been around for thousands of years, but the proto-Muppets that began to appear on *Sam and Friends* were different. Kermit was there, looking and sounding much as he would later (until his death Henson always animated Kermit and provided his voice). Typical hand puppets have solid heads, but Kermit's face was soft and mobile, and he could move his mouth in synchronization with his speech; he could also gesticulate more facilely than a marionette, with rods moving his arms. For television, Henson realized, it was necessary to invent puppets that had "life and sensitivity." (Henson sometimes said Muppet was a combination of puppet and marionette, but it seems the word came to him and he liked it, and later thought up a derivation.)

Throughout the early 1960s, the Muppets made appearances on the *Today* show and a range of variety programs. Then, in 1969, came *Sesame Street*. Henson was always careful not to take the credit for *Sesame Street's* achievements. It was not his program,

hosts, and the show launched the career of Miss Piggy, the vain, *très sophistiquée* female who was besotted with Kermit.

The beauty of the Muppets, on both *Sesame Street* and their own show, was that they were cuddly but not too cuddly, and not only cuddly. There are satire and sly wit; Bert and Ernie quarrel; Miss Piggy behaves unbecomingly; Kermit is sometimes exasperated. By adding just enough tartness to a sweet overall spirit, Henson purveyed a kind of innocence that was plausible for the modern imagination. His knowingness allowed us to accept his real gifts: wonder, delight, optimism.

Henson was a kind, infinitely patient man. Those who worked for him say he literally never raised his voice. Frank Oz, the puppeteer behind Bert, Miss Piggy and many others, was Henson's partner for 27 years. "Jim

| | | |
|---|---|---|
| **BORN Sept. 24, 1936, in Greenville, Miss.** | **1955 Creates Kermit, his alter ego** | **1976 Launches The Muppet Show, starring Kermit and Miss Piggy** |

**1936** ———————————————————————— **1990**

| | | | |
|---|---|---|---|
| **1954 Gets first TV job as a puppeteer on a local Maryland station** | **1959 Marries Jane Nebel** | **1969 Sesame Street appears on PBS, introducing Bert, Ernie and Big Bird** | **1990 Dies suddenly in New York City on May 16** |

after all—the Children's Television Workshop hired him. In fact, Henson hesitated to join the show, since he did not want to become stuck as a children's entertainer. Nonetheless, few would disagree that it was primarily Bert and Ernie, Big Bird, Grover and the rest who made *Sesame Street* so captivating. Joan Ganz Cooney, who created the show, once remarked that the group involved with it had a collective genius but that Henson was the only individual genius. "He was our era's Charlie Chaplin, Mae West, W.C. Fields and Marx Brothers," Cooney said, "and indeed he drew from all of them to create a new art form that influenced popular culture around the world."

SINCE *SESAME STREET* HAS BEEN ON THE AIR FOR 30 years and has been shown in scores of countries, Henson's Muppets have entranced hundreds of millions of children. And the audience for the Muppets has not only been huge; it has also been passionate. In fact, given the number of his fans and the intensity of their devotion, Kermit may possibly be the leading children's character of the century, more significant than even Peter Pan or Winnie-the-Pooh.

But despite the Muppets' success on *Sesame Street* and their demonstrated appeal to adults as well as children, no U.S. network would give Henson a show of his own. It was a British producer, Lew Grade, who finally offered Henson the financing that enabled him to mount *The Muppet Show*. The program ran in syndication from 1976 until 1981, when Henson decided to end it lest its quality begin to decline. At its peak it was watched each week by 235 million viewers worldwide. Stars from Steve Martin to Rudolf Nureyev appeared as guest

was not perfect," he says. "But I'll tell you something—he was as close to how you're supposed to behave toward other people as anyone I've ever known."

The only complaint of his five children seems to be that because Henson was so busy, he was unable to spend enough time with them. They often accompanied him while he worked, and he once even took his eldest daughter along when he held a meeting with the head of a movie studio. That child, Lisa, is now a powerful producer in Hollywood; Henson's elder son Brian runs the Jim Henson Co.; and another daughter, Cheryl, also works there. However gentle, Henson was not a complete naif. He liked expensive cars— Rolls-Royces, Porsches—and after he and Jane separated in 1986 (they remained close and never divorced), he dated a succession of women.

In the '70s and '80s, Henson produced innumerable films and TV shows with and without the Muppets. Some were dark, like his adaptations of folktales and myths in the ingenious TV series *Jim Henson's The Storyteller*. Then in 1990, at age 53, Henson suddenly died after contracting an extremely aggressive form of pneumonia. He remains a powerful presence, though, on account of *Sesame Street* and the Henson Co., whose next venture will be a worldwide family-entertainment network called the Kermit Channel. Because the works we encounter as children are so potent, Henson may influence the next century as much as this one, as his viewers grow up carrying his vision within them. ∎

*James Collins is TIME's TV critic. His household includes two Kermits and an Elmo.*

# Oprah Winfrey

## She didn't create the talk-show format. But the compassion and intimacy she put into it have created a new way for us to talk to one another

### By DEBORAH TANNEN

THE SUDANESE-BORN SUPERMODEL ALEK WEK STANDS poised and insouciant as the talk-show host, admiring her classic African features, cradles Wek's cheek and says, "What a difference it would have made to my childhood if I had seen someone who looks like you on television." The host is Oprah Winfrey, and she has been making that difference for millions of viewers, young and old, black and white, for nearly a dozen years.

Winfrey stands as a beacon, not only in the worlds of media and entertainment but also in the larger realm of public discourse. At 44, she has a personal fortune estimated at more than half a billion dollars. She owns her own production company, which creates feature films, prime-time TV specials and home videos. An accomplished actress, she was nominated for an Oscar for her role in *The Color Purple;* in 1998 she starred in her own film production of Toni Morrison's *Beloved.*

But it is through her talk show that her influence has been greatest. When Winfrey talks, her viewers—an estimated 14 million daily in the U.S. and millions more in 132 other countries—listen. Any book she chooses for her on-air book club becomes an instant best seller. When she established the "world's largest piggy bank," people all over the country contributed spare change to raise more than $1 million (matched by Oprah) to send disadvantaged kids to college. When she blurted that hearing about the threat of mad-cow disease "just stopped me cold from eating another burger!" the perceived threat to the beef industry was enough to trigger a multimillion-dollar lawsuit (which she won).

**Winfrey teamed up with Steven Spielberg in *The Color Purple***

**BORN**
**Jan. 29, 1954, in Kosciusko, Miss.**

**1954**

**PRODIGY**
**She was a veteran speaker at 4**

**1971 Competes in Miss Black America pageant**

**1973 First black and first woman hired to anchor TV news in Nashville, Tenn.**

**1977 Starts co-hosting *People Are Talking* morning show in Baltimore, Md.**

**1986 *The Oprah Winfrey Show* goes national; Oscar-nominated for *The Color Purple***

**1996 Launches book club**

**1998 Produces, stars in Toni Morrison's *Beloved***

# " More than a great star, you are a 20th century political figure. Your good works have touched all of us. "

PHIL DONAHUE, when Oprah received an Emmy for Lifetime Achievement

Born in 1954 to unmarried parents, Winfrey was raised by her grandmother on a farm with no indoor plumbing in Kosciusko, Miss. By age 3 she was reading the Bible and reciting in church. At 6 she moved to her mother's home in Milwaukee, Wis.; later, to her father's in Nashville, Tenn. A lonely child, she found solace in books. When a seventh-grade teacher noticed the young girl reading during lunch, he got her a scholarship to a better school. Winfrey's talent for public performance and spontaneity in answering questions helped her win beauty contests—and get her first taste of public attention.

Crowned Miss Fire Prevention in Nashville at 17, Winfrey visited a local radio station, where she was invited to read copy for a lark—and was hired to read news on the air. Two years later, while a sophomore at Tennessee State University,

**"Girlfriend!"** Women relate to Oprah because she speaks their language

she was hired as Nashville's first female and first black TV-news anchor. After graduation, she took an anchor position in Baltimore, Md., but lacked the detachment to be a reporter. She cried when a story was sad, laughed when she misread a word. Instead, she was given an early-morning talk show. She had found her medium. In 1984 she moved on to be the host of *A.M. Chicago*, which became *The Oprah Winfrey Show*. It was syndicated in 1986—when Winfrey was 32—and soon overtook *Donahue* as the nation's top-rated talk show.

Women, especially, listen to Winfrey because they feel as if she's a friend. Although Phil Donahue pioneered the format she uses (mike-holding host moves among an audience whose members question guests), his show was mostly what I call "report-talk," which often typifies men's conversation. The overt focus is on information. Winfrey transformed the format into what I call "rapport-talk," the back-and-forth conversation that is the basis of female friendship, with its emphasis on self-revealing intimacies. She turned the focus from experts to ordinary people talking about personal issues.

Girls' and women's friendships are often built on trading secrets. Winfrey's power is that she tells her own, divulging that she once ate a package of hot-dog buns drenched in maple syrup, that she had smoked cocaine, even that she had been raped as a child. With Winfrey, the talk show became more immediate, more confessional, more personal. When a guest's story moves her, she cries and spreads her arms for a hug.

I WAS LUCKY ENOUGH TO APPEAR ON BOTH *Donahue* and *Oprah* when my book *You Just Don't Understand: Women and Men in Conversation* was published—and to glimpse the difference between them. Winfrey related my book to her own life: she began by saying she had read the book and "saw myself over and over" in it. She then told one of my examples, adding, "I've done that a thousand times"—and illustrated it by describing herself and Stedman. (Like close friends, viewers know her "steady beau" by his first name.)

Winfrey saw television's unique power to blend public and private; while it is a medium that links strangers and conveys information over public airwaves, TV is most often viewed in the privacy of our homes. Like a family member, it sits down to meals with us and talks to us in the lonely afternoons. Grasping this paradox, Oprah exhorts her viewers to improve their lives and the world. She makes people care because she cares. That is Winfrey's genius, and will be her legacy, as the changes she has wrought in the talk show continue to permeate our culture and shape our lives. ∎

*Deborah Tannen, a professor at Georgetown University, is author of* The Argument Culture.

# An Influence Beyond Words

Television was a technology in search of its destiny: these pioneers helped the tube discover its voice

### Edward R. Murrow

A hard-edged war journalist on radio, he took on tough subjects, including Joseph McCarthy, on his TV show *See It Now*. But his popular *Person to Person* was the show celebrities angled to do long before anyone had heard of Barbara Walters—or Oprah.

### Ed Sullivan

For 23 years, the least telegenic man in America slumped and slurred through Sunday's "rilly big shew," a vaudevillian mix of high and low culture. When Elvis and then the Beatles appeared on his stage, they instantly found mainstream fame.

### Johnny Carson

More than funny, Carson was likable and acutely aware of America's mood: when he backed young black comics, the nation accepted them too. When he made jokes about Watergate, Nixon knew it was time to get out of town.

### Howard Cosell

Loved and hated, endlessly imitated for his abrasive drone, Cosell redefined TV sportscasting. His self-promoted quest to "tell it like it is" brought a refreshing skepticism to the bland idolatry of "color" commentary.

# Bart
# Simpson

Talk about arrested development—
this kid has been 10 for 11 years!
We hope he stays there: deplorable,
adorable, Bart is a brat for the ages

**By RICHARD CORLISS**

**H**E MUST STAY AFTER SCHOOL, EVERY SINGLE EPISODE of his life, to write a homily on the fourth-grade blackboard (e.g., "The Pledge of Allegiance does not end with 'Hail, Satan'"). In a family of very noisy eaters, he is perhaps the loudest, at least in decibel-to-kilogram ratio. He has a few weaknesses: exposing his buttocks, sassing his father, making prank calls to Moe's Tavern ("Is Oliver there? Oliver Clothesoff?") and speaking like a Cockney chimney sweep. One of the few trophies on his bedroom shelf is labeled EVERYBODY GETS A TROPHY DAY.

Bart Simpson is an underachiever—"and proud of it," as a million T shirts read, back when *The Simpsons* began its run on Fox and he was the first fad of the '90s. Remember "Eat my shorts"? Recall "Cowabunga" and "Ay, caramba"? His fame skyrocketed in no time; burnout was virtually ensured.

Ah, but this young Springfieldianite has staying power: staying in the fourth grade, to the endless vexation of his teacher and his principal; staying glued to the living-room tube to watch his idol, Krusty the Clown; staying for years in the hearts and humors of a fickle, worldwide TV audience. This young scamp—with his paper bag–shaped head, his body's jagged, modernist silhouette, his brat-propelled skateboard—may be "yellow trash" to the town gentry, but to his mother and everyone else, he's our special little guy.

It's true that a few other cartoon characters might try to claim Bart's place of honor. This century is gaily strewn with them, from Winsor McCay's benign Gertie the Dinosaur (cinema's first animated icon) to Fox's other cartoon glory, *King of the Hill*. The Warner menagerie— Bugs, Daffy, Tweety, Wile E. Coyote—energized three decades of Saturday matinees. And when cartoons invaded TV, creatures from Bullwinkle Moose to Tex Avery's Raid insects kept alive a hallowed comic tradition. Bart fits in snugly here. As he once cogently boasted, "I'm this century's Dennis the Menace."

That Bart is a cartoon character—a sheaf of drawings animated by smart writing and the unique vocal stylings of Nancy Cartwright—makes him both "real" and surreally supple. Cartoon figures can do more things, endure more knocks on the noggin, get away with more cool, naughty stuff than the rest of us who are animated only by a telltale heart. The face-offs

MATT GROENING

**164**

> ❝ I will not sell miracle cures... I did not see Elvis... The truth is not out there... I will never win an Emmy. ❞
>
> **BART SIMPSON, on the Springfield Elementary School blackboard**

of Bugs and Daffy in Chuck Jones' cartoons of the '50s involved many shotgun blasts and rearranged duckbills, but the humor and humiliation, the understanding of failure and resilience were instantly translatable to kids and adults alike. The injuries were fake. The suffering, pal, was genuine.

Suffering and failure are at the core of *The Simpsons,* which was created by newspaper cartoonist Matt Groening as crudely drawn filler material for the *Tracey Ullman Show* in 1987, then went weekly in 1990. A *Honeymooners* with kids, the series features a man in a deadening blue-collar job (Homer, the nuclear-plant safety inspector), his epochally exasperated wife (Marge of the mountainous blue hair) and three conflicted kids. Bart, 10, is clever and cunning but addled in class; Lisa, 8, is a near genius whose intelligence deprives her of friends; year-old Maggie expresses frazzled wisdom beyond her years with the merest suck on her pacifier.

Springfield boasts a teeming gallery of low- and medium-lifes—surely the densest, funniest supporting cast since the '40s farces of Preston Sturges. The church, school and pub are places of refuge and anxiety. But home, 723 North Evergreen Terrace, is where the show's heart is, where everyone's despair is muted by familial love. Homer (whom the writers hold in a sort of amazed contempt) bumbles into some egregious fix. Marge fusses and copes. Lisa sublimates her rancor by playing her sax. And Bart is ... Bart.

Lisa, when not condemning Bart and all his works (she once called him "the devil's cabana boy"), tries to explain him. "That little hell raiser," she recently ranted, "is the spawn of every shrieking commercial, every brain-rotting soda pop, every teacher who cares less about young minds than about cashing their big, fat paychecks. No, Bart is not to blame. You

Like their painting, life with the Simpsons is slightly askew

can't create a monster and then whine when he stomps on a few buildings." Nice try, Lisa, but not quite. He's not Bartzilla. The kid knows right from wrong; he just likes wrong better.

His rude streak is indeed stoked by cartoons. After savoring some impossible TV torture that Itchy the mouse has wreaked on Scratchy the cat, Bart says, "Lisa, if I ever stop loving violence, I want you to shoot me." (Lisa: "Will do.") Maybe the Simpson home carries its own germ of carnage. In the episode where evil old Mr. Burns adopts Bart as his heir and whisks him away, sweet Lisa is seen ripping off strips of wallpaper. Confronted by Marge, Lisa explains that she is "just trying to fill the void of random, meaningless destruction that Bart's absence has left in our hearts."

We'll admit this: Bart has a riven soul. He needs to be loved ("Tell me I'm good!" he pleads of his friend Milhouse's mom). But do hold the pathos. The reason for his appeal is that he's so brilliant at being bad; his pranks have a showman's panache. When he drives off in what is touted as Hitler's car, he chortles, "It's Führer-ific!" After impishly filling Groundskeeper Willie's shack with creamed corn, he listens to Willie curse, "You did it, Bart Simpson!" and murmurs, with practiced modesty, "The man knows quality work." So do we.

One of Bart's blackboard punishments was to write, "I am not delightfully saucy." But he is, he is—a complex weave of grace, attitude and personality, deplorable and adorable, a very '90s slacker who embodies a century of popular culture and is one of the richest characters in it. One thinks of Chekhov, Céline, Lenny Bruce, little boy lost. Anyway, we love the kid and his endlessly terrific show; so here he is in the TIME 100.

Congratulations, Bart. For once, you've overachieved. ∎

---

*TIME senior writer Richard Corliss has been an animated cartoon fan for nearly 50 years.*

# Index

# Index

# Photo Credits

Photo credits read left to right and from top to bottom of page, except as noted.

## Cover

Photo-illustration by Sanjay Kothari. Photographs: Churchill by Yousuf Karsh/Woodfin Camp, Map by The Stock Market, Atom by Gilbert/ Photo Researchers, Princess Diana by John Stilwell/PA, Armstrong by Eliot Elisofon/LIFE©Time Inc., Model T by Ford Motor Co., Picasso by Edward Quinn/Camera Press/Retna, Vietnam by Eddie Adams/AP/Wide World, F.D.R. by George Skadding/LIFE, Fiber Optics by Hamblin/Gamma Liaison, Dolly by Chris Buck/Outline, Hitler by Archive Photos, 3-D Theater by J.R. Eyerman/LIFE©Time Inc.

## Contents

**iv** Brown Brothers, FPG, Fred Ward/Black Star, Farnood/Sipa Press **v** Gjon Mili/LIFE©Time Inc., no credit, Ken Regan/Camera 5, Archive Photos

## Leaders & Revolutionaries

**1** Louise Gubb/The Image Works, George Skadding/LIFE©Time Inc., Giansanti/Sygma **2-5** Illustrations by Luba Lukova **6** PACH/Corbis **7** Corbis-Bettmann **8** UPI/Corbis-Bettmann, Museum of the City of New York/Archive **9** Photoworld/FPG **10** UPI/Corbis-Bettmann **11** Yuri Ryazanov **12** Sovfoto (2) **13** Sovfoto, *Paris Match*, Edgar Snow, UPI/Corbis-Bettmann **14** UPI/Corbis-Bettmann **15** UPI/Corbis-Bettmann, Sophia Smith Collection/Smith College **16** Dillip Mehta/ Contact Press Images, David Rubinger, Anthony Suau/Gamma Liaison **17** Melvyn Calderon/Gamma Liaison, J.B. Diederich/Contact Press Images **18** FPG **19** Archive Photos, Franklin D. Roosevelt Library **20** U.S. Army **21** U.S. Navy **22** Corbis-Bettmann **23** UPI/Corbis-Bettmann, AP/Wide World (2), John Dominis/LIFE©Time Inc. **24** Popperfoto/Archive Photos **25** Schall-Daniel/Time Inc. **26** Hugo Jaeger/LIFE©Time Inc. **27** Heinrich Hoffmann Collection/LIFE©Time Inc., Pictures Inc.©Time Inc. **28** *News Chronicle*-London **29** Wide World Photos **30** UPI/Corbis-Bettmann **31** UPI/Corbis-Bettmann **32** UPI/Corbis-Bettmann, Larry Burrows©Larry Burrows Collection **33** AP/WideWorld, Archive Photos **34** Thomas McAvoy/LIFE ©Time Inc. **35** Franklin D. Roosevelt Library, Popperfoto/Archive Photos **36** Leonard McCombe/LIFE **37** Martha Holmes/LIFE **38** Margaret Bourke White/LIFE©Time Inc., DPA/The Image Works **39** Courtesy Apple **40** DPA/The Image Works **41** Popperfoto/Archive Photos **42** Elias Gilner **43** Archive Photos **44** UPI/Corbis-Bettmann **45** Hulton Getty/Gamma Liaison, no credit, Andrew St. George, AP/Wide World **46** Reni Burri/Magnum Photos **47** Keystone Paris/ Sygma **48** Courtesy of Chiang Ching, A.T. Steele **49** Brian Brake **50** Charles Bonnay/Black Star **51** AP/Wide World Photos, Bibliothèque Nationale-Paris **52** Martin Luther King Jr. Center for Nonviolent Social Change **53** Bob Adelman/Magnum Photos **54** Charles Moore/Black Star, Bob Adelman/Magnum Photos **55** Bob Fitch/Black Star **56** Sygma **57** David Burnett/Contact Press Images **58** Gamma Liaison, Preisig (SIZ Mag.)/Magnum Photos **59** Alon Reininger/Contact Press Images **60** Express Newspapers/Archive Photos **61** ©Nigel Parry/CPI **62** Peter Jordan, *Daily Express*/Archive Photos **63** Shepard Sherbell/ Saba Press **64** David Burnett/Contact Press Images, Micha Bar'Am/ Magnum Photos **66** Michael Evans/Contact Press Images **67** Archive Photos **68** Tass/Sovfoto **69** Peter Souza/Ronald Reagan Library **70** Alain Nogues/Sygma **71** Philippe Ledru/Sygma **72** ADN/Zentralbild **73** Michael O'Neill/Outline **74** Tass/Sovfoto **75** Gedda/Sygma **76** Alon Reininger/Contact Press Images **77** Sygma **78** Stuart Franklin/Magnum Photos **80** Bernie Boston

## Artists & Entertainers

**81** Ken Regan/Camera 5, John Engstead/The Kobal Collection, Jerry Cooke **82-85** Illustrations by Luba Lukova **86** Robert Capa/Magnum Photos **87** Pablo Picasso: *Les Demoiselles D'Avignon*, Paris (June-July 1907) Oil on Canvas, 8'x7'8" (243.9 x 233.7 cm) The Museum of Modern Art, New York. Acquired through the Lillie P. Bliss Bequest. Photograph © 1998 The Museum of Modern Art, New York., Courtesy Sir Roland Penrose-London **88** D. Young **89** Pages/*Paris Match*, Robert Capa/

Magnum Photos **90** Henri Matisse: *Dance* (first version). Paris (March 1909) Oil on Canvas, 8'6 1/2" x 12'9 1/2" (259.7 x 390.1 cm) The Museum of Modern Art, New York. Gift of Nelson A. Rockefeller in honor of Alfred H. Barr, Jr. Photograph ©1988 the Museum of Modern Art; Marcel Duchamp: *Nude Descending a Staircase*, Philadelphia Museum of Art: The Louise and Walter Arensberg Collection **91** Jackson Pollock: *Autumn Rhythm (Number 30)*, The Metropolitan Museum of Art, George A. Hearn Fund, 1957; (57.92) Photograph ©1980 The Metropolitan Museum of Art/ARS, New York.; Robert Rauschenberg: *Monogram*, Moderna Museet, Stockholm ©Robert Rauschenberg/Licensed by VAGA, New York.; Andy Warhol: *One Hundred Cans* ©The Andy Warhol Foundation for the Visual Arts/ARS, New York./Art Resource. **92** Paul Strand: *The White Fence, Port Kent, NY, 1916*, ©1971, Aperture Foundation, Inc., Paul Strand Archive.; Edward Weston: *Pepper #30* The Lane Collection/Courtesy Museum of Fine Arts, Boston **93** Henri Cartier-Bresson: *Valencia*, Magnum; Robert Frank: *Parade—Hoboken, N.J.*, ©Robert Frank/Courtesy Pace MacGill Wildenstein; W. Eugene Smith: *Minimata* © Aileen M. Smith/Black Star; Cindy Sherman: *Untitled Film Still*, Courtesy Cindy Sherman and Metro Pictures **94** Roberto Schezen/Esto Photographics **95** Jean Lattes, Ezra Stoller/Esto Photographics **96** Peter Mauss/Esto Photographics, Scott Frances/Esto Photographics **97** Ezra Stoller/Esto Photographics, no credit, Jeff Goldberg/Esto Photographics **98** White Studio/Collection of Martha Graham **99** ©1994 Barbara Morgan/Willard & Barbara Morgan Collection/Time Inc. is the Licensee **100** Jim Wilson/ The New York *Times*, Burt Glinn/Magnum Photos **101** Archive Photos, John Engstead/MPTV, Martha Swope/©Time Inc., Ted Thai for TIME **102** no credit, Hulton Getty/Gamma Liaison **103** Mark Shaw/Photo Researchers **104** Douglas Kirkland/Sygma **105** Paul Himmel **106** Mark Summers **107** Corbis-Bettmann, Poetry/Rare Books Collection/SUNY/ Buffalo **108** Gisele Freund/Photo Researchers **109** no credit, Hulton-Deutsch Collection/Corbis, George Karger/LIFE©Time Inc., Ben Martin, Carlos Angel/Gamma Liaison **110** no credit, Hulton Getty/ Gamma Liaison **111** Larry Burrows ©Larry Burrows Collection **112** Myron Davis/LIFE ©Time Inc. **113** European, Eric Schaal, Eileen Darby, no credit, S. Girella/Fotostudio **114** no credit **116** Corbis-Bettmann, Photofest **117** Camera Press/Retna, UPI/Corbis-Bettmann **118** Ralph Camping/Arizona *Republic* **119** Gregory Heisler/Outline Press **120** Photofest (2) **121** David James/DreamWorks/Photofest **122** Keystone/FPG, MPTV, Paramount/MPTV **123** Brian Braker/Rapho/ Liaison, MPTV, Bruno Barbey/Magnum Photos **124** Steve Schapiro/ Gamma Liaison **125** John Engstead/Time Inc. **126** Holland/Retna, Gamma Liaison **127** MPTV, Everett Collection (2), Warner Brothers/ MPTV **128** Cornell Capa/Magnum Photos **129** AP/ Wide World, Corbis-Bettmann **130** ©1956 Bob Willoughby **131** no credit **132** ©1956 Bob Willoughby **133** Gordon Parks, Yale Joel/LIFE©Time Inc., Eliot Elisofon/LIFE©Time Inc., Guy Le Querrec/Magnum Photos **134** Ken Veeder/Capitol Records/MPTV **135** Bill Dudas/MPTV, Sid Avery/MPTV **136** Illustration by James McMullan **137** no credit, Cornell Capa/Magnum Photos **138** George Karger/LIFE©Time Inc., Gjon Mili/LIFE©Time Inc. **139** Gjon Mili/LIFE©Time Inc., Photofest **140** Billy Rose Theater Collection/NYPL for the Performing Arts, Elliot Erwitt/Magnum Photos, Gordon Parks/LIFE©Time Inc. **141** R. D'Asaro, W. Eugene Smith/Black Star, Henry Grossman, Billy Rose Theater Collection/NYPL for the Performing Arts **142-43** Stan Wayman/LIFE ©Time Inc. **144** Phillip Jones Griffiths/ Magnum Photos, Express Newspapers, ©Time Inc. **145** Jim Marshall, Henry Grossman **146** Alice Ochs/Michael Ochs Archive, Charles Trainor **147** Neal Preston/Corbis (2), John Roca/Corbis **148** no credit **149** Ted Russell/Sygma **150** Danny Lyon/Magnum Photos, Ken Regan/ Camera 5 **151** ©1986 Delta Haze Corp. All Rights Reserved. Used by Permission, Frank Driggs Collection, Dennis Stock/Magnum Photos, Guy Le Querrec/Magnum Photos **152** David Gahr **153** Larry Busacca/ Retna, David Redfern/Retna **154** Gabi Rona/CBS/MPTV **155** The Kobal Collection, MPTV **156** MPTV (2) **157** Photofest (2) **158** William Coupon/ Gamma Liaison **159** Jim Henson Productions **160** Illustration by Robert Risko **161** Gordon Parks, no credit **162** Terry Thompson/Sipa Press **163** Everett Collection (4) **164-65** The Simpsons™©20th Century Fox Film Corp. All Rights Reserved.